The Principal As Steward

by
Jack McCall

EYE ON EDUCATION
6 Depot Way West, Suite 106
Larchmont, N.Y. 10538

ISBN 1-883001-32-3

Library of Congress Cataloging-in-Publication Data

McCall, John R.
    The principal as steward / by Jack McCall.
        p.   cm.
    Includes bibliographical references.
    ISBN 1-883001-32-3
    1. School principals—United States. 2. Educational leader-
ship—United States. 3. School management and organization—
United States. I. Title.
LB2831.92.M22 1997
371.2'012—dc20   96-34173
                                                          CIP

Editorial and production services provided by:
Bookwrights
1211 Courtland Drive
Raleigh, NC 27604

Published by Eye On Education

LEADERSHIP
ADMINISTRATOR'S GUIDE TO SCHOOL-COMMUNITY RELATIONS
by George E. Pawlas

THE EDUCATOR'S BRIEF GUIDE TO COMPUTERS IN THE SCHOOLS
by Eugene F. Provenzo, Jr.

HANDS-ON LEADERSHIP TOOLS FOR PRINCIPALS
by Raymond Calabrese, Gary Short, and Sally Zepeda

INSTRUCTION AND THE LEARNING ENVIRONMENT
by James W. Keefe and John M. Jenkins

INTERPERSONAL SENSITIVITY
by John R. Hoyle and Harry M. Crenshaw

LEADERSHIP: A RELEVANT AND REALISTIC ROLE FOR PRINCIPALS
by Gary M. Crow, L. Joseph Matthews, and Lloyd E. McCleary

LEADERSHIP THROUGH COLLABORATION:
ALTERNATIVES TO THE HIERARCHY
by Michael Koehler and Jeanne C. Baxter

MOTIVATING OTHERS: CREATING THE CONDITIONS
by David P. Thompson

ORAL AND NONVERBAL EXPRESSION
by Ivan Muse

ORGANIZATIONAL OVERSIGHT:
PLANNING AND SCHEDULING FOR EFFECTIVENESS
by David A. Erlandson, Peggy L. Stark, and Sharon M. Ward

THE PRINCIPAL'S EDGE
by Jack McCall

SYSTEMIC REFORM
BLOCK SCHEDULING: A CATALYST FOR CHANGE IN HIGH SCHOOLS
by Robert Lynn Canady and Michael D. Rettig

DIRECTORY OF INNOVATIONS IN ELEMENTARY SCHOOLS
by Jane McCarthy and Suzanne Still

EDUCATIONAL TECHNOLOGY: BEST PRACTICES FROM
AMERICA'S SCHOOLS
by William C. Bozeman and Donna J. Baumbach

INNOVATIONS IN PARENT AND FAMILY INVOLVEMENT
by J. William Rioux and Nancy Berla

RESEARCH ON EDUCATIONAL INNOVATIONS
by Arthur K. Ellis and Jeffrey T. Fouts

RESEARCH ON SCHOOL RESTRUCTURING
by Arthur K. Ellis and Jeffrey T. Fouts

THE SCHOOL PORTFOLIO:
A COMPREHENSIVE FRAMEWORK FOR SCHOOL IMPROVEMENT
by Victoria L. Bernhardt

SCHOOLS FOR ALL LEARNERS: BEYOND THE BELL CURVE
by Renfro C. Manning

SCHOOL-TO-WORK
by Arnold H. Packer and Marion W. Pines

QUALITY AND EDUCATION: CRITICAL LINKAGES
by Betty L. McCormick

TRANSFORMING EDUCATION THROUGH TOTAL
QUALITY MANAGEMENT: A PRACTITIONER'S GUIDE
by Franklin P. Schargel

TEACHING AND LEARNING
BRINGING THE NCTM STANDARDS TO LIFE:
BEST PRACTICES FROM ELEMENTARY EDUCATORS
by Lisa B. Owen and Charles E. Lamb

THE EDUCATOR'S GUIDE TO IMPLEMENTING OUTCOMES
By William J. Smith

HANDBOOK OF EDUCATIONAL TERMS AND APPLICATIONS
by Arthur K. Ellis and Jeffrey T. Fouts

MATHEMATICS THE WRITE WAY:
ACTIVITIES FOR EVERY ELEMENTARY CLASSROOM
by Marilyn S. Neil

THE PERFORMANCE ASSESSMENT HANDBOOK
Volume 1 Portfolios and Socratic Seminars
Volume 2 Performances and Exhibitions
by Bil Johnson

TEACHING IN THE BLOCK: STRATEGIES FOR ENGAGING
ACTIVE LEARNER
by Robert Lynn Canady and Michael D. Rettig

TABLE OF CONTENTS

Stew-ard *n.* A leader who serves

What they're saying about THE PRINCIPAL AS STEWARD

"Jack McCall is at once inspiring, entertaining, and brilliant. He has a unique ability to weave together various threads of thought and make them relevant to all school leaders. Those of us who are lucky enough to know him personally appreciate his powerful common sense. In this book, you will hear that same voice of intelligence and clarity."

> Michael Ward
> Superintendent of Public Instruction
> North Carolina

"This book is filled with simple, accessible stories which shed penetrating light on the kinds of things which are at the heart of what school leadership is all about."

> Jerry Weast, Superintendent
> Guilford Public Schools

"THE PRINCPAL AS STEWARD is Jack McCall's best book yet."

> Dianne Ashby, Executive Director
> Illinois Women Administrators

FOREWORD

This book is a sequel to *The Principal's Edge*. In the previous book I covered the first nine of the 21 Domains of Knowledge and Skill required in the preparation and on-going training of public school principals, according to a study from The National Policy Board for Educational Administration. In a study (*Principals For Our Changing Schools*) this group answered the question: "What essential knowledge and skills do school principals need to function effectively as leaders?" My claim in the previous book was that principals who mastered the first nine domains would have an edge in accomplishing the difficult task of leading schools in a period of rapid change and renewal. They would be able to change their schools into true Learning Organizations.

In the present book, I have written about the next nine domains of knowledge and skill necessary for a practicing principal. The unifying theme in the previous book was "the Learning Organization," while the theme in this book is Stewardship. I cover in it the following nine domains:

Student Guidance and Development

Staff Development

Measurement and Evaluation

Resource Allocation

Motivating Others

Interpersonal Sensitivity

Oral and Nonverbal Expression

Written Expression, and

Philosophical and Cultural Values.

Principals' role as leader expressed in terms of Stewardship will demand that they become more proficient in these domains of knowledge and skill.

In my decade of teaching principals, I have noticed that their tasks have become more complicated and demanding than ever. No longer is it merely a matter of exerting more direct control over the stakeholders. The role of the principal is changing in many ways, but perhaps most importantly in the way the principal exercises "power." In the old days, the principal would get his or her marching orders from the Central Office and relay them to the troops (teachers and students) with the assurance that they would be carried out. Today's principals are fully aware that this is no longer the situation. The principal is called upon to be a "site manager," which means a decision maker who decides with all the stakeholders what the shared vision of the school will be. Parents, business people, politicians and other interested parties want to have some input into the running of the school. The principal finds himself or herself in the role of facilitator rather than dictator. The idea of a Steward epitomizes this new role.

Stewardship is an umbrella idea that offers the means of achieving fundamental change in the way we govern our institutions (schools included). Stewardship means to hold something in trust for another. The principal no longer owns the school. Originally, a Steward protected a kingdom while those rightfully in charge were away, or, more often, governed for the sake of an under-aged king. Throughout history we have had cases in which the king is a child, and the Steward manages the kingdom for him until he reaches an age at which he can take over. What is immediately apparent is that Stewardship is a position of great trust. Principals really manage the schools for the sake of students and their parents. Secondly, the Steward is definitely not the king, rather he is a servant, a servant-leader. Here is a new way of thinking about the use of power in school management. It is quite different from a Machiavellian approach in which the unjust Steward would immediately get control of the military, and thus usurp the power. In writing about the nine domains, I try to show principals how mastery of these domains of knowledge and skills will equip them to be good Stewards, capable of turning the schools into Learning Organizations in which all the stakeholders feel they share in the ownership of the enterprise.

Stewardship, according to Peter Block, author of the best selling, *The Empowered Manager*, is the willingness of the leader— the principal, in our case—to serve for the well-being of the school, rather than control the stakeholders. Put simply, the principal as Steward promises to be accountable without control or compliance. No one claims that this will be easy, but I do claim that it is the best leadership stance principals can take. In a Learning Organization, all the stakeholders should be working toward a shared vision. If in such an organization *all* the stakeholders are working toward a Shared Vision, creating the institution's future, it is a learning organization. If they are committed to Personal Mastery, if they continually join in Team Learning, if they are willing to shatter some of their Mental Models, and, if they take a Systemic approach to school renewal, then the principal's role will be that of a Steward-servant leader, rather than a taskmaster pushing people who are motivated by their own individual visions. The Steward Principal's task is to get all the stakeholders to take responsibility and become accountable for the school. Problems are no longer the principal's problems alone; they are the systemic obstacles that interfere with the accomplishment of the Shared Vision. They are everyone's responsibility. If schools are for children, even children must learn to take more responsibility for their schools. The spirit of Stewardship should permeate the rank and file as well as the leader.

DEDICATION

This book is dedicated to Gordon Smith III, who has been like a son to me. He is a global educator living in Raleigh, North Carolina, where he founded Exploris, a delightful children's museum, about the world. He is presently starting a charter middle school whose students will act as docents to younger students visiting Exploris.

1

THE STEWARD PRINCIPAL GIVES TOP PRIORITY TO THE STUDENTS' DEVELOPMENTAL NEEDS

"He who stops learning is old at 20 or 80." —*Henry Ford*

The lesson of Domain 8, Instruction and the Learning Environment, in *Principals For Our Changing Schools*, is that we cannot create a school culture for learning without recognizing the developmental needs of students. Author Fenwick English and his team noted that the recognition of students' developmental needs is key to a principal's communication with colleagues. In our first chapter we start with Domain 10: Student Guidance and Development from *Principals For Our Changing Schools*.

Co-leaders, Albert W. Edgemon and David A. Erlandson, have given us a full explanation of the knowledges and skills that principals need if they are to be successful in handling Student Guidance and Development. I would recommend that each principal carefully study the material found in Domain 10, since it is essential for the establishment of a Learning Organization.

WHEN AND WHY DID WE UNCOUPLE FEELING AND THINKING?

Living as we do very near the end of the Twentieth Century, we have inherited a set of beliefs that have been so integrated into our social thinking that we just assume they are true. Most of the great thinkers who have fed our minds in the last century have drunk deeply from the enticing waters of the Age of Enlightenment. They told us, " School is for the mind. Schools are to teach reasoning and thinking. The only safe way to do that is to make a clear distinction between thinking and feeling. Let the family take care of their children's personal and emotional development. We school people will handle students' intellectual development."

One philosopher summarized well the thinking of the Enlightenment. Condorcet, a French philosopher of the 18th century, summarized the optimism and faith in human reason that was characteristic of that movement. In tracing man down from the dawn of history, he emphasized the liberation of mankind from ignorance, tyranny, and superstition by means of his science and reason. He then sketched a hopeful future in which mankind would be free, enjoy sexual equality and be equal in wealth and education. Finally, he envisioned a moral, intellectual, and physical improvement, indeed a perfection of humanity that would come about through better instruction, laws, and institutions.

Those promises ring hollow today. Principals know only too well that the Enlightenment failed to deliver on its promises. Human development is not and cannot be compartmentalized. The various facets of development are interdependent. School leaders must address the whole developmental process as well as the whole developing child or adolescent. Nevertheless, some principals and parents act as if they believe that by focusing on core academics alone, the school can accomplish its goals. These are the people who think that time for student guidance, development, and activities is an infringement on the time for core academics and should be cut out.

PRISONERS OF TIME

In the recent report of the National Education Commission on Time and Learning entitled *Prisoners of Time*, we get a more balanced view.

> "The traditional school day, originally intended for core academic learning, must now fit in a whole set of requirements for what has been called 'the new work of the schools'—education about personal safety, consumer affairs, AIDS, conservation and energy, family life, driver's training—as well as traditional nonacademic activities, such as counseling, gym, study halls, homeroom, lunch, and pep rallies. The school day, nominally six periods, is easily reduced at the secondary level to about three hours of time for core academic instruction.
>
> "Most Americans believe these activities are worthwhile. But where do schools find the time? Within a constrained school day it can only come by robbing Peter to pay Paul." (1)

It is becoming imperative that Steward Principals ask for a longer school day and a longer school year so they can accommodate both the "academic day" and the "school day." As good stewards, principals know that they can't cut the "academic day" anymore than it has already been cut. As it is, only about 40% of the present school day is devoted to core academic instruction. Nor can they deny that many of society's problems have found their way into the schools. Physically and emotionally hungry students can't learn. Principals know they must make room for and give time to student guidance, or the limited time devoted to core academics will be wasted.

STUDENT DEVELOPMENT NEEDS

As I write this, today's newspaper informs me that one of the giants in the field of human development passed away at 91 years of age. Erik H. Erikson, the psychoanalyst, who profoundly reshaped views of human development, was a thinker whose ideas had effects far beyond psychoanalysis, shaping the emerging field of child development and life-span studies, and reaching into the humanities. Over thirty years ago, I was teaching his eight stages of human development. The students in the turbulent 60's were rebellious and opposed to authority (many were returning Vietnam vets), but they listened attentively and appreciated the teachings of Erikson. For some reason, Erikson seemed to be able to help them make sense of their own rather turbulent progressions.

Today, as we think of the place of student development needs in the school, we can still profit from reviewing Erikson's treatment of the early steps of childhood and adolescent development.

ERIKSON LENDS A HAND

Erikson sought to broaden psychoanalysis to account for changes in personality that resulted from developmental and environmental influences. He insisted that the qualities of the society in which a person lived influenced the way he or she negotiated the eight crises that marked the stages of human development. In his old age Erikson pointed out that children growing up in the 20th century were living with widespread violence that was unheard of in prior ages.

Students have egos that can be greatly influenced by their life experiences, and school is one of their very important life experiences. Erikson would encourage principals to take into consideration the stresses under which many students are being reared. Families, churches, and neighborhoods no longer seem to buffer the stresses or give the support they once did.

Erikson outlines eight stages: **infancy** in which the emotional conflict is between basic trust and mistrust; **toddler** in which autonomy ("No, I want to do it myself.") conflicts with shame and doubt; **Dennis the Menace** (elementary school stage) where the conflict lies between initiative and guilt; **early middle school** where the positive component is industry and the negative is inferiority; **adolescence**, where the identity crisis occurs leading to either role confusion or the beginning of having a "voice" or an identity; **young adulthood** in which intimacy vies with isolation; **adulthood** in which the crisis pits generativity (having the power to produce) against stagnation; and finally **retirement** (old age) when despair threatens ego integrity.

If we understand Erikson correctly, it would be wrong for schools K-12 to disregard the total development of their students. From age four or five until eighteen, students spend a large portion of their waking hours in school learning to handle their developmental tasks. If some students have not resolved or only partially resolved their early crises of trust—mistrust, autonomy vs. shame, and between initiative and guilt—they are going to bring these unresolved conflicts into the school. It may have been possible fifty years ago to assume that the majority of students would have resolved the first four stages of development successfully before they came to school. In that case, they would still need help with their developmental needs for the next two stages. However, in our times many students have been unsuccessful in resolving their early developmental crises. They come to school exhibiting behavior characterized by mistrust, shame and doubt, guilt, inferiority, and role confusion. It is difficult for such children to learn to read by the end of third grade without being given special guidance and support.

I wish we had time to go more deeply into the work of Erikson. I believe further study of his theory could help principals do a better job in handling student developmental needs. I am convinced that the source of most violence in our world comes from what Erikson calls shame. When young children have been abused they suffer deep shame. In his book, *Childhood and Society*, first published in 1950, he says,

"Shame is early expressed in an impulse to bury one's face or to sink, right then and there into the ground. But this, I think, is essentially rage turned against the self. He who is ashamed would like to force the world not to look at him, nor notice his exposure. He would like to destroy the eyes of the world. Instead he must wish for his own invisibility. This potentiality is abundantly used in the educational method of 'shaming' used so exclusively by some primitive peoples." (2)

In the latest theory on violence, James Gilligan M.D., head of the Center for the Study of Violence at Harvard Medical School, states in his book *Violence*, "The emotion of shame is the primary or ultimate cause of all violence whether toward others or self." (3) I recommend *Childhood and Society (1950)* and *Violence (1996)* to principals who are trying to guide students coming from harsh, neglectful, and abusive residences.

STUDENT GUIDANCE AND COUNSELING

Principals For Our Changing Schools defines Student Guidance and Development in this way:

> "**Student Guidance and Development**: Understanding and accommodating student growth and development; providing for student guidance, counseling, and auxiliary services; utilizing and coordinating community organizations; responding to family needs; enlisting the participation of appropriate people and groups to design and conduct these programs and to connect schooling with plans for adult life; planning for a comprehensive program of student activities." (4)

The authors, Edgemon and Erlandson, go on to explain that effective student guidance and development requires connecting four major initiatives involving institutional and community life. We will develop these later.

Principals know they have to find time and resources to address both the academic and nonacademic needs of the students. But they feel overwhelmed by the demands this puts on school personnel and the already crammed day. The Development Team offers principals an attractive alternative: use of community organizations.

Recently, I did a workshop for a principal, John Frazier, who is very creative. A couple of years ago he got some of his teachers interested in forming a year-round school that is now running successfully. More recently he has discovered how to create more time using the year-round format. He wisely discerned that if he could get community agencies that are presently mandated to serve the needs of school-age children to come to his school, they could serve the children and families without stealing time away from the academic teachers. They would have more time to teach the "liberal arts" of reading, writing, speaking, listening, thinking and understanding, which are the keys to all learning. The school cannot meet the ever increasing developmental needs without outside help. Even with outside help, the needs can't be met without shortchanging academics unless the day and year is lengthened. With year-round schools, many students are coming to school over 200 days a year.

Here is John's explanation of the program, "More and more, the students were bringing in developmental problems, which interfered with their learning. Hunger takes precedence over learning, so we had to take care of this need. Other students came in with needs and disabilities of various kinds, which demanded immediate attention. The time for academics was shrinking but there was nothing we could do about it. The teachers were forced to do triage."

In John Frazier's school, like most year-round schools in North Carolina, they simply rearrange the school calendar for a very good purpose. The schools run on 45-15 plan, with children attending school for 45 weekdays, then exercising options for the 15 weekdays of intersession. These added 15 days can be used for enrichment or vacation or completing remediation requirements if they fail the end-of-quarter tests. Now with the "extended day" from 7 AM to 6 PM and the "year-round" with its three-week periods of intersession, many students go to school on the bus and take advantage of the services of many community agencies as well as the schools' offerings of enrichment or remediation. John Frazier now sees his teachers able to spend a lot more time on core academics. Believe me, he has a busy school but a happy one. Some of the outside agencies bringing their services to the school include: social workers, mental health workers, parks and recreation specialists, dental technicians, nurses, and workers from many other community agencies committed to the needs of children.

How did this alert principal marshal the resources of the community while running an elementary school with four times its share of students with special needs? He realized he couldn't do it by himself, so he applied for a grant that allowed him to hire a full-time social worker. Most school social workers cover four, five, or six schools. This worker has only one school, and the difference is amazing. Doctors and dentists in private practice have also volunteered time. The principal makes sure that the social worker, and all agency members or volunteers who come to assist, are introduced to the teachers and the parents of the children served. In no way does the school staff abrogate its responsiblity for meeting the students' developmental needs. Each teacher is fully aware of and involved in the services to his or her students, as are the parents. I interviewed the social worker and learned that she was delighted with the cooperation of agencies, volunteers, teachers, parents, and students.

STUDENTS DON'T QUIT CLASS, THEY QUIT SCHOOL

There is always a danger that in our effort to meet the extraordinary developmental needs, we may bring in outside experts and shunt the students off to them. It is important to keep in mind that the family is primarily responsible for the meeting of these needs whether the child is in school or at home. When the children are in the school, the principal, teachers, and other school staff are deputized by the parents to be responsible for their children's needs. The community agencies, who send workers to help in this process, should never be given the impression that the school is abrogating its responsiblity. For this reason, the social worker sees to it that the outside service deliverers are careful to make sure that the students' teachers are fully informed about what is going on with their students. Developmental needs are too important to be the sole domain of nonacademic specialists.

Practically all of the 2500 public school principals I have taught expressed a desire to have more guidance counselors and/or school psychologists. This is proof that the developmental needs of the students are becoming more and more urgent, and the principals feel guilty that they don't have the resources to cope with the increase. John Frazier experienced the same problem and found a way to solve it. Blessed with more time, his school is coming closer to meeting both the academic and nonacademic needs of children, their ordinary and extraordinary

developmental needs. He learned the truth in the African prov-
erb, "It takes a village to bring up a child."

No longer is it sufficient for a teacher to say, " I do my job. I
teach the students in my classroom and I teach them well." As
we said above, students don't quit class, they quit school—and
you can be sure that what makes them quit school is a feeling
that they don't belong. No teacher at any level can refuse to take
part in shaping and forming the school climate so it will be con-
ducive to learning. Every student in the school has a right to be
responded to in a caring way by every adult who works in that
school. When classroom teachers set the tone not just for the
class but for the whole school, they must take the initiative in
finding out what is being done for their students by the outside
specialists. Ideally, the school guidance counselor should coor-
dinate regular meetings that include the social worker, outside
specialists, students, parents, and teachers. When a village takes
on the responsibility of bringing up children as every good village should, the villagers must ensure that no one is left out of
the communication loop.

It is important to note that intellectual needs are serious developmental needs as well. They are best met by teaching the
academic core subjects with plenty of coaching and seminars as
well as lectures and group projects. The students' needs are not
compartmentalized, they are inter-related and interdependent.
In assuring that all the developmental needs are met, the principal does all he or she can to make time become the servant of
meeting student needs, rather than the reverse. The members of
the National Education Commission on Time and Learning concluded that in order to meet all the needs of today's students,
schools will have to remain open longer during the day, and
some schools in every district will have to remain open throughout the year.

THE COMER PROCESS IS ONE WAY TO MEET STUDENT AND FAMILY NEEDS

James P. Comer, a psychiatrist, who teaches at the Yale Medical School and is the director of the University's Child Study
Center, decided to devote his life to helping those children with

limited opportunities for success. He dedicates his life to helping "at risk" children, believing this is the most important task
facing the nation today.

Comer's philosophy, which appeals greatly to me, can be
summed up in six words, "*Human beings thrive in supportive environments.*" Comer notes that these supportive environments
or communities are becoming increasingly rare. The only adults
that many children see at work up close are their teachers and
principals. The school's authority figures model what an adult
should be and take the place of an actual community. Comer
wonders how we can get children to interact with a variety of
adults acting as legitimate authority figures. Unless children
experience a supportive environment supplied by many responsible adults (not just teachers), they will never be able to successfully navigate the crises of childhood between trust vs. mistrust, autonomy vs. shame/doubt, initiative vs. guilt, industry
vs. inferiority and when they reach adolescence, identity vs. role
confusion. Without this immersion in a community of responsible and responsive adults, the children will be unable to move
successfully through the developmental steps leading to an adult
maturity characterized by integrity.

Comer set out to change the school environment so it could
meet the developmental needs of children "at risk." He first
stressed to principals and teachers the fact that learning involves
more than native ability. Success in school is a product of overall development, made possible to a large extent by a child's
ability to internalize the values and ways of significant adults.
That is why he wanted more responsible adults connected with
the school, who model essential social values along with the
teachers and principal.

Comer started by upsetting the traditional, insensitive hi-
erarchical management system and involving the entire community in the running of the schools. He suggested that each
school have a "governing council" of teachers, counselors, and
parents, headed by the principal. He wanted to bring parents
actively into the life of the school and thus create a "shared sense
of purpose between parents and staff." In the Comer approach,
parents are a part of the governing council, but their participation in social events is equally important because this provides

the opportunity for parents and teachers to interact in relaxed and positive ways, where social differences can be minimized. Parents are also encouraged to become classroom assistants, tutors, or aides. Comer wisely points out that it is important for "at risk" children to see their parents taken seriously by mainstream institutions.

For me, the crown jewel in the Comer approach is contained in his next step. He wanted the partnership between parents and staff to become more knowledgeable and effective by establishing a "mental health" team to assist the governing council in each school. The mental health team consists of guidance counselors, social workers, school psychologists, special education teachers, nurses, and classroom teachers. It meets regularly to discuss the developmental needs of individual children and study the best ways to cope with these needs. It is interesting to note that Dr. Comer has been successful in implementing these ideas in over 100 schools around the country. To learn more about James Comer's program, write to the School Developmental Program, Child Study Center, 230 South Frontage Road, P.O. Box 3333, New Haven, CT 06510-8009. (5)

THE FOUR WHEELS OF EFFECTIVE STUDENT GUIDANCE AND DEVELOPMENT

Doctors Edgemon and Erlandson have provided principals with an excellent overall approach to Student Guidance and Development. They make their points with clarity and precision. In explaining their process model, they state their case as follows.

"Effective student guidance and development requires connecting four major intitiatives involving institutional and community life. These include:
1) determining student and family needs;
2) involving school staff and community organizations;
3) understanding both student growth and the educational program, and their interrelationships; and
4) providing a comprehensive student guidance and activities program designed to meet student and family needs."

It is worth noting that the material in Domain 10 fleshes out the principles offered by Comer and others. As we enter the 21st century we must recapture what was well known in the first half of the 19th century and before. It is impossible to meet students' needs without taking into consideration not only family needs but also family choices.

As we look at Figure 1, the Process Model (6), we note that the four boxes are linked by arrows pointing clockwise around the figure. Family and student needs in box #1 are identified by those participants in box #2: school professionals, community organizations, and other appropriate persons and groups. (Here I would include representatives of parents, as Comer does.)

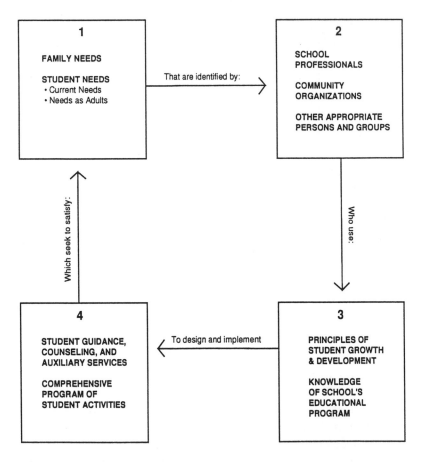

Figure 1. Guidance Process Model

These participants use the contents of box #3: Principles of student growth and development and knowledge of the school's education program. Principals should note that those adults from outside the school need time and coaching to be helped to understand the school's education program. It may take a village to bring up a child, but it is equally important that the adults involved get the training they need to work intelligently with developing children in a school setting. Equally important, school professionals, community organizations, parents and other volunteers who work together to meet students' developmental needs, require solid understanding of student growth and development.

In the last 20 years, we have learned a lot about how young people develop. There is much illuminating brain research that has not yet been brought to the attention of the people who work most closely with the developing students, for instance. As we move to the next box (#4) to design and implement the student guidance, counseling, and auxiliary services and a comprehensive program of student activities, we become aware that we must know more about the youngsters whom we are trying to help. We need to know so much more about the world in which they are developing with its special tensions and stresses. We need to listen to the youngsters as they try to explain to us how they perceive their world. There is no way we can complete the circle around the four boxes and go back to box #1 unless we get continuous feedback from students, parents, and school staff. If we dared to think of the families and students as clients or customers, the identifiers and designers in box #2 would realize how impossible it is to use the principles of student growth and development or knowledge of school's educational program without a continuous dialogue in which all stakeholders take part.

THE LOGIC OF A MAD TEA PARTY

We create a false dilemma when we ask if the school can offer the necessary time to address ever-increasing family and student needs, while simultaneously increasing time for the core academic studies in the confines of the current day and calen-

dar year. False dilemmas create false choices. In the field of public education, we can no longer make believe that the average
kindergarten child comes to school ready to follow a serious
curriculum of core academic studies for the next 13 years. We
cannot neglect the needs that families and children bring into
the school. Unless many of these needs are met, any success at
core academics becomes impossible. These needs can be met at
the school, but not by the teachers who are commissioned and
trained to teach core academics, and not in the confines of the
six-hour school day and 180-day school year. When will our society break away from "Mad Tea Party" thinking?

> "At the Mad Tea Party, the Hatter broke the silence. 'What
> day of the month is it?' he said, turning to Alice: he had
> taken his watch out of his pocket, and was looking at it
> uneasily, shaking it every now and then, holding it to
> his ear.
>
> Alice considered a little, and then said, 'The fourth.' 'Two
> days wrong!' sighed the Hatter, 'I told you butter
> wouldn't suit the works!' he added looking angrily at
> the March Hare.
>
> 'It was the best butter,' the March Hare meekly replied.
> 'Yes, but some crumbs must have got in it as well,' the
> Hatter grumbled: 'you shouldn't have put the butter in
> with the breadknife.'
>
> The March Hare took the watch and looked at it gloom-
> ily: then he dipped it into his cup of tea and looked at it
> again: but he could think of nothing better to say than
> his first remark, 'It was the best butter, you know.'
>
> Alice had been looking over his shoulder with some cu-
> riosity. 'What a funny watch!' she remarked. 'It tells the
> day of the month, and doesn't tell what o'clock it is!'
>
> 'Why should it!' muttered the Hatter, ' Does your watch
> tell you what year it is?' 'Of course not,' Alice replied
> very readily: 'but that is because it stays the same year
> for such a long time together.'

'Which is just the case with mine,' said the Hatter. Alice felt dreadfully puzzled. The Hatter's remark seemed to her to have no sort of meaning in it, and yet it was certainly English. 'I don't quite understand you,' she said, as politely as she could.

The Chairman of the National Education Commission on Time and Learning, John Hodge Jones, was recently quoted in the Murfreesboro, Tennessee and the national press as saying, "By living with the constraints of yesterday's school calendar, our nation is committing slow-motion social suicide. Our schools and the people involved with them—students, teachers, administrators, parents, and staff—are prisoners of time, captives of the school clock and calendar."

We will consider further conclusions of the National Commission on Time and Learning in the following chapters. Suffice it here to say, the aim of this excellent study was to find more time in the school day and year for the pursuit of core academic subjects. They discovered that U.S. students spend less than half as much time in core academic instruction as their international peers. On average, U.S. students can graduate if they devote 41% of their school time to academic subjects. Milton Goldberg, Executive Director of the Commission's study of Time and Learning states, "If reform is to truly take hold, the six-hour, 180-day school year should be relegated to museums—an exhibit from our educational past."

It is a "Mad Tea Party" idea to think that the best principal can marshal resources in the school using only present staff under current time constraints, and meet the needs presented by families and students while giving adequate time to academics. If we are to meet these needs, we will have to lengthen the school day, the school year and bring in auxiliary resources.

Looking again at Figure 1 we see that if the family and student needs increase (box #1), then the school professionals, community organizations and other appropriate persons and groups (parents included) in box #2 will have to expand resources to respond to these increases. When a school district is rapidly increasing, the school board must listen to the demographers and other futurists to find out how many schools must be on the drawing board to meet the growth. Similarly, if a school or school system is being inundated with increasing social problems caused by unemployment, overcrowding, mobility, child abuse and neglect, racism, drugs, violence and sexually transmitted diseases, it should ask specialists to help it plan to meet these crises. Are there any "Mad Tea Party" people who really believe we can have open-door public schools and refuse to cope with the serious developmental problems the children bring with them? Are there any Tea Party dreamers who think we can take time to handle these problems without seriously cutting into academic instruction? Do any think the teachers and staff can handle all the specialized problems without help from outside specialists? Are there any Mad Hatters and March Hares who believe that the six-hour day, 180-day year will suffice?

There may be a minority still at the Mad Tea Party, but we have good news. After nearly 40 years of opposing a longer school year, 52 percent of Americans now favor students spending more time in school. A plurality (52 percent) favor increasing the number of days in the year. A large majority (62 percent) support providing after-school care for the children of working parents. Americans have finally reached a national consensus on the importance of pre-school programs to help low-income and minority children get ready for school. In a recent poll, 85 percent supported the idea of pre-school for those who need and want it. Head Start is picking up speed again. In France, all children are offered a quality pre-school experience regardless of parent's ability to pay. The costs are on a sliding scale.

AMERICAN PSYCHOLOGICAL ASSOCIATION OFFERS SOME HELP

In my experience, many principals complain that they received very little in-depth training in the psychology of student development. As a Clinical Psychologist, I have spent a lot of time working with school guidance and counseling personnel, as well as school psycholgists. Even these more highly trained specialists express a strong desire to learn more and more about human growth and development.

I am somewhat ashamed to think how little my field of clinical psychology has done to help public school practitioners. Only in the last couple of years have the psychological faculties in undergraduate and graduate departments begun to realize how negligent they have been in working with school personnel.

I was proud a couple of years ago to receive copies of *Learner Centered Psychological Principle: Guidelines For School Redesign And Reform*. (7) This 16-page document was distributed by the American Psychogical Association. I was relieved to see that the APA, an organization to which I have belonged for over 45 years, was reaching out to offer direct help to public school practioners. The dozen principles contained in the document represent both an ideal vision and an accumulation of ongoing practice and research. The purpose as stated by the authors was to provide significant information consistent with research generated by psychologists and educators in the areas of learning, motivation, and human development.

In the last 10 years, psychologists have mined rich veins of knowledge, much of which has relevance to school-age children. If educational reforms proceed by setting standards for schools without taking into account these research findings, reform efforts will fail. Adding more time to the school day and year while continuing to teach in the same ineffective way will do more harm than good. The findings in psychology can help us teach and learn better. *Learner Centered Psychological Principles* was published by the American Psychological Association, 750 First Street N.E. Washington D.C. 20002-4242 (Third Draft-1992).

A Dozen Learner Centered Psychological Principles

The following twelve principles taken from the APA document are relevant to the academic and non-academic developmental needs of school age children. The twelve principles should be understood as a whole and not treated in isolation. We could all profit from a deeper understanding of these principles.

"**Principle #1: The Nature of the Learning Process.** Learning is a natural process of pursuing personally meaningful goals that is active, volitional, and internally mediated; it is a process of discovering and constructing meaning from information and experience, filtered through each individual's unique perceptions, thoughts, and feelings."

"**Principle #2: Goals of the Learning Process.** The learner seeks to create meaningful and coherent representations of knowledge regardless of the quantity and quality of data available."

"**Principle #3: The Construction of Knowledge.** The learner organizes information in ways that associate and link new information with existing knowledge in uniquely meaningful ways."

"**Principle #4: Higher-Order Thinking.** Higher-order strategies for thinking about thinking—for overseeing and monitoring mental operations—facilitate creative and critical thinking and the development of expertise."

"**Principle #5: Motivational Influence on Learning.** The depth and breadth of information processed, and what and how much is learned and remembered, is influenced by (a) self-awareness and beliefs about personal control, competence, and ability; (b) clarity and saliency of personal values, interests, and goals; (c) personal expectations for success or failure; (d) affect, emotion, and general states of mind; and (e) the resulting motivation to learn." (Note how closely the pursuit of core academic instructions is aligned with the successful resolution of the stages of human development, self-awareness, goals, expectations, emotion, and motivation. How did we ever think we could separate core academics from the whole developing child or adolescent?) This is my quote in parentheses.

"**Principle #6: Intrinsic Motivation to Learn.** Individuals are naturally curious and enjoy learning in the absence of intense negative cognitions and emotions (e.g. insecurity, worrying about failure, being self-conscious or shy, fearing corporal punishment or verbal ridiculing or stigmatizing labels.)"

"**Principle #7: Characteristics of Motivation—Enhancing Learning Tasks.** Curiosity, creativity, and higher order thinking processes are stimulated by relevant, authentic learning tasks of optimal learning difficulty, challenge and novelty for each student."

"**Principle #8: Developmental Constraints and Opportunities.** Individuals proceed through identifiable progressions of physical, intellectual, emotional, and social development that are a function of unique genetic and environmental factors."

(Why did we set schools up as if we believed that all students progressed through these stages in lock step? Why didn't we realize that under certain distressful social conditions the navigating of some of these progressions become so difficult that many youngsters need special help to make it through the childhood crises?) This is my quote in parenthesis.

"**Principle #9: Social and Cultural Diversity.** Learning is facilitated by social interactions and communication with others in a variety of flexible, diverse (cross-age, culture, family background, etc.) and adaptive instructional settings. "(In this multicultural country of ours, we should have an advantage, since learning is enhanced when practiced in the midst of cultural diversity. To segregate children or adults is to rob them of shared riches in learning.) Quote in parenthesis is mine, not to be attributed to the American Psychological Assocation.

"**Principle # 10: Social Acceptance, Self-Esteem, and Learning.** Learning and self-esteem are heightened when individuals are in respectful and caring relationships with others who see their potential, genuinely appreciate their unique talents, and accept them as individuals."

"**Principle #11: Individual Differences in Learning.** Although basic principles of learning, motivation, and effective instruction apply to all learners (regardless of ethnicity, race, gender, presence or absence of physical handicaps, religion or socioeconomic status), learners differ in their preferences for learning mode and strategies, and unique capabilities in particular areas. These differences are a function of both environment (what is learned and communicated in different cultures or social groups) and heredity (what occurs naturally as a function of genes and resulting differential capacities)." (With these individual differences so apparent, it makes little sense to hold time constant in schools and let standards of learning vary. Isn't it time we opted for high standards of learning and decided to give each student the time and special help he or she needs to reach those standards?) Quote in parenthesis is mine.

"**Principle #12: Cognitive Filters.** Personal thoughts, beliefs, and understandings resulting from prior learning and unique interpretations become each individual's basis for constructing reality or interpreting life experiences."

THE STEWARD PRINCIPAL SEES EACH STAKEHOLDER AS A UNIQUE TREASURE

If there is one word that is repeated over and over again in these 12 principles, it is the word "unique". When these principles are applied in school redesign and reform, they lay stress on individual differences in the students. Steward Principals are aware that students don't develop in exactly the same way and certainly not at the same time. Students have different strengths, weaknesses, preferences, and dislikes. In addressing both academic and developmental needs, it is the wise principal who listens to students and families and gets the staff to do the same. It is the wise principal that realizes that time must be the variable in dealing with developmental and academic needs. Some students need plentiful student activities, some only a few. All students are seeking to realize their own uniqueness but also belong to social groups that are developing along with them. They want so much to be accepted for who and what they are as unique individuals. They fear shaming and rejection, and flourish in an atmosphere of respect, acceptance, and love. School climate is crucial for meeting all developmental needs, and teachers and principals who are able to integrate these psychological principles into their school day will help many children.

True Steward Principals are aware of these student developmental needs and strive to manage scarce resources in a way that will enhance the learning of each unique child. Stewardship begins with the willingness of the principal to be accountable for each child in the school. When the Steward Principal consistently places service over the pursuit of self-interest, he or she is developing a community or learning organization. When principals are true servant-leaders choosing service over self-interest, they are saying they are willing to be accountable without choosing to control the world around them. To be a Steward Principal requires a level of trust that we are not used to holding.

Stewardship forces principals to yield on their desire to use good parenting as a basic form of governing. They already know how to be good parents at work. They enter into real learning when they opt for the alternative of parenting, which is partnership. It is difficult. Parenting and its close relative patriarchy are so much a part of our ordinary way of exerting power, it takes constant vigilance to change and play the role of servant leader—one seeking to partner rather than parent. Principals serve best through partnership, rather than patriarchy. In true stewardship there is no room for dependency. All stakeholders become interdependent as they take responsibility for themselves and the whole school. When Steward Principals are able to empower teachers, staff, students, parents, community supporters, great things happen as they did with John Frazier in his school.

SUMMATION

The principal as chief steward has the duty to respond to the needs of the other stewards on the school staff, as well as families and children who attend the school. As chief steward, the principal cannot decide what the needs of these two groups are, rather he or she must do a needs analysis and listen to them as they express their needs. I developed the idea of probing in the third chapter of my earlier book, *The Principal's Edge*. Principals and teachers must become good probers if they are to find out what the real needs of students and families are. With experience, the principal learns that the needs of staff, students, and parents include skills in thinking and in handling emotion. The Steward Principal is aware that it will take more time in the school day and year to adequately respond to these needs. Studying Erikson's stages of life development, the Steward Principal realizes that students, staff, and parents are all going through developmental stages. The principal realizes that it is impossible to do an adequate job on core academic instruction without also taking into account the developmental needs of all concerned. He or she knows that the climate of the school is determined to a large extent by the quality of student guidance and student activities. Unless, as Comer says, the students feel that they belong in a safe and protective environment, they will not and cannot learn the core academics. Studying the Process Model, the principal sees in a graphic manner the way family and student needs have to be identified by school professionals, community agencies, and other appropriate persons (including parents), who must use principles of student growth and development as well as the knowledge of school's educational program to design programs in student guidance, counseling, auxiliary services, and comprehensive programs of student activities.

The Steward Principal refuses to play the illogical game demonstrated at the Mad Tea Party. The principal joins Alice in saying politely, "I don't quite understand you."

As Steward Principals strive to increase school time and other resources in order to meet the needs of each unique student, they will find support and justification in the dozen Learner Centered Principles offered by the American Psychological Association.

QUESTIONS FOR REFLECTION

1. What do we mean when we say, "Human development cannot be compartmentalized?"

2. When and why did we uncouple feeling and thinking?

3. Why has humanity failed to attain perfection in spite of all the improved instruction, laws, and institutions?

4. How could a review of Erikson's Eight Steps help principals in their efforts to further the full human development of students?

5. Principals know that they must find time and resources to address both the academic and nonacademic needs of students. How can they do this when only 40% of the present school day is devoted to core academic work?

6. How did John Frazier try to solve this problem?

7. How does Dr. Comer's insistence that humans thrive only in a supportive environment force principals to take Guidance and Development seriously?

8. How can the Four Wheels of Effective Student Guidance help you as a principal to meet the needs of students?

9. Why is it a "Mad Tea Party" idea to think that principals can meet student needs simply by using present school staff and working under current time constraints?

10. Among the 12 Learner Centered Principles choose those that seem most helpful to you and explain how they help principals and teachers meet the academic and nonacademic developmental needs of students.

2

WHAT THE STEWARD PRINCIPAL NEEDS TO KNOW AND DO TO MEET THE STAFF'S DEVELOPMENTAL NEEDS

*Staff members who think they have all the answers
have surely missed the questions.*

Of the many roles the principal must play, the role as the director of staff development deserves the highest priority. Wise principals know that the quality of their school reflects the quality of their personnel. The freshly developing knowledge and skills of the teachers are essential to the learning of the students. In forming and maintaining a true Learning Organization, the actual process of learning that teachers go through is as important, if not more important, than the teaching they do in the classroom. *Students learn only from teachers who are themselves in the process of learning.* The same can be said about parents. Only parents who give their own learning a high daily priority can model for children the value of learning. Parents and teachers who put a low priority on their own learning are poor models for children. With children, the question is never "Do you want to be good? "It is rather, "Who do you want to be like?" If children have adults around them who relish learning, the children will take to learning like ducks take to water. If the teachers and parents are not interested in actively pursuing learning or improving themselves, the children won't make sacrifices to engage in serious learning.

My father graduated from elementary school at 13 and immediately went to work in a factory to support the family. He never set foot in a day school thereafter, yet he attended night school classes for nearly twenty years. All the years I was in elementary, high school, and even some of my college years, he continued to attend night classes. He would repeat the same accounting course hoping to raise his mark to 90. He took all the courses offered. It appeared to me that learning was my father's most valued activity. It was his hobby. This love of learning rubbed off on me. I wanted to be like him. I still do, and at 76 after I teach and write during the day, I go to the local community college Monday nights to take art classes. It's not a burden. Arts training is helping me to appreciate the "beautiful." Now I sketch that I may see. Learning invigorates me as it did my dad.

Senge in *The Fifth Discipline* (8) defines a "Learning organization" as an organization that is continually expanding its capacity to create its future. In the Learning Organization, "survival learning" is necessary but not sufficient. Joined to "adaptive or survival learning," the members of a true "Learning Organization" pursue "generative learning", learning that enhances their capacity to create. My father wanted our family to become a Learning Organization. Likewise, the smart principal, while trying to turn the "factory" school into a "Learning Organization," is perfectly aware that the secret to success lies in good staff development. If the staff is learning, the students will learn.

DEVELOPING THE PERSONAL AND PROFESSIONAL LIVES OF SCHOOL STAFF

In *Principals For Our Changing Schools*, a team of educators from Utah under the leadership of Lloyd E. McCleary laid out for principals a more complete Staff Development Schematic. They have taken an extremely complex subject and given us a clear and concise way of dealing with it. They offer a definition of staff development that can serve to start us off on this chapter.

> "**Staff Development:** Working with faculty and staff to identify professional needs; planning, organizing, and facilitating programs that improve faculty and staff effectiveness and are consistent with institutional goals and needs; supervising individuals and groups; providing feedback on performance; arranging for remedial assistance; engaging faculty and others to plan and participate in recruitment and development activities; and initiating self development." (9)

School staffs need to renew themselves in order to remain vital and effective. If teaching school today saps the energy of the teachers to such an extent that they have no energy left to read a book, design new learning experiences for their students, plan team teaching experiences with other teachers, attend workshops, participate in professional seminars, and work with other teachers improving the school learning environment, then we must make major changes in the way teaching is practiced. Is the problem the overcrowded classroom, the jammed schedule? Is it a lack of intellectual curiosity on the part of the staff? Is it because staff development programs are designed and implemented poorly? Is it possible we suffer from a misconception about teaching and learning? Did we assume teachers went to college to learn how to teach and what to teach, then simply taught what they had been taught? Is it really teaching to repeat the same material to each new class of students? Could it be that we have underestimated what continual staff development entails?

If we assumed that machinists, tool makers, accountants, dentists, physicians, insurance adjusters, and paralegals already know all they needed to know, we would be laughed out of court. We are in the midst of an information explosion and a technical deluge that renders skills, instruments, and procedures obsolete in months. One cannot store up a body of knowledge in any profession, craft or trade during the apprenticeship years and then merely apply that knowledge for the next 10 years. In every other profession, such misbehavior would be spotted and punished quickly. The practitioner would look silly for using outmoded methods. Customers would complain about the plumber using techniques from the 60's to repair toilets in the 90's.

Is it possible that parents give high marks to their local school only because they are unaware of how much things have changed in education? To take one example, the research on the brain has been extremely fruitful since the 60's, and yet little of this new knowledge is incorporated in teacher training or curriculum development. How can we get school staffs to recognize that they need to renew themselves in order to remain vital and effective? Staff development is an integral part of this process, as McCleary and his team point out. The principal has the responsibility to see that well-designed programs that teach new skills and knowledge are available. The staff, on the other hand, has the obligation of realizing the need of upgrading and renewal. How many learned ten years ago about Howard Gardner's seven intellectual competencies? How little do most of us know about the new brain research and its applications in learning? There is so much more to be learned if we, as educators, want to be worthy of our trust. Staff development needs should take priority over all else.

TIME FOR STAFF DEVELOPMENT

One of my favorite literary characters is Don Quixote de la Mancha (10). This self-proclaimed knight with an old horse, a loyal squire named Sancho, and some beat-up armor, set out to right the ills of his time. As he rode along, he caught sight of 40 windmills on a wide Spanish plain. In his mind, made feverish by reading too many "Romances of Chivalry," he thought the windmills were giants. Sancho tried to convince him that they were really windmills, but Don Quixote would have nothing of it. He said, "They are giants, surely you see their long arms flailing at us." Sancho tried to tell him they were the whirling arms that make the windmills work. But Don Quixote clapped his spurs on his poor old horse and went out to do battle with the giants. He galloped up to the nearest windmill and thrust his lance through an arm. The lance broke and the windmill arm lifted Quixote up into the air. Round and round he whirled until at last he tumbled down onto the plain in Spain. How many principals know that feeling of frustration?

Sometimes I think public school principals are like Don Quixotes. Educational reform, starting with the 1983 Carnegie Report, *A Nation At Risk,* has been piling on these principals new measures of accountability, new policies and programs to ensure higher academic outcomes, new ways to develop the staff, and countless suggested remedies for all the acknowledged ills of our schools. Worthy principals have complied. Like Don Quixotes, they have jumped on their weary old horses and tried to attack all the ills (40 windmills). No wonder Don Quixote and every idealistic principal has found himself or herself thrown back time and again by the same giant. In every case the invincible giant was "time." One can't do all things in no time.

In *Prisoners of Time,* the recently released report of the National Education Commission on Time and Learning, we read, "Given the many demands made of schools today, the wonder is not that they do so poorly, but that they accomplish so much. Our society has stuffed additional burdens into the time envelope of 180 six-hour days without regard to the consequences for learning." The report goes on to say,

"The degree to which today's American school is controlled by the dynamics of clock and calendar is surprising, even to people who understand school operations:

♦ With few exceptions, schools open and close their doors at fixed times in the morning and early afternoon.

♦ With few exceptions, the school year lasts nine months, beginning in late summer and ending in late spring.

♦ According to the National Center for Education Statistics, schools typically offer a six-period day, with 5.6 hours of classroom daily.

♦ No matter how simple or complex the school subject— literature, shop, physics, gym or algebra—the schedule assigns each an impartial national average of 51 minutes per class period, no matter how well or poorly students comprehend the material.

◆ The norm for required school attendance, according to the Council of Chief State School Officers, is 180 days.

◆ Secondary school graduation requirements are universally based on "Carnegie units," a standard of measurement representing one credit for completion of a one-year course meeting daily.

◆ Staff salary increases are typically tied to time—to seniority and the number of hours of graduate work done.

◆ Despite the obsession with time, little attention is paid to how it is used: in 42 states examined by the Commission, only 41 percent of secondary school time must be spent on core academic subjects. The results are predictable. The school clock governs how families organize their lives, how administrators oversee their schools, and how teachers work their way through the curriculum. Above all, it governs how material is presented to students and the opportunity they have to comprehend and master it." (11)

The Commission's fifth recommendation states, "Give teachers the time they need." Not only are we shortchanging our students on time for core academics, we are badly handicapping our teachers when we make no provisions during the school day for the teachers to engage in staff development. Presently, there is too little time for staff development. *Without major structural changes in school scheduling, any effort at improving staff development is doomed to fail.* To quote a corollary to Murphy's law, "Everything takes longer than you expect." Providing serious staff development opportunities will take a lot more time than school boards, superintendents, Central Office staff, principals, staff, students, and parents realize. If staff development is the most important of the principal's roles, then the first duty of the principal is to fight for more time for quality staff development.

Again, in *Prisoners of Time*, we read the following:

"The daily working life of most teachers is one of unrelieved time pressure and isolation; they work largely alone in a classroom of 25–30 children or adolescents for hours every day. Unlike teachers in many systems overseas, who can take advantage of continuous, daily opportunities for professional development, American teachers have little time for preparation, planning, cooperation, or professional growth. The Commission believes that time for planning and professional development is urgently needed—not as a frill or an add-on, but as a major aspect of the agreement between teachers and districts." (12)

Members of the Commission on Time and Learning make it clear that staff development includes time to develop effective lessons; to assess students in meaningful ways and discuss the results with students individually; to talk with parents and other family members; to read professional journals and interact with their colleagues; to watch outstanding teachers demonstrate new strategies; and to participate in seminars with peers and recognized scholars in education and other fields.

TIPS FOR EFFECTIVE STAFF DEVELOPMENT

My experience tells me that the best principals play a very active role in staff development programs. Realizing that their school reflects the quality and training of their personnel, they are at pains to increase the quality and quantity of staff development. In some cases, the principal will actually take a direct role in delivering the staff development. At the Principals' Executive Program at the University of North Carolina at Chapel Hill, we have found that training principals to lead seminars with and for their staffs is one excellent way to assure good staff development. For example, a principal could lead a seminar using Prisoners of Time. (The National Education Commission on Time and Learning, *Prisoners of Time*. This 56-page booklet can be purchased for $5.50 from the U.S. Government Printing Office. Write to: Superintendent of Documents, P.O. Box 371954, Washington, D.C. 20402-9328 and ask for item 065-000-00640-5).

In order to grasp the process of staff development more completely, it will help if principals study the Staff Development Schematic produced by McCleary and his team and taken from

Domain 11, *Principals For Our Changing Schools* (13), reproduced below (cf. Fig. 2).

The schematic makes the necessary distinction between the roles of the district (school system or LEA) and the school itself in staff development. The staff of the local school must be trained to read from the same sheet of music as the whole district, but the school staff must also have staff development tailored to its unique role and mission.

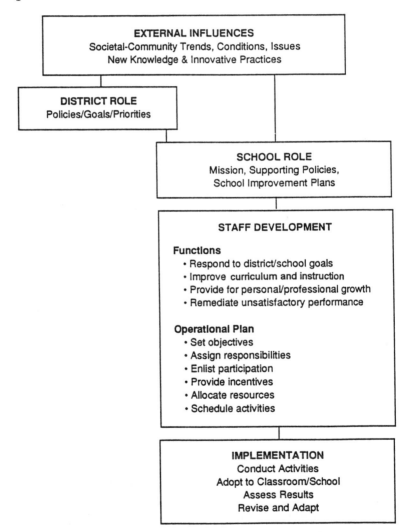

Figure 2. Staff Development Schematic

In this schematic we see that several elements are included. The authors caution us to look at the elements in an interactive and interdependent manner rather than linear. Principals are aware of the external influences on staff development both from community trends, political climate, etc. Next, the role of the Central Office must be taken into consideration. Only then can the Steward Principal and the stakeholders—taking into account the school's mission, supporting policies, and improvement plans—integrate these into their staff development plans. The authors highlight functions and offer the outline of an operational plan for staff development.

EFFECTIVE STAFF DEVELOPMENT DEPENDS ON GOOD ADULT LEARNING PRACTICES

When I think of adult learning, the name Malcolm Knowles comes immediately to my mind. He is a pioneer who did much to improve our appreciation of the way that adults learn. Knowles never tired of stating that because of their life experiences, adults and children approach learning differently. Children are quick and bright, but they suffer from having had so few life experiences. Mortimer Adler used to say we shouldn't look for wisdom from anyone until he or she is 60 years of age. Like Knowles, he was stressing the necessity of a variety of experiences as a prerequisite for profound insight. I think many staff development programs fail precisely because the leaders carry over the teaching techniques they use with children to teaching the staff. The rich experiences of the staff are wasted and insight development is postponed. When principals take charge of the staff development needs of their schools, they should review some findings from the field of adult education.

One of Malcolm Knowles' prize students, Jane Vella, is a colleague and friend of many years. She wrote a book, *Learning to Listen, Learning to Teach* (14). In chapter one, Vella offers twelve principles for effective adult learning. I recommend that principals read the whole book as a preparation for their role in leading staff development. I have, with the author's permission, reduced her twelve principles to eight tips for teaching adults, adapted for principals who are directing staff development.

EIGHT TIPS FOR EFFECTIVELY TEACHING ADULTS

1. Probe the Staff to Discover Its Development Needs.
Underlying all others is a basic assumption that adult learning
is best achieved in dialogue. That is why the seminar approach
is effective. But even prior to using seminars, it would be wise
for principals to involve the staff as they plan for staff development programs. Adults have experience and we presume some
self-knowledge, so we can consult them to find out what it is
they need for staff development. I like the story about the Boy
Scout who helped an old man across a street only to find out he
never wanted to go there in the first place. The Boy Scout should
not get a merit badge for performing an unwanted service. I
have seen many attempts at staff development go awry because
the planning was done by central office or the principal without
consulting the participants. The big questions are: how and what
does the group want and need to learn? What do its members
know? What parts of the planned program really fit their situation? What parts would be superfluous?

We suggest that principals form a small group of staff members who will do a "needs analysis" of the staff. I have always
thought of staff development as a two-pronged operation. On
one prong, the whole staff needs to be developed together as a
team to better accomplish the school vision. On the other, the
individual staff members should have their own professional
developmental needs addressed. The principal is responsible for
both prongs.

A metaphor may make it clearer. When most of us open up a
box containing the parts of a jigsaw puzzle, we are careful to
hold onto the boxtop because it contains a picture of the puzzle
completed. It is possible to put together a jigsaw puzzle without
seeing what the completed picture will look like, but it is much
harder. When a principal and his or her staff development team
start thinking about designing staff development programs, it
is imperative that they have a picture of what the school will
look like when the staff continues to develop. Put in another
way, without a vision of what the school is trying to become, it
is almost impossible to do effective staff development planning.
Staff development is only one part of the big picture. Beyond
asking the staff what they think they need to learn, we should

also ask them how they will use what they learn in order to implement the school's shared vision and their own professional careers.

It becomes apparent that central office most certainly can and should help with staff development to make sure the schools are moving in the direction that the school system or district is going; however, it is mandatory that central office or other consultants see clearly the picture on the jigsaw puzzle box. Site management demands a shared vision, and the staff development must always be tailored to that mission or vision.

On the individual level, I often think a principal would do well to spend more time with individual staff members helping them to express their own personal visions. What is it they want to accomplish in the field of education? In my experience, the majority of teachers and other staff have spent little time thinking about their own professional development goals. Up until now in school work, the only way to be promoted was to become a principal. How often have we seen excellent teachers leave the classroom only to become mediocre administrators? There are many master teachers who don't care to go into administration, preferring to stay on as teachers; but for financial reasons, they have to give up classroom teaching to take the only ladder upward.

As schools become Learning Organizations in the 21st century, teachers and staff will find many new professional employment opportunities. There will be master teachers with limited classroom duties who spend half their time in training and developing other teachers. There will be teachers who spend a large portion of their time with parents. Others will be working with local business representatives to ensure that schooling is in alignment with employment opportunities. Some staff will be educational designers who spend time helping improve the learning environments in the school. Once we discover that the time frame can be changed in schools, many good things will happen. Teachers won't need to spend the lion's share of their time standing in front of 25–30 students controlling their behavior. We'll discover that children can take a more active role in teaching and class management. Just as in the delivery of health services, we will begin to allow adults with less training than our present teachers have to assume many of the duties now restricted to teachers. Like John Frazier, we'll learn that nurses, park rangers, recreation specialists, landscape gardeners, fire fighters, police officers, and city planners can educate outside the classroom. Then we will begin to have a system that will allow the staff to think more precisely about what part of the educational jigsaw they would like to be able to fill.

Suppose we discovered that there were 21 domains of knowledge and skill that a teacher should have? It wouldn't be surprising if some teachers did better in one set of seven while another functioned more comfortably in a different set of seven. Not all doctors perform major surgery, and not all dentists do root canals. Many teachers who are good "coaches" are poor lecturers. Must every teacher lecture, even those who find it next to impossible? Why can't they spend their time coaching or leading seminars, or devising new experiences for team learning? Even now, steward-principals are taking more time to listen to the staff individually and in groups. They want to design staff development to make it fit into the big picture. When we have cooperative learning, team teaching, flexible scheduling and integrating themes, we will get much better performances from our staff. In preparation for that day, good principals are helping individual staff members to better understand where their strengths and weaknesses lie. They are helping them to craft a career in education that will enhance their own gifts and talents and dovetail into a team approach. Without the picture on the box, it is difficult to know where we are going and how to get there. The staff as a whole and the individual staff members will be trained best if they are asked to look at the big picture and determine where they need staff development at the district, school site, and personal level.

2. The Quality of the Relationship Between Learner and Leader Is Key to the Success of Staff Development. In teaching adults (staff development), we often fail to realize that the quality of the relationship between the leader and the other learners is as important, if not more important, as it is between younger students and their teachers. Because the staff is made up of experienced adults who can accurately judge the competence and compassion of the lead-learner, it is important that the principal and staff choose a trainer who can establish rapport with adult learners.

Staff wants to be assured that the lead-learner is capable of designing a learning experience in which all participants will feel safe. Teachers are extremely sensitive about being put in a position in which their lack of knowledge or skill becomes apparent to others in the group. One of the difficulties with some staff development leaders is their insensitivity to the teachers' need for safety and security. They show this by setting objectives that are unreachable, and sending negative messages to the participants. Sometimes a visiting Ph.D. with a huge briefcase and a 24-page resume assumes specialized knowledge the participants don't have. He or she talks over their heads using incomprehensible technical jargon. The expert never allows the staff to work in small groups where they have a chance to find their voices and get support in the unfamiliar territory. Such staff development is worse than a waste of time.

One of the defects I have witnessed in staff development arises when the lead-learner starts off in the middle of a complex theory, skipping over the early stages in the development of the theory, body of knowledge, or set of skills. He or she doesn't begin with simple, clear, and reasonably easy approaches to the subject, instead intimidating the participants the way some math teachers do by assuming that the in-between steps are just obvious. This type of lead-learner fails to sequence the material. It is a fatal flaw.

Others neglect the current experience of the staff. Experts sometimes forget that all learning goes from the known to the unknown. The lead-learner needs to devote sufficient time to listening to the participants and finding out what they know. Suppose a lead-learner is discussing the theory of Multiple Intelligence. He or she should begin with a brief overview of the seven intellectual competencies in the theory. Then it would be helpful to allow the participants to break up into small groups in which they can connect their teaching experience to the theory. A good lead-learner will make sure that the staff members feel safe as they expand their teaching techniques to take advantage of the seven intelligences. The lead-learner affirms the contributions of those who are willing to speak up in the large group. He or she admits the group is dealing with new material, but shows how teachers have used some of it for many years. In quality staff development, the lead-learner is a compassionate, competent communicator who knows that the staff will teach each other if the atmosphere is safe, interesting, entertaining, engrossing, non-threatening, and very affirming. The visiting expert may do all these things and do them well. On the other hand, there are often staff members in your schools who, with some coaching, could be very effective lead-learners. Much of their effectiveness would derive from the positive relationship they already have with other staff members.

3. Good Staff Developers Use Sequence and Reinforcement. Whether the lead-learner who conducts the staff development is an expert from over 100 miles away carrying a fancy leather attache case, or a member of the local staff, the need for sequence and reinforcement is the same. In adult education there is an axiom: do it 1,142 times and you have learned it. That used to be an axiom for all education at the skill level, but now we live in an "instant jello" age in which all repetition is boring. Where is the old adage, *Repetitio est mater scientiae*—Repetition is the mother of knowledge? A good lead-learner makes sure that in staff development the programming of knowledge, skill, and attitudes is designed in an order that goes from simple to complex, and from group supported to solo. This assures the feeling of safety in the participants. When the participants have time to assimilate the new learning into their own patterns, they are highly motivated and manifest enthusiasm and a readiness to achieve.

Principals have the obligation to make sure that the lead-learners who conduct staff development follow the very clear guidelines that make adult learning effective. Sequencing and reinforcement are essential parts. Both presuppose that we accept the definition of teaching as showing someone how to do something. Good staff development calls upon coaching and seminar teaching as means of sequencing and reinforcing.

4. Good Staff Development Rests on a Foundation of Praxis. As a principal you know from experience that any learning worth its salt includes the element of *praxis*. *Praxis* is a Greek word that means "action with reflection." Gabriel Moran's definition of teaching—showing someone how to do something—implies that someone is actively doing something, and the learning comes about because the doing is reflective. When your staff takes part in staff development, the lead-learner should design the learning experiences in such a way that each of the participants is working on a project, either alone or with other team members. Learning is possible only if the learner or learners are actively engaged in doing something. They must have a fairly clear idea of what it is they are trying to accomplish, and they need feedback on how they are progressing. Only with reflection after some coaching will the learners begin to grasp the total process.

Once a week I play the role of student by attending a community college for a three-hour session called "Expressions in Oil Painting." I am one of a dozen students ranging in age from mid-twenties to the late seventies. In the first class of each quarter our lead-learner gives a 30-minute lecture. After that he does no didactic teaching. He spends all his time coaching us individually. He comes over and sits next to us as we paint. When he is coaching one of us and wants to impart some information to the whole group, he simply raises his voice and briefly notes something he believes will help all of us. He has taught us in sequence to crawl, creep, walk, and run. He reinforces us by commenting on how well our paintings are progressing, even as he makes a suggestion here or there to improve something like a shadow. For most of us, this is just a pleasant way to spend an evening. There are a few who really catch fire and spend much time outside class reading books and practicing color mixing, brush strokes, composition, sketching, etc. As the classes progress, a more experienced student, one who has caught fire, will come over, look at my painting, compliment me, and show me how to get a certain effect by using a little yellow ochre. The attitude in the class is not competitive but rather that of a team trying to help all the members learn more. The teacher always tells us to get our pictures framed and bring them back to show him and the class. He makes sure that our hard-won successes become reinforcing agents that fuel our enthusiasm. I would be surprised if my art teacher, a musical director in a Methodist Church, could spell out the principles of adult learning, but he surely practices them very well.

Too often in staff development the leader acts as if deductive learning is all that is required. In a lecture, the leader imparts knowledge, reviews the deductive reasoning that led to the conclusions, and gives the participants a pep talk on why they should follow the conclusions. Unfortunately, in this setting it is all too easy for the participants to miss the point.

For this reason experts in this field stress the importance of *Praxis*. *Praxis* is doing with built-in reflection. It beautifully choreographs the dance of inductive and deductive forms of learning. The skilled lead-learner makes certain that the participants are actively using *inductive* learning, which moves from the particular to the general, as well as *deductive*, which moves from the general to the particular situation. When the lead-learner sets a group of adults to practicing a skill and invites them to analyze the quality of their experience, that moves the learning forward to *praxis*, and elicits the principles of all adult learning: reflections on the action, connecting it to past experience, and sharing with peers.

When principals at the Principals' Executive Program work cooperatively on School Improvement Plans, it leads to *praxis*, which opens new approaches to future learning. Principals know they have good *praxis* when participants are reflecting on these four questions:

1. What do you see happening here ? (description)
2. Why do you think it is happening? (analysis)
3. When it happens in your school, what problems does it cause? (application)
4. What can we do about it? (implementation)

5. Make Room for Ideas, Feelings, and Actions in Staff Development. The skilled lead-learner stresses learning with the mind, emotions, and muscles—or attention to the cognitive/affective/psychomotor aspects of adult learning. Frequently, schools hire a famous educator to give a half-day program. He or she lectures for three hours as if in a graduate class at the university to a staff of two hundred sitting in an auditorium. They are presented a mass of very erudite cognitive matter: information, data, and facts. It is all good stuff, but the staff just can't assimilate it and make it relevant to what they do. This formal lecture approach is not an efficient way to do staff development.

Most learning involves more than cognitive material. It should take into consideration feelings and activities. We are run by our emotions more often than by our ideas. Finally, nothing happens with the "learning" unless it is put into action. The guest professor should have designed the session so that staff could have had time in small groups in which they consider conceptual, affective and psychomotor aspects of the material. One reason seminars work so well is that they seem to allow room for all three dimensions. The same can be said about cooperative learning, and other well-led small group work.

6. The Best Staff Development Puts Emphasis on Immediacy. Like most children, every night my father asked me, "What did you learn in school today?" I found it hard to answer, because, although we had been exposed to a mass of cognitive material in a variety of subjects, I was at a total loss as to what relevancy any of it had to my life as an 11-year-old boy, or to my father who to me knew practically everything in the world. More often than not I solved the problem by saying, "Nothing spectacular." He then countered with the question, "Why do you go to school then?" Again with some pain I would answer, "Because you make me go. It is the law." He invariably laughed and let the matter drop. Now, 65 years later, I think I know why I couldn't give a better answer. We learn things without even knowing that we learned them. I'm sure that if we had studied the state capitals that day, and if my father had asked me, "What is the capital of New York State?", I would have been able to answer.

Of course, I learned something in school everyday, but I didn't grasp the *connectedness* between what the teacher was professing and the rest of my life. If I had a project which entailed finding a way to get a free map of New York State, with some coaching I would have found that Albany was the capital and that the New York State Tourist Department in the Department of Commerce was located there. Using the ZIP Code book I would have discovered the address and ZIP Code. If I had done all that, I am sure I would have told my father all about it. I would have told him how I found a way to learn the capital of every state and how to get free maps from their travel bureaus. Best of all, I would show him the map of New York State when it came. It was true of you and me as kids, and it is still true: we learn by doing something real.

Of course, we have to make time for staff development, but when we do have the time we have to use it sensibly. Too much staff development in the past lacked immediacy. The staff didn't see the immediate usefulness of the new learning. Most adults don't have time to waste. If they are going to devote time to staff development, they want to get something out of it that will improve what they are doing. They want to see something in hand as soon as possible. The participants will continue to be motivated only with some immediate results that can be applied in the real world of the school or classroom. Good lead-learners end each session with a question like this: "How can you use this new skill, knowledge, understanding to improve your professional work?"

7. When the Roles Are Clear, Staff Development Rolls Smoothly. Malcolm Knowles has always insisted on another vital principle in adult education. Success of adult education depends on the clarity of roles in communication between lead-learner and the other learners. The lead-learner may want to have a dialogue with an adult learner, but if the learner sees the leader as "the professor" with whom there can be no disagreement, no questioning or challenging, then dialogue is impossible. In staff development, it is imperative that the participants and the lead-learner function as equals. It is not a power relationship.

One of the highlights in my life was teaching in the same program as Mortimer Adler at the University of North Carolina at Chapel Hill. Adler is a scholar-educator now in his 90s, a man for whom I have had the utmost respect for over 50 years. I have seen him conduct seminars with principals and observed him openly disagreeing with the opinion of one of them, hoping it would lead to dialogue. Instead, the principal buckled, giving in to the "expert," which disappointed Adler. On the other hand, I have seen Adler conduct a seminar on Hamlet with fifth graders in which students unaware of Adler's prestige, wisdom, and experience would boldly state their own reasons and battle for them in opposition to Adler. The wise old man, because of age and poor health, is no longer able to lead seminars but how he loved the give and take of good dialogue. I know it isn't easy for teachers to confront each other in public, but if dialogue is the key to good staff development, we need to encourage the leader and the participants to dialogue politely and civilly as equals.

When Mortimer Adler was in his late 80s, he still came to speak at the University of North Carolina, but he refused to give a talk that lasted more than 20 minutes. However, he would answer questions for over an hour after his mini-lecture. I have learned a great deal from sitting in on these illuminating discussions. They were made possible because this great intellectual luminary lived out his belief that dialogue depends on clear roles of equality between lead-learner and all others. This is the secret of good staff development. Dialogue among equals is not a pooling of ignorance. It is the beginning of learning for understanding for the participants and leader.

When selecting lead-learners, principals will do well to note how skillful the lead-learner is in getting dialogue flowing. When you ask the participants to evaluate a session of staff development, you will invariably find that the high marks go to the lead-learner who can put the participants at ease and get them into a lively dialogue. This takes real skill, humility, and self-discipline.

8. Accountability Is the Key to Good Staff Development. When a lead-learner designs a session of staff development, he or she must be accountable to the learners. What is proposed to be taught must be taught; what was meant to be learned must be learned; the skills intended to be mastered must be manifest in all the learners; the attitudes taught must be apparent in the behavior of the learners; and the knowledge conveyed must now be discernible in the language and reasoning of the participants.

I have been writing as if all the responsibility for staff development rested with the principal. This is not the case at all. If the principal is functioning as a steward, then he or she will be dealing with the stakeholder as partners. Partners have emotional responsibility for their own present and their future. When teachers are participants in staff development, they have responsibility and accountability for the process just as the principal does.

The outcomes and quality of cooperation within a school are everyone's responsibility. Each is responsible for maintaining faith, hope, and spirit. The Steward Principal is not solely responsible for morale, learning, or career development of the stakeholders. As partners in running the school, teachers are partners in running the staff development. They should be on the lookout for the best lead-learners available and suggest that the principal try to enlist their services. When we talk about accountability in a true partnership, we must conclude the principal, teachers and other staff all bear accountability for the success or failure of staff development.

When we talk about a servant-leader, we have to realize that it will take time for us to assimilate all the meaning contained in that juxtaposition of words. Instinctively we think of a leader as one who has power and gives orders to servants whose job it is to obey the orders complying with the mandates. This new way of thinking about leadership will take some getting used to. At first glance servant-leader appears to be an oxymoron. We have lived through a period of history in which our leaders have for the most part tended to be autocratic and impersonal. Now as we move into the knowledge society, we realize that the leaders who succeed in the 21st century will be cut from a different bolt of cloth. There won't be much room or need for autocratic bosses in the knowledge society when human talent (knowledge and skills) will become the coin of the realm. They will be much more humane, inclusive, participative, personally and culturally sensitive, and committed to a cooperative rather than a competitive approach to work. We will measure the success of leaders not merely by quarterly profits, but by how much followers reach their potentials. As long as land, machines, and capital are no longer in the driver's seat, leaders will have to recruit talented workers and treat them the way football or basketball coaches treat their star players.

SUMMATION

In Chapter 1, we have pointed out the importance of the principal's role in staff development. It is helpful to have a source like Domain 11 in *Principals For Our Changing Schools* to give us a framework. If principals study this material, they will understand what they need to know and be able to do in order to effectively direct staff development. The comprehensive definition offered by McCleary and his team, coupled with the Staff Development Schematic, cover the parameters of staff development well.

Granting the importance of staff development as stated in Domain 11, we demonstrated the hypocrisy of admitting the importance of staff development while at the same time refusing to set aside the time, money, and effort necessary to make it effective. For Total Quality staff development, time must be set aside for the work, and the best planning and talent must be utilized.

We offered the Eight Recommendations from the report of the National Education Commission on Time and Learning in support of this approach with special emphasis on Recommendation Number Five, "Give Teachers Time." Over the last 25 years, schools have accepted more responsibilities without expanding time or staff to handle them. Some educators believe that the encroachment on staff development has been one of the most serious effects of this crunch. Teachers need time for development daily, weekly, and monthly.

Recognizing that the school district has a role in staff development as well as the school itself, we offered principals and central office personnel some effective tips on improving staff development based on research in adult education. It will do no good to merely increase the time set aside for staff development if we maintain flawed approaches. Finally, the "Eight Tips On Effective Adult Learning" should be helpful to the principal as well as Central Office personnel as they try to improve the quality of training. No school is better than the quality of its staff development.

QUESTIONS FOR REFLECTION

1. Why should every school strive to be a Learning Organization?

2. Do you agree that the first priority for a Steward Principal should be staff development? If so, why so; if not, why not?

3. Why should the first step in staff development consist in "needs analysis"?

4. In *Prisoners of Time* the National Commission on Time and Learning recommends that we allow to teachers the time they need for staff development. Why don't we take this seriously?

5. Jane Vella insists in her book *Learning to Listen, Learning to Teach* that the quality of the relationship between the staff and the Learner-Leader is of paramount importance. Do you agree? Why?

6. What do we mean when we say good staff development rests on a foundation of *praxis*?

7. Any staff development session which doesn't include: mind, emotion, and muscle shortchanges the staff? Is this true?

8. Why is the use of the seminar or dialogue method so apt for teachers' staff development?

9. Staff development seems to go best when all the staff members grasp the connection between what is going on in the session and their actual daily practice. Why is this immediacy so important to teachers?

10. "When the roles are clear, staff development rolls smoothly." What happens when the roles aren't clear in staff development?

3

THE STEWARD PRINCIPAL
USES ASSESSMENT
WISELY

The wise tailor measures twice and cuts only once.

Principals know they need to use assessment to measure each student's progress as a thinking, social, responsibly self-assured person. Schools try to produce educated persons who as productive members of society will work efficiently and effectively, vote wisely, and engage in lifelong learning. What if the means of assessment used by the schools actually interfered with the progress of the student's thinking as a social, responsible assured person? A most interesting headline appeared in our local paper as I was finishing this chapter. The headline read: "Teachers Seek Oasis of Learning for Test-Worn Students." The article reported that a group of 100 instructors were selected by the North Carolina Governor's Standards and Accountability Commission to ensure that students learn the state curriculum, not just ways to pass a battery of exams. The 100 instructors are to prod other teachers to rethink the way students are judged, moving away from merely number of tests. Students in the last decade have spent an unprecedented amount of time filling in answer sheets, but more testing has not produced more learning. "It never will," according to Grant Wiggins a consultant

with the governor's office. Wiggins said, "Students need ongoing assessment of their work, and testing doesn't do that. Testing is little more than a classroom audit." He insists that testing
should become one step in the learning process rather than the
end point of the lesson. The end point should be the mastery of
a skill regardless of how long that might take. A skill might take
some students a day or two to master, while requiring a week or
more for others. Some students might need more hours in the
day or even extra Saturday sessions in order to meet the higher
goals. Better prepared students might delve deeper into some
subjects, or spend the extra time on subjects in which they are
weaker.

I have noted in the last decade more principals are complaining that deeper student understanding is often sacrificed in favor of preparation for tests measuring factual retention. Some
say it is a case of the tail wagging the dog. Testing that should be
a means to improve the ability of the students to think and understand instead becomes an obstacle to this end. Yet it may not
be easy to get teachers to give up their practice of teaching for
the tests.

Ruth Mitchell in her fine book *Testing for Learning* (15) tells
us that retooling the school system will entail changing assessment. Of course, we need good assessment to know how we are
doing but if we are using faulty assessment and if assessment
drives instruction, then some assessment could be doing more
harm than good. Mitchell points, "Between 1955-1986, the dollar volume of sales of tests at the elementary and secondary level
grew by 400 percent and are probably now 1/2 billion dollars a
year." (16) The baby boom—1946 to 1964—started a wave of demographic growth in the schools that might account for the increase in standardized multiple-choice testing. This type of test,
which entails choosing a single answer from among a small
number of prepared possible answers, has had a bad effect on
instruction. Administrators and politicians care about the results
of these tests because they are concerned with how their district
or school looks to the outside world. Of course, the teachers are
pressured into teaching for the tests. This type of test and that
type of teaching does little to help a student become a thinking,
social, self-assured person with a deep love of learning.

The story of Herb may make this more clear. Herb is a rather talkative high school principal who made a valiant effort to dominate a recent discussion in one of my classes. The class of principals was discussing the advisability of introducing flexible scheduling to give teachers an opportunity to use different teaching styles such as seminars and team teaching, and to offer students an opportunity to deepen their understanding of concepts. Flexible scheduling which allows for two-hour blocks of time, makes it possible for teachers to spend time on planning, student and parent interviews, etc. Most of the principals were favorable to the idea, but Herb offered his argument against flexible scheduling. He announced to the class that his best teachers were against this innovation because it could take control away from them making it more difficult to prepare their students to do well on the tests. They couldn't take the risk with flexible scheduling and seminars, etc. Granted, the students might improve their understanding of the concepts; nonetheless, this gain wouldn't be reflected on the test results. Depth of understanding is not measured on these tests. As a result, their own rating as teachers might go down. So Herb warned us to avoid wasting our time encouraging teachers to change their teaching styles to increase student understanding. The "best" teachers, whose "best" rating is determined by the success of their students on end-of-the-year tests, are wise enough to see that the status quo is their best assurance that they will retain their high rating. Why, asked Herb, would teachers who are successful want to change their procedures?

One of the most cynical remarks I ever heard about school reform was made to me by a veteran superintendent who was about to retire. He said, "I learned one thing about reforming the school system or any particular school. You can change anything in the system or a school if it doesn't inconvenience any adults." Like Herb, this superintendent was aware that the system was the problem. The "good" teachers did what the system demanded: teach for tests. When an innovation like seminars or flexible scheduling was introduced that might help the students learn for understanding, the teachers were unmotivated because they knew the system would not reward them for what couldn't be measured on the multiple-choice tests. It is a Catch-22.

Accountants and other financial managers have a saying, "What is measured tends to improve." There is some merit to this dictum, but there is also a hidden trap. What is measured tends to improve only if what is measured is given higher priority than the measurement itself. I have seen companies taken over by the Chief Financial Officers fail. Although they made sure that everything measurable was measured accurately, they missed the point that some of the most important things were not amenable to measurement. It is very difficult to measure commitment, creativity, morale, loyalty, etc. Yet most companies succeed if they share these qualities and fail without them even if they measure everything else accurately.

In the fall of 1989, the National Governor's Association met with President Bush at an "educational summit" in which they agreed that there was a national emergency in the field of education. In the spring of 1990, the National Governors' Association announced the national goals for American education. It was called Goals 2000, because it promised "every school in America will ensure that all students learn to use their minds well so they may be prepared for responsible citizenship, further learning, and productive employment in our nation's modern economy." The Governors are quite aware that this goal will not be met in 2000.

When tests are limited to measuring the retention of facts or test-taking skills that are the most ephemeral of all outcomes, and fail to assess knowledge and understanding that will have sustained value, we had better re-examine the roles of tests, measurement, assessment, and evaluation in our schools.

TESTS ARE ONLY ONE OF THE NECESSARY MEANS TO ASSESS LEARNING

Domain 12 in *Principals For Our Changing Schools* is a gold mine for our discussion on assessment in the schools and especially the role the principal must play in this process. Richard J. Stiggins and Judith A. Arter as leader and associate leader have provided principals with an excellent review of the knowledge and skills they need in order to assure sound assessment in an effective school. The first service they and their team members provide is a definition.

Measurement and Evaluation: Determine what diagnostic information is needed about students, staff, and the school environment; examining the extent to which outcomes meet or exceed previously defined standards, goals, or priorities for individuals or groups; drawing inferences for program revisions; interpreting measurements or evaluations for others; relating programs to desired outcomes; developing equivalent measures of competence; designing accountability mechanisms. (17)

If we accept this omnibus definition, we find Steward Principals should have knowledge and skill in seven areas.

1) Principals should be able to determine what diagnostic information is needed about students, staff, and school environment.

2) Principals should be able to examine the extent to which outcomes meet or exceed standards, goals, and priorities for individuals and groups.

3) Principals should be able to draw inferences for program revisions.

4) Principals should be able to interpret measurements and evaluations for others (students, parents, teachers, business community representatives, Central Office, etc.).

5) Principals should be able to relate programs to desired outcomes.

6) Principals should be able to develop equivalent measures of competence.

7) Principals should be able to design accountability mechanisms.

Take a moment to assess yourself as a principal or aspiring principal on each of these seven skills and knowledges. Rate yourself from 1–15 on each with "1" being almost no knowledge and skill in the area, and "15" indicating total mastery of the area. Add them up and you will find your total mark. It would be a rare principal who scores above 70. Why? Because principals have not been prepared in this area. Years ago I taught courses in Educational Statistics and Tests and Measurements. Teachers and principals were less than enthralled by these subjects. Although principals today are much more knowledgeable, they still don't have sufficient preparation to accomplish the seven tasks above. In my experience, the principals look to experts at Central Office to help them understand new assessment methods. If we look at the last three tasks, "relating programs to desired outcomes, developing equivalent measures of competence, and designing accountability mechanisms," I believe most principals would admit they feel inadequate in these areas. What to do? Central Office should offer more help to teachers and principals so they can exert more influence on the way assessment is used. With more input from knowledgeable principals and teachers, we will integrate assessment into the process of teaching rather than using it like an IRS audit aimed at monitoring the administrator and teachers. To accomplish this, both principals and teachers need to learn how to develop equivalent measures of competence, and design their own accountability mechanisms.

Developing a challenging curriculum and high academic standards for all students may help us to find the proper place for measurement and evaluation at the district and school building level. Teacher-made tests, and tests that don't count (coaching guides) are two ways that many teachers use assessment and evaluation as tools for improved learning, as a means to relate programs to desired outcomes. However, tests are often used improperly and sabotage the educational system. If children K–4 are so demoralized by their poor test results that thereafter they lack the self-assuredness necessary to take the risks involved in new learning, we have created a monster. If Herb is right, if his "best" teachers teach only for the tests and will not improve students' learning at the risk of lowering their own ranking, then we have much work to do. Principals in my opinion want to know more about how to use measurement and evaluation better. They are angry because so much of the assessment comes from the state or district level, and seems to be blind to the impact of demographics on a school. They are aware that many teachers teach for tests, and they see many students lost in the process.

THE PRINCIPAL WEARS THREE ASSESSMENT HATS

What should a principal know about the testing that is taking place in his or her school, district, state, and country? It all depends upon which of the three hats the principal is wearing at the time. The principal has three roles: *instructional leader, instructional manager, and communication facilitator.* A framework of assessment competencies should reflect current thinking about the three roles.

- ♦ As instructional leaders, principals have prime responsibility for developing and implementing a vision of assessment integrated with classroom instruction.

- ♦ As instructional managers, they must be informed users of assessment in their management of the decision making process.

- ♦ As communication facilitators, principals must promptly and accurately deliver sound assessment information to those who make decisions within and beyond the school building (teachers, students, parents, district personnel, community members, etc.).

To help the process even more, principals have to address this question: does assessment as now practiced in your school primarily serve as a monitor, or as an aid to improve student outcomes?

A BROADER AND BETTER VIEW OF ASSESSMENT

Principals know that many students come to school unprepared to learn. They have little or no intellectual stimulation at home. They seldom eat a sit-down meal with both parents and siblings. They have no time or place set aside to do homework. The parent or parents seem uninterested in their children's academic success or failure, and hold out no expectations that their children will graduate from high school. The home is without books or magazines, yet the TV is never off. The conversation is banal, totally lacking in mental stimulation. The daily schedule is unpredictable. The children can stay up as late as they wish, and they often oversleep in the morning and miss school.

Many principals would agree with William A. Henry III, the late theatre critic of *Time* magazine. He died last year at 44 years of age just after finishing his book, *In Defense of Elitism*. He died fighting what he believed to be the assault on the intellectual attributes he valued most: "respect and even deference for leadership and position; esteem for accomplishment, especially achieved through long labor and rigorous education; reverence for heritage, particularly history, philosophy, and culture; commitment to rationalism and scientific investigation; upholding of objective standards; most important, the willingness to assert unyieldingly that one idea, contribution, or attainment is better than another." My father, who had only eight years of formal schooling, held the same belief system. So did my grandfather, who went to school for only four years. They lived in a society that respected these intellectual attributes, and did all in their power to get them for their sons and daughters. Principals realize that if these attributes aren't modeled in the home, the students will have to look to society. If society is cavalier about these attributes, holding for high standards only for the Baseball and Football Halls of Fame and the Oscars and Tonys, how can the youth of the country be expected to come to school motivated to work hard to accomplish academic greatness?

Many principals say, "You can't teach students to espouse these intellectual virtues if they don't get them at home or in society. And it doesn't help when the school uses most of its academic time preparing students to give the correct test answers rather than to pursue excellence in searching for the truth."

In an earlier book, I alluded to a freshman class at Harvard in which the professor asked this question, "How many of you think there is one answer to every question and the teacher or professor knows what that answer is?" To his amazement all 35 students raised their hands. Then he inquired, "Are you kidding me? Do you really mean to say that for every question there is one answer and some authority figure knows what that answer is?" Speaking out almost the way a Greek chorus does, they answered, "That is what got us here." These bright young students knew they had played the game to perfection, satisfying the most demanding admission officers in the country. They were aware that for the most part they had been given little or no time for reflecting, observing, theorizing, seeking, discussing, and exploring around and behind concepts. Instead, they memorized facts and sharpened their test-taking skills. It worked. They were at Harvard.

Now in college, would it be more of the same? Or would they be allowed to satisfy their repressed intellectual cravings? Would they now have a chance to approach concepts leisurely— something you can't do preparing for a timed multiple-choice test?

Most principals are aware that full understanding of a concept of any complexity cannot be restricted to a single mode of knowing or way of representation. Suppose someone were to ask you if you understood the meaning of democracy. I would reply that I was first exposed to the concept in the early 1920s when I went into first grade. Though even before that I can remember, if vaguely, that my mother and father talked about democracy in my presence. I remember my father was a registered Democrat. My mother was not registered to vote when I was born because women weren't allowed to vote until November 1920. If I am not mistaken, my mother registered as a Democrat when she got the franchise to vote. I knew that in the U.S. democracy in which we lived, there were three parties: Democratic, Republican, and Socialist. Our mayor was a member of the Socialist party. I realized that in a democracy a citizen could choose to vote for the party of his or her choice. That still wasn't much knowledge about democracy.

Later when I studied Greek, I learned that the word "democracy" comes from the Greek word "demos," which signifies the common people, and "cracy," which means to rule or govern. So democracy means a government by the people, exercised directly or through representatives. It was in high school when I was elected president of the freshman class that I got a deeper understanding of what it meant to be elected to represent someone else. I had to campaign against others who were seeking the position. Then I had to abide by the vote of my classmates. When they chose me, as they did for four years, I tried to represent them well. I realized I served at their pleasure.

Now in my 77th year, I have voted in about 98 percent of the possible elections. I have read reams of material on democracy, and I have a fuller understanding of what it means to live in a democracy. Having visited the former USSR and other non-democratic countries, I know a little more about what a democracy is not. Yet I am still trying to understand the concept better. If I can live ten more years, I will better understand democracy. Just as it has taken decades to understand democracy, it would take multiple methods across many disciplines to assess my knowledge of this concept. Mortimer Adler has chosen 102 great ideas as the basis for a liberal education. Democracy is one of them.

How can some teachers say, "Oh, we covered democracy in sixth grade and it was tested on the End-of-Grade exam." If I were given a standardized test with one multiple-choice question on democracy, the test would not determine my grasp of this complex concept. It could check my ability to spell "democracy" but not much more. If you sat down with me and asked me oral questions about democracy, and we had an hour or more to talk, you could get some idea of the depth and breadth of my understanding of the subject. Whether it is democracy, pleasure/pain, or concepts like liberty, religion, and temperance, one needs experience—some glad, some sad—to fully understand. Tests that can be machine scored cannot measure the grasp one has on these ideas.

APPROPRIATE ASSESSMENT CAN AID LEARNING FOR UNDERSTANDING

Howard Gardner in his *The Unschooled Mind* (18) offers some very helpful ideas on learning for understanding. I found his Five Entry Points very helpful.

Gardner tells us that even students who are well trained, who exhibit all the signs of success—faithful attendance, high grades, high test scores, praise from teachers—typically do not display an adequate understanding of the material and concepts with which they have been working. He says teaching for understanding must have the highest priority. If teaching is merely aimed at getting students to score well on standardized tests, then we are working at cross purposes. The student needs to learn for understanding if he or she is to make it in the highly competitive global marketplace. If we teach for tests that can't measure deeper understanding, and if we reward and punish students on the results of such tests alone, we fail in our main goal to maximize students' learning.

Of course we need assessment in schools. But what kinds of assessment? How much of them? When? For what purposes? By what means? To whose advantage? Under what circumstances? At what cost?

There seems to be little debate about the fact that some of our American colleges and universities are world-class. In these excellent institutions, there are students who are able to learn for understanding. They will be able to compete well in the world market. Unfortunately, many college graduates have not gained these higher thinking skills. In my opinion, too many of our college students have not been challenged to learn for understanding. What is even more appalling is the amount of remedial work colleges must do, and the plight of 70 percent of our students who won't graduate from any college. They will lack the skills to learn for understanding. How can we start earlier in K-12 to stress learning for understanding? Improving assessment may be the first step.

Dennie Wolf of Harvard has referred to the performance assessment movement as "the flying wedge of school reform." Howard Gardner makes it clear that five-year-olds entering school for the first time have theories and hold dearly to them. They are *intuitive learners* who are superbly equipped to learn language and other symbolic systems, and who have evolved serviceable theories of the physical world and of the world of other people. Once in school these *intuitive learners*—creative, universal, natural and naive thinkers—quickly become traditional students, or *scholastic learners*. From age seven to 12 or 13, they are forced to learn the literacies, concepts, and disciplinary forms of school. At this stage in their young lives, they seem to split into two people. In school they act as *scholastic learners* (this is true whether they are successful or not in producing standard performances). Outside school on the other hand, they respond in similar ways to preschool or primary school youngsters as *intuitive learners.* When schools begin to use better performance assessment, they will help students connect their intuitive learning with their scholastic learning. The newer ways of assessing that include portfolios, seminars, projects etc. will help students and teachers to assess for both surface and natural knowledge.

Surface knowledge is anything a robot can be programmed to know. There is very little connectedness with other knowledges, with social and emotional issues or with other aspects of the learner's psyche. On the other hand, *natural knowledge* seems to have real significance to the learner. Every individual brings to every learning situation a font of knowledge that is personally meaningful. It is perceptual knowledge, the kind that people use to organize their grasp of the world in which they live. Every school subject can enhance the capacity of students to "read" their world. We must both teach and assess students in a way that points out real relationships and connections between the subjects and the students' present life experiences. Good teachers have always taught that way but they couldn't assess that way. Children from five to 15 need to be exposed to educational experiences both inside and outside school, which will activate *scholastic knowledge* and *intuitive learning* for understanding. The first step in this revolution demands that we find means of assessment that don't prejudice teaching in the direction of merely *scholastic knowledge*—presented as *surface knowledge*. Without assessment, there is no guarantee that learning for understanding has taken place. Now our task is to discover as many ways as possible to help students assess themselves and learn from feedback filtered through others how much they are learning for understanding. The ultimate aim of all assessment is to lead learners to that stage of development in which they can reliably and validly assess themselves. As we discover better ways to assess learning for understanding, we will begin to teach in ways that will help students use all seven intelligences in a creative and exciting way.

WAYS TO ASSESS LEARNING FOR UNDERSTANDING

The best assessment is and has always been self-assessment. The Greek philosophers have told us from the beginning to know ourselves. Genuine disciplinary experts (masters of their fields who have deep understanding of their world and of other people), exhibit superb gifts of self-appraisal or -assessment. They know what they know and what they don't know. They rate each of their performances against high standards, and tend to mark themselves lower than their audiences do. They are brutally honest with themselves, but with a sense of balance. They improve with new experiences precisely because of their ability to self-assess. In school, we should be coaching students to do exactly what the masters do—assess themselves. The younger the student, the more coaching he or she will need. Using seminars and portfolios are two ways in which the students are aided in self-appraisal. They can see their own progress, but also compare it with the standards that are held up to the class. Good assessment may well be the best motivator for learning.

The next best type of assessment is coaching. By adding a coach who can mirror the performance and intervene with suggestions on how the performer can gain more understanding, we have both subjective and objective appraisal. When teachers spend twice as much time coaching as they do lecturing, they function as user-friendly assessor. These coach-teachers will not have to rely as much on standardized tests because they are assessing their students daily in a personalized manner. The assessment in this case is intrinsic to the learning, not an outside audit done on a sample of behavior that is torn out of the normal fabric of learning.

PORTFOLIOS

One method of assessment friendly to learning for understanding follows the lead of artists and art schools. In a typical portfolio, a student artist assembles her best works and presents them to the admissions office of the art school. Or an aspiring commercial artist will take his or her best work and present it to a potential employer. The theory behind this type of assessment is quite simple. What you have already done gives some indication of what you might be able to do in the future with some more teaching and coaching.

Many principals are experimenting with the use of portfolios in a variety of subject areas other than art.

Similar to the portfolios described above are the process-folios that represent an effort by teachers to capture the steps and phases through which a student advances in the course of developing a project, product, work of art, piece of music, booklet, lecture, etc. Even in projects carried on in small groups, this process-folio's approach has some merit for judging learning for understanding. If the Federal Government mandates that every student with special needs should have an IEP (Individual Education Plan), why should this not be the rule for all students? In these IEPs, we could add more samples of the students' stages of learning development. We could use a camcorder to give us a running record of the advances a student makes. A recorded performance of a student in a high school debate could be a better predictor of college success than some standardized test.

Ruth Mitchell in *Testing for Learning* (19) makes it clear that no other form of performance assessment is as widespread as portfolios. She says they are in use from kindergarten through graduate school. Portfolios are more likely to be used to inform the student of progress and provide feedback on teacher's instructions. More and more, however, portfolios are being scored and used as a percentage of monthly or semester marks.

The California English/language arts teachers have developed a list of 35 purposes for which portfolios can used. Ruth Mitchell refers to this list in her book and indicates that other discipline groups are doing similar exercises.

Would that a simple switch to portfolios would change the linear "curriculum, instruction, assessment" tradition. We learn from Bil Johnson in both volumes of his *Performance Assessment Handbooks* that these three elements should be thought of as dynamic and interdependent. He notes in *Performance Handbook # 1—Portfolios & Socratic Seminars*, "Changing assessment practice requires a total rethinking of how we organize curriculum, instruction, scheduling, and a host of other institutional issues." (20)

Portfolios can fulfill any and all of the purposes for educational assessment, but they demand that the users undergo a paradigmatic shift in their view of classroom teaching and learning. If teachers can make this mental shift and use portfolios, seminars, performances, and exhibitions as forms of assessment, they will be integrating the curriculum with instruction and assessment in a dynamic trio. This will enhance learning for understanding.

SOCRATIC SEMINARS: DISCUSSIONS WITH A DIFFERENCE

The National Paideia Center is located here at the University of North Carolina at Chapel Hill. When Mortimer Adler taught here with us he was active in the Paideia Center and his reputation and influence helped the center to preach the gospel of seminars and discussions as potent ways of learning for understanding with built-in assessment.

Mortimer Adler in *The Paideia Proposal* notes:

"Teaching by discussion imposes still other requirements. For older children, it calls for more than a fifty-minute class period. It calls for a room in which the participants in the discussion sit around a table instead of in rows. The teacher is one of the participants, not the principal performer standing up in front of the group. The teacher's role in discussion is to keep it going along fruitful lines— by moderating, guiding, correcting, leading, and arguing like one of the students! The teacher is first among equals. All must have the sense that they are participating as equals, as is the case in a genuine conversation." (21)

Having observed Mortimer Adler directing seminars with fifth graders, high schoolers, and adults, I have come away with the conviction that the method is not only a great learning aid, but it is an accurate means of assessing the knowledge of the participants. In my own experience directing seminars for the National Paideia Center I am convinced that Bil Johnson has it right when he says,

"As with all the performance assessments, Socratic Seminars start with outcomes. Clearly focusing on what it is the student should know and be able to do during and after the seminar is the first step in the designing process. What makes this particular form of assessment valuable is the variety of outcomes that can be achieved through its use—offering the assessment designer the opportunity to use this method instruction any number of times. In fact, Adler makes a case for instituting at least one day each week in which all students participate in seminar. Some schools have done just that while others leave it to the discretion of individual teachers or teams of teachers. The significant note to be taken here is that Socratic Seminar should be a recurring practice in a classroom or school. It is an effective performance assessment because of the numerous outcomes it can address, thereby creating a consistent method of achieving diverse goals." (22)

Johnson points out that an array of critical thinking skills can be approached through the seminar method—analysis of text, synthesis of ideas, evaluation of concepts, inferential reason, etc. The seminar can also be used to develop reading comprehension skills—comprehension exhibited through application, analysis and so on. It is obvious the seminar is a great developer of speaking and listening skills. In my experience, if you use the Socratic Seminar regularly you will help the shy students to get a voice. It will help the vociferous ones to learn to discipline themselves and take turns in holding the spotlight.

PERFORMANCES AND EXHIBITIONS AS ASSESSMENT AIDS

For fuller understanding of the Socratic Seminar as a performance assessment aid along with portfolios, performances, and exhibitions, I suggest you read both of Bil Johnson's *Performance Assessment Handbooks*—the first covering portfolios and Socratic Seminars and the second, performances and exhibitions.

We will look briefly at an example of a performance and an exhibition taken from the books by Bil Johnson. When I look back to my elementary school experience 65 years ago, there is one thing I remember vividly. In grade five or six, the teacher had us put on a play based on the building of the Panama Canal. I played the role of the doctor who helped them combat malaria. I will never forget this learning experience because my own activity in the cast left an indelible trace on my brain. I have been aware all my life that fighting the malaria bearing mosquitos was one of the biggest obstacles to building this man-made wonder of the world. I am sure each of you can recall a similar example in your schooling. What is pitiful is the fact that it happened so seldom. Most of my early years of schooling were spent in passivity. It was only when I was allowed to perform that I actively engaged in the learning so deeply that it has stayed with me for these 65 years.

Bil Johnson gives an example of a Social Studies performance assessment from a private school in South Carolina.

> "The students are studying the French Revolution and the performance involves teams of students writing and publishing a pamphlet on the French Revolution. The first and most important step is taken by the teacher who designs 'Essential Questions' whose aim is to go to the heart of the discipline—there are no right or wrong answers only the creation of more questions that demand deeper study. They are questions that have relevancy to the students. That is, they engage students' curiosity. This doesn't mean they have to be immediate to the student's life but are challenging in a way that demands a response because the question has a strength and relevance to all our lives. One of the essential questions is 'Why do revolutions occur?' Essential questions cause students to ask more questions and direct their work as those questions emerge. They provoke 'higher-order' thinking, demanding analysis, synthesis, and evaluation of problems—students have to go beyond simple fact-gathering and rote recall."(23)

The students in teams are encouraged to pursue essential questions while they are learning about important content outcomes. The focus on student-active, student-constructed products and performances creates the point of departure from the traditional study of the French Revolution. Additionally, we see a conscious effort by the teaching team to promote habits of sound learning in their students. The students are given strict parameters as to the structure of the pamphlet they are to produce, but they are given wide latitude in style and approach. According to Bil Johnson, this example of performance assessment works because the desired skills and habits are presented to the students before the "Body of Knowledge" to be learned. You can find many other examples in both of Johnson's handbooks.

When we come to exhibits, "Science Fairs" come to mind. Many of our top scientists today started as youngsters presenting their work as high school students at "Science Fairs." I can remember one specific learning experience in high school that stands out. I now realize it was an exhibit. Our French teacher, Miss Bushnel, gave us an assignment that consisted of each student designing the outside cover of a menu for an upscale French Restaurant. Of course, the wording had to be in French and in acceptable grammar. The art work was left to each student's ingenuity. I still remember the name of my restaurant: Haut Chapeaux. Of course I got it wrong. I put the adjective in the wrong place but I still remember the experience with some pleasure. The art work was displayed in the classroom for a week.

Bil Johnson gives an example of a high school that decided to have quarterly exhibits, which they called Heroes Exhibition. The essential questions were stated: What kind of heroes would you prescribe for our society? After whom should we pattern our lives? For the exhibition, the students were expected to create and justify a collection of heroes for our time and culture. They had to define the idea of hero for the late 20th century. They had to select a group of persons—mythic or real, living or dead, famous or only known to a few—who exemplify that definition. The students were given wide latitude in the format. They could choose an anthology of stories and poems, a series of monologues, an expositor speech, an illustrated calendar, a set of trading cards, an illustrated magazine or comic book, a hypercard stack, or mural. The students are told in the beginning how their work will be judged but the student is the responsible party throughout. Such exhibits call on higher-order thinking and allow for analysis, synthesis, and comparative evaluation. The teachers mark them not only on the final product, but what must have been done to reach the point at which the final product could be made. The students did a tremendous amount of serious work on their own or in teams and they showed real maturity in the way they handled the tasks.

The problem we face at present is designing the kinds of assessment that will be able to measure the complexities and idiosyncrasies of learning for understanding. Once we plumb below surface knowledge, we begin to see that a grasp on the meaning of a concept is usually unique and difficult to pigeon-hole. The learner needs time to express his or her understanding in a variety of symbol systems. The examiners need to have a variety of doorways through which to enter as they assess a person's understanding. If we persist in using only standardized tests with very tight time requirements, we will continue to measure test-taking skills instead of natural knowledge and encourage teaching for surface knowledge. We can do better. We must do better if we are to prepare our students for the global marketplace.

It remains for district office test specialists, principals, teachers, and parents to get together to rethink the purposes of assessment—the Why, How, When, By what means, For whose benefit, Under what circumstances, etc. I encourage principals to study the newer performance assessment approaches presented by Johnson and Mitchell in their books. This will help principals discern how assessment must be changed if it is to serve as an aid to learning for understanding. Like daily school scheduling, curriculum and assessment must become the servants of the teachers and learners not their masters.

SUMMATION

We accepted the definition of Measurement and Evaluation offered in *Principals For Our Changing Schools* and developed some of its components. Following the work of Stiggins, Arter and their development team, we described the three assessment hats that the principal must wear: instructional leader, instructional manager, and communication facilitator. Some principals are less than enthusiastic about the way tests are being used in their schools. They grant that assessment is necessary, but they think the present process should be rethought with more input from principals and teachers. Some principals feel that much testing is interfering with preparing the students to learn for understanding. The tests nudged the teachers in the direction of teaching surface knowledge—the kind the tests measure—rather than going for deeper understanding and mastery of basic concepts and skills.

Even when principals feel negatively about tests they don't feel adequate to criticize them head-on because of their own lack of expertise in the highly specialized field of Measurement and Assessment.

Most principals agree that learning for understanding should take precedence over testing for surface knowledge. We briefly outlined some means of assessing that would make it possible for teachers to teach for understanding without giving up entirely on assessment. We offered a broader and better view of assessment, and with the help of authors Ruth Mitchell and Bil Johnson, we discussed means of assessing deeper learning and the skills of analysis, synthesis, and evaluation. We offered examples of portfolios, the Socratic Seminar, performances, and exhibitions, noting the advantages these assessment procedures have in integrating curriculum and teaching with assessment. We concluded that the performance assessment movement is the flying wedge of school reform. Steward Principals will lead the way as we improve the way we assess learning for understanding.

QUESTIONS FOR REFLECTION

1. Managers and accountants love to say, "What gets measured tends to improve." Why is it that giving more and more tests in school doesn't necessarily improve learning?

2. The Steward Principal has sufficient knowledge and skill in the area of assessment when he or she has mastered the seven key steps contained in the definition of Measurement and Evaluation contained in Domain 12. Do you think most principals have this kind of mastery in all seven steps?

3. How can Steward Principals help teachers use assessment as an aid to students learning for understanding?

4. Why are Howard Gardner's Five Doors to understanding so important if we are to avoid teaching merely for test results?

5. What does Dennie Wolf mean when she says the performance assessment movement is "the flying wedge of school reform"?

6. How would you compare and contrast "surface knowledge" with "natural knowledge"?

7. How could the use of portfolios in assessment aid a more creative approach to teaching and learning?

8. Explain how the use of Socratic seminars could not only enhance learning for understanding but also offer a better approach to assessment.

4

THE PRINCIPAL AS STEWARD OVER SCARCE RESOURCES

The Multiplication of the Loaves and Fishes

Lincoln, as a member of Congress, opposed the Mexican War. He thought it was a war of aggression motivated by America's greed. He said, "It was like the farmer in his Illinois district who claimed he wasn't greedy for land—he only wanted the land that abutted his."

Many principals in the past have felt that one of their most difficult tasks was to allocate resources. Resources for schools have often appeared to principals to be a day late and a dollar short. They felt as if they had to distribute a few loaves and fishes and make them stretch to fit the needs of hundreds of recipients. Principals had to "make do" with supplies that never seemed to last through the school year. The principal had to be the "procurer" (the one who gets the supplies), the apportioner (the one who gives them out), the monitor (the one who looks after the supply room and watches to see that staff uses these scarce supplies judiciously), the accountable one (the one who has to answer to Central Office when problems arise), and the planner (overseer at the end of the year who checks to see what— if anything—is left), and tries to "guesstimate" what added resources will be needed next year. It was never an easy job, but today the principal's task of resource allocation is more difficult than ever. Today, the principal is called upon to be a true steward and to motivate the staff to exemplify the same good qualities of a steward.

To get a more accurate idea of the role the principal plays in this area, we look to *Principals For Our Changing Schools*. In Domain 13, Barbara Y. La Cost, team leader, and her development team have presented a clear and logical summary of this role.

> **Resource Allocation:** Procuring, apportioning, monitoring, accounting for, and evaluating fiscal, human, material, and time resources to reach outcomes that reflect the needs and goals of the school site; planning and developing the budget process with appropriate staff. (24)

This is a more complex picture than the one I presented above. In this excellent definition, we find a different spin on the role of principal as resource allocator. First, "procuring" in this definition means more than the principal getting supplies from the Central Office. Many of today's principals and teachers are learning to write grants, create programs, and get them funded by community businesses, discovering new ways of gaining financial support for the school. No longer is the principal the sole provider. Second, resources today are much more broadly defined. They include more than supplies, human resources, space, time, etc. LaCost and her development team wisely note that the time of parents and students are important unpurchased resources. In times of scarcity, all stakeholders should act as wise stewards utilizing all resources in the most efficient way possible. As more non-parent adults volunteer their time to help schools, principals should graciously and prudently use this excellent source of talent.

In dealing with resources, the principals must take into consideration the needs and goals of their particular schools. In order to accomplish this, the principals must work to get all the stakeholders to buy into the goals of the school. With the goals in mind, they can make sensible decisions about what resources will be necessary to meet them. Resources are always means to an end goal. If the stakeholders share the school's goals, they will be in a better position to plan for and use resources in an intelligent manner. Not only are principals supposed to be wise stewards, so also are the teachers, staff, and students. The Japanese third graders I saw cleaning their classrooms and corridors before leaving the schools certainly were more careful about littering in school than students whose messes are cleaned by custodians each night. Studying La Cost's exposition on this domain makes it eminently clear that the use and abuse of resources is definitely an educational outcome. Good principals know that modeling good stewardship in handling resources may be one of the most leveraged activities they perform.

The principal should make a plan that includes necessary resources for the coming year, and develop a budget process with the assistance of appropriate staff. If all the school's stakeholders share the same vision and work toward realizing the acknowledged school goals, it would seem logical that all the stakeholders should share the responsibility for the procurement, allocation, apportionment, monitoring, and accounting of resources. To do this, a team of stakeholders should be co-planners and co-executors with the principal for both the budget and the handling of resources.

When stakeholders play a meaningful role in the planning of the budget, they feel the sense of ownership that makes joint projects succeed. *The budget is key because it encompasses the financial crystallization of an organization's intentions.* With this in mind, we see that the principal becomes a team leader who helps the stakeholders commit to a shared vision for the school. This results in a sense of co-ownership of the venture. Under these circumstances, the stakeholders no longer think of resources as belonging to the principal, who then apportions them to the teachers, custodians, students, etc. Rather, the stakeholders act as if the resources belong to the whole school and are the means necessary for accomplishing the goals of the school, in line with realizing the shared vision. The judicious use of resources becomes a *desideratum* for everyone. It is no longer the sole responsibility of the principal.

When I saw young Japanese school children serving their peers a full four-course lunch and later cleaning the school, I began to realize what was meant by the team approach to the use of resources. I wondered out loud to one of the teachers if the students didn't resent the work involved. On the contrary, she told me, "The children look forward to the physical work they do in teams. It isn't punishment to them. Rather, to be made to sit alone while the others are working together, that is punishment. They are used to working together at school because they see their schooling as a great gift. They love their school and want to make it beautiful."

Someone will object and say you can't do that with American children. My rejoinder is: What our grandparents did as students cleaning the one-room school house, can be done by our grandchildren in their high-tech schools. Does it add to pupils' maturity to be waited on and catered to by hired help, or might it not be advantageous to have them pitch in and share the work? Principals reflecting on the use of resources should give some thought to ways in which schools can educate young students to be good stewards over resources.

THE STEWARD IS A SERVANT-LEADER

The principal as steward is a concept that has captured my imagination since I read a book by Robert K. Greenleaf, *Servant Leadership: A Journey in the Nature of Legitimate Power and Greatness*. (25) This book, published in 1977, started many of us thinking about the role of leadership in a different way. Greenleaf takes a rather novel approach to leadership. He recommends that leaders, in our case principals, should be servant-leaders who will serve with skill, understanding, and spirit. He further suggests that followers should only be responsive to able servant-leaders who are committed to lead them. He notes that discriminating and determined servant-followers (all other stakeholders in the school) are as important as the servant-leader. Most importantly, he notes that from time to time everyone in the organization will serve in both roles. There are occasions when the principal should play the role of servant-follower while another stakeholder acts as servant-leader. In the classroom, there are times when the children should play the role of servant-leader as the teacher plays the role of servant-follower.

THE SERVANT AS LEADER

While we are discussing the role of the principal in presiding over scarce resources, we can further delve into Greenleaf's concept of servant- leader. He got the idea from reading Hermann Hesse's *Journey to the East*. In this story, a band of men are on a mythical journey. The central figure of the story is Leo, who accompanies the party as the servant who does the menial chores, but who also sustains them with his spirit and his song. He is a person of extraordinary presence. All goes well on the journey until Leo disappears. Then the group falls apart and the journey is abandoned. They cannot make it without their servant Leo. After some years of wandering, the narrator, who is one of the party, finds Leo and is taken into the Order that has sponsored the journey. There he discovers that Leo, whom he had known as a servant, was in fact, the head of the Order, its guiding spirit, a great and noble leader. Greenleaf says the meaning of the story is clear. Leo the great leader is seen as a servant first, and that simple fact is the secret to his greatness. Leo was actually the leader all the time, but he was servant first because that was what he was, deep down inside. Leadership was bestowed upon a man who was by nature a servant. His servant nature was the real person, assumed, and not to be taken away. The principal who is a servant first, upon whom leadership has been bestowed, will be the greatest leader. If we apply this to the management of resources the servant-leader—in our case the principal—serves the community he or she leads by helping them acquire the means to accomplish their shared vision. This is what Leo was doing with his group on the journey. The resources are collected, preserved, monitored, accounted for only as a means of making it easier for the other stakeholders to continue on this journey. The journey of every school is the same: to improve the instructional climate so the students can learn. The handling of resources should be accomplished in a way that is convenient for those who use them.

SQUIRRELS IN THE SUPPLY ROOM

Perhaps a story related to me recently by Ann, a veteran principal, will illustrate this better. Many years ago, when she was first appointed principal of an elementary school, she noticed among other things that each teacher had to make out a requisition slip at the end of the school day indicating what supplies she would need for class the next day. A typical sheet would list 28 pieces of construction paper, six bottles of glue, four boxes of

50 crayons, etc. This slip had to be on the desk of the school secretary by the end of the day if the supplies were to be delivered from the storage room in time for class the next day. Ann, who had the principalship bestowed on her, was deep down a servant and reasoned that this procedure was cumbersome for the teachers and the secretary. The secretary spent hours filling the orders and delivering them to the classrooms. Ann wondered if the teachers wouldn't prefer to go to the storage room themselves, and pick up what they needed when and as they needed it. She was not naive. It didn't surprise her that many teachers suffered from the "squirrel syndrome." Like the squirrel who lays in a supply of nuts for the whole winter, some teachers have the tendency to do the same with school supplies. Being a servant-leader, Ann felt that if that happened, she could go around to some of the teachers' rooms and reclaim the excesses. Soon most teachers learned that there was no need to stockpile in their classrooms because the supply room was open and continuously supplied. The few remaining squirrels hoarded less. The secretary picked up two extra hours a day during which she could serve the more important needs of the stakeholders. Ann's story illustrates the way a principal who is a servant-leader operates. Every great principal I know is a servant-leader. They are stewards.

RESOURCE ALLOCATION MODEL FOR STEWARDS

La Cost and her team give us a most helpful process model. They conclude that the principal, like a good steward, in partnership with the stakeholders is required to do the following:

- ◆ to identify needs and determine goals for a specified time cycle;
- ◆ to recognize that resources are defined in many ways;
- ◆ to plan strategies that result in a budget and the allotment of time, ways, and means to accomplish goals;
- ◆ to identify sources of resources and procedures for procuring them;
- ◆ to procure appropriate resources to meet goals or satisfy needs, apportion resources to site locations, programs and personnel groupings;

♦ to manage resources using accounting, monitoring, and reapportionment, such as Ann's trips to retrieve excess supplies;

♦ to evaluate effects of resource apportionment;

♦ to judge the validity and implications of evaluation results.

DETERMINATION OF NEEDS AND GOALS AT SCHOOL SITE

In Figure 3 the La Cost team has produced a flow chart that makes the whole process logical and manageable. If you study the Resource Allocation Model carefully, you will see how the principal could be more effective functioning as a steward. Like the servant-leader, the steward is able to convince the stakeholders to take more responsibility for resources. In this model, the drive that pushes the process comes from the determination of needs and goals at the site. The allocation of resources becomes one of the principal's most important duties when seen in its true light as a step toward the school's shared vision. With all the stakeholders committed to the same vision, they have the perfect starting point for determining what resources are needed to realize the vision. The Steward Principal doesn't allocate resources to the other stakeholders like a parent distributing cookies to children. Steward Principals don't conceive of the resources as given into their keeping, so they don't micromanage their use by the stakeholders. *The first principle of stewardship is to maximize the number of choices for those closest to the actual work.*

As the stakeholders do their work designing the goals of the school the principal as steward will help with the overall vision. He or she leaves the decisions about type and amounts of construction paper, crayons, and computer printing paper in the hands of the stakeholders who will be working most closely with students. The Steward Principal acting as a servant-leader will encourage core workers, including the students, to control resource costs and improve operations so that the shared vision may be realized. The principal offers choices to the other stakeholders, and herein lies the accountability. It is shared as the vision is shared.

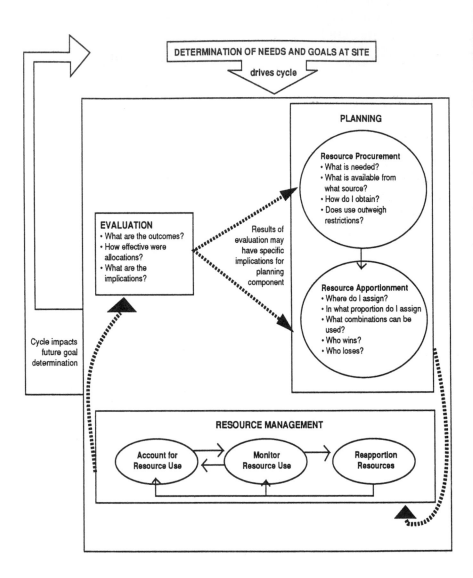

Figure 3. Resource Allocation Model

I can't resist an anecdote. When I finally got my driver's license, I would periodically ask my father if I could borrow the family car for some big event like a prom. When he agreed to let me use the car, he always went through the same ritual. He would solemnly hand me the keys while saying, "Drive the car the way you would if it were your own." I only vaguely understood what he meant, since I owned precious little at that time. Yet it did impress me, and as a result I drove the car in a careful and controlled way. I remember some of my friends riding with me complained that I drove like an old man. I treated that car as if it were made of gold. I wouldn't park near other cars. When I got home I gave the car a good cleaning. It looked better after I used it than it did before.

Over the years as I have owned and loaned my own cars, I have begun to see more clearly what my father meant. He was a good steward and knew that people treat things they own with more care than they do public property. Many police departments have discovered this truth. The patrol cars last twice as long when the officers are given total control of a vehicle and told they are responsible for maintaining it. Why should it be any different with resources in the school? When the stakeholders share a vision for the school and commit to pursue it, they use scarce resources with great care and economy, aware that they have to "make do" until the end of the year and that the vision depends on it. Stewardship aims at helping all stakeholders to govern themselves in a way that creates a strong sense of ownership and responsibility. Everyone is responsible for the outcomes of the school from the bottom up. The buck stops with every one of the stakeholders at every level.

In a school district about an hour and a half ride from where I live, they have preserved a one-room school house from the last century. Two teachers are assigned to it, and they demonstrate daily lessons to mixed classes of visiting elementary and middle school youngsters. The children are always amazed at how much responsibility they share. They seem to have a real sense of ownership for the building: serving the lunch, tending the fire, getting water, cleaning the chalk boards and emptying the trash. More importantly, the older students carry on tutoring duties with the younger ones and exert a level of discipline and control. It seems as if all the participants are cooperating toward a mutual goal. Younger and older students really like the experience. They discuss it with enthusiasm when they get back to their own schools. They say they enjoyed being taken seriously and being treated as partners in the enterprise. They felt more grown up.

STEWARDS INVOLVE ALL PARTICIPANTS IN RESOURCE PLANNING

This stage includes the procurement and apportionment of resources that will meet the goals and needs established over a one-to-five-year cycle. The Steward Principal makes sure that the planning is accomplished with input from everyone who will use resources. No longer does the principal do all the planning. Each stakeholder is asked to look ahead and determine what will be needed to carry on the functions of the school. What is needed? What is available from last year? What sources will need to be tapped? How can resources be procured? How stored? How monitored and accounted for?

This idea of stewardship in the management of resources demands a paradigmatic change in school governance. The principal and all others must make a new approach to the handling of resources. The Steward Principal must be willing to be accountable for results without using control or caretaking as the means to bring the results about. It takes a lot of trust on his or her part. When the principal acts in this manner, he or she chooses to govern relying on the strategies of partnership and empowerment. It is a powerful way to improve the learning climate of the school. Responsible use of resources may well be one of the most important skills needed for success in adult life.

In the past when the principal did all the planning and caretaking, a school had a high control environment. Principals enjoyed the security that came from this environment. Unfortunately, this type of governance did little to develop the character of the teachers, who almost invariably treated their students in the same way they were treated by the principal. The teachers complained that the students had no sense of responsibility and had to be spoon-fed. The principal told the superintendent that the teachers showed no signs of initiative. They seemed to shirk responsibility. It was a vicious circle.

The Steward Principal assumes, on the other hand, that both the teachers and the students long to invest themselves in something that really matters. The Steward Principal believes the antidote to self-interest is commitment to a "cause." If the teachers and students are consumed with a desire to work on something they really care about, they will be motivated by the spirit of Stewardship. They will understand immediately that the "cause" is so important, it is necessary for everyone to work together using resources wisely to accomplish the desired end.

Deeply committed people honor what has been given to them (resources), strive to use what power they have with a sense of grace, and pursue purposes that transcend their short-term self-interest. In such a case, teachers and students are imbued with the spirit of Stewardship and feel responsible for procuring, monitoring, using, conserving, and accounting for resources to accomplish the shared vision—better learning.

When this happens, the stakeholders feel that they own their own actions. This is the opposite of a high control environment. Since they own their own actions and share a common vision, they can be expected to act with a generosity and desire to serve. Even in this case, the Steward Principal is still responsible for results, but since the stakeholders are thought of as partners rather than employees, the principal expects that they will act with responsibility, and in most instances they do just that. I like the way the late Sam Walton, founder and owner of Wal-Mart, decided to treat his workers. He made sure that everyone who worked with him in this shared vision would be called an associate and treated like one. It seems to be working well at Wal-Mart. It can and does work well in any organization. A Steward Principal creates a marvelously freeing environment in which the associates, including the students, honor what is given them and use the resources to bring about the accomplishment of the shared vision.

PROCUREMENT

Traditionally, teachers have expected the principal to make sure that the school received enough supplies or other resources.

Yet in the best of times, teachers have regularly spent from $200 to $1,000 of their own money to make up for resource shortages. I know many principals and teachers who besides paying for supplies have kept a large jar of peanut butter and a loaf of bread in their desks to feed hungry kids whose parents failed for one reason or another to fill out the necessary paperwork for the free breakfast and lunch program. Most teachers have subsidized their own classes with supplies they paid for themselves. How often do the employees at Microsoft, IBM, or Xerox do that? The teachers are already partners and enjoy being treated as such.

When we start to think of the principal as steward and realize that all the stakeholders are stewards as well, we begin to think differently about procurement. If the principal is supposed to know about funding sources, know how to purchase and requisition resources, know how to tap community resource pools (e.g. volunteers, parents, college students, elderly, community businesses, social agencies, etc.), know how to shop for the best buys, know how to "make do," then in a true Stewardship the stakeholders including children should know these things as well. It is a truism: we learn to love the organization for which we have to scrounge to make sure it meets its goals. I don't mean that school children or teachers should be going door-to-door selling things to supply basic school needs. I do mean that if all the stakeholders make real sacrifices and try to discover ingenious ways to get more and better resources, they will grow in love for their school, become wiser consumers, and will waste less. It is time for us to take a broader view of the role of procurement in a school. Of course the principal is ultimately responsible, but just as in a family so also in a school: when the members take responsibility for the resources they need, the outcomes improve.

APPORTIONMENT

We all know that a principal should be fair in the distribution of resources. Many disagreements between teachers and principal and among teachers arise when some feel they are treated unfairly in the apportionment of resources. How often have you heard a statement like this in a high school faculty room? "If you aren't in the English Department in this school

you pretty much get the 'leftovers.' I asked our assistant principal for a fairer distribution of the 'goodies,' e.g. the better classrooms, better class hours, some new supplies, more computer
time etc. She said, 'Sorry, the English Department always gets
the first choice.' You can hear similar complaints in middle and
elementary schools. The teachers claim the principal isn't fair.
The real problem is that the school is being run in a patriarchal
manner, which always leads to teachers' dependency. Such dependency reduces one's sense of responsibility and often leads
to a sour resentment of authority. Teachers can't help students
learn responsibility if they are acting irresponsibly themselves.

On the other hand, when the Steward Principal empowers
teachers by giving them more experience procuring and appor-
tioning the resources, the staff begins to function in a mature
and responsible manner. The principal no longer functions as a
parent, and the staff no longer acts like a group of spoiled children. There will always be problems involved in the apportionment of scarce resources; that is a given. However, a staff
accustomed to acting as both servant-leaders and servant-followers working with a Steward Principal can settle disputes
quickly and move on to more important matters.

A Steward Principal chooses to empower all the stakeholders rather than encourage dependency. People who are dependent believe that there are people in charge who know or should
know what is best for others, including themselves. They think
the task of the boss or leader is to create a world (school) where
the stakeholders can live a life of safety and predictability. Everything will be fair and just; and if it isn't, the fault will lie with
the principal. Teachers, parents, and students working in a control-oriented environment—a paternalistically run school for
instance—hold the principal responsible for the way they feel
about themselves, the school, and the amount of freedom they
have. The longer a staff functions in this type of control-oriented
organization, the more the feeling of dependency is fostered.
Teachers working in that milieu inevitably treat their students
in a way that fosters their dependency. *Responsibility is conta-
gious, so is irresponsibility.*

In the last 12 years, I have witnessed a wonderful change in
the way schools are being led by principals. Today, fewer princi-

pals encourage dependency. They just don't have the time to be non-delegating, paternalistic or maternalistic, control-driven, micro-managers. As the Central Office delegates more to the principal in site management, so the principal is encouraged to share the responsibility and power with all the staff. The procurement and apportionment of resources is one of the most obvious places in which to share duties.

Most of the principals I teach today are learning to empower the stakeholders by encouraging them to believe that the solution of the problem of resource apportionment and many other problems lies within each of us. As Pogo says, "We have met the enemy and they is us." Once the stakeholders grasp the fact that the resources belong to all of them, they begin like wise consumers to use ingenious methods of stretching a dollar and making do. They care more for the good of the whole school, rather than battling to win the lion's share for their own department or class. This is the mark of a Learning Organization and the foundation for a Learning Community.

In the last chapter, I claimed that American schools are poised to make a giant leap forward in the process of educating youth. Although the management of resources may not seem to have a very high priority, the use of resources by the principal and all the stakeholders, including students, may be one of the most important components of school reform. Good things are happening because the stakeholders are beginning to realize that when they share purpose, power, and prestige, cooperative learning becomes possible. Slowly we will learn to share space and time as well as we do other resources. The act of learning, like the allocation of resources, is improved drastically when all the stakeholders take responsibility for outcomes. When the Japanese third graders take responsibility for serving the lunch at school, there is an expected amount of horseplay but they waste or misuse very little food. The after-meal clean-up is a piece of cake. "After all, tomorrow my team will be serving and cleaning up. I know how hard it is to clean a mess. I don't want to make it more difficult for today's team. That is why I am careful with the food," explained one of the Japanese students, recognized as one of the class cut-ups.

MANAGEMENT OF ACQUIRED RESOURCES

In Domain 13, the authors place three subheadings under Management of Resources. These include accounting for, monitoring, and reapportioning resources as necessary during a specified time cycle. As principals you are aware of the complexity involved. When I try to explain the principal's job to those unfamiliar with the way schools run, I use a metaphor. A middle school in late August or early September starting the school year with 1000 students and a staff of 120 is like a ship pulling out to sea. The principal is the captain. He or she must be sure that the ship is stocked for a nine-month tour of duty. The principal's chief concern is signing on a top-notch crew (staff). The student passengers are not selected by the principal. Some feel they were shanghaied. Much of the success of the cruise will depend on the behavior of the students, and the principal hopes the students will be easy to deal with. The supplies on the ship must include food, drink, medicine, books, papers, crayons, computers, chalk boards, recreational equipment, plumbing, heating, electricity, air conditioning, telephones, faxes, and 1400 other incidentals. If the principal is the chief resource allocator, this can be a huge time-consuming responsibility. Steward Principals wisely decide to delegate. If they fail to delegate and spend too much time on the management of resources, they will neglect more important instructional duties.

Good principals spend a lion's share of their time in planning, improving instruction, contacting outside agencies, speaking to civic groups, working with parents and the Central Office, and collaborating with business leaders, principals and other educational administrators around the state and country. Principals for our changing schools will be aware of the great need to manage resources well, but will also focus on the ends, goals, and visions for which the resources are to be used: to improve instruction and the learning climate of the school.

PARTNERSHIP IN ALLOCATING RESOURCES

Peter Block in his book *Stewardship* encourages the heads of organizations to choose partnership over patriarchy in the way they govern. When a principal chooses patriarchy, implicit is the belief that those at the top are responsible for the success of the organization and the well-being of its members. This leads to dependency on their part. When it comes to allocating resources, the stakeholders assume the principal will stock the ship at the start of the cruise, and it will be his or her responsibility to make sure there is enough of everything for everybody for the duration. This kind of assumption is perfectly fine for an able-bodied seaman on a ship. He can assume that the supplies will be taken care of by the captain. Not so with the stakeholders in a school. When stakeholders in a school tend to blame the principal for all shortages, we may or may not have a poor principal, but we certainly have a poor example of governance.

The alternative to patriarchy or parenting is partnership. The Steward Principal chooses partnership. In this form of governance the principal gives up some of his or her control to the stakeholders. This may mean less consistency and predictability in the school but the increase in stakeholders' empowerment and shared responsibility more than compensate for the loss. In partnership or steward-type governance, the principal intends to balance power with the stakeholders. The principal knows that when the stakeholders become partners, they become self-motivated and much more creative, committed, responsible, and accountable.

The work of a school is learning. A partnership in the allocation of resources for learning makes sense. Teachers and students have to feel a sense of ownership for the resources if they are to use them to the best advantage. The way they get this sense of ownership is by being included in the processes by which resources are procured, maintained and used. This is what takes place in a partnership. Used by a principal in the management of resources, it may be one of the best ways to help students learn how to manage scarce resources for life. When I hear the call, "Back to basics," I can't think of anything more basic that learning to be a wise consumer and provident Steward.

LIFE IS A SERIES OF GUESSTIMATIONS

Domain 13 indicates that evaluation is a must in the allocation of resources. When stakeholders plan for the procurement of resources, they have to have knowledge of what changes have taken place or will take place during the planning cycle. To accomplish this, the stakeholders must collect highly objective data to determine what changes have taken place and will occur in specified areas. Principals and other stakeholders need to know how to develop surveys that accurately assess attitude changes among students as well as demographic shifts. In my city, 4000 new students move in each year, which means we have to build seven or eight new schools annually. It is a repeat of what happened in California. We have to read the future as best we can.

At least as important, the principal and stakeholders need to determine whether the use of the resources are bringing about improvement in learning outcomes. A knowledge of student attendance, suspensions, expulsions, staff absenteeisms, and teacher turnover are also part of the evaluation of the use of resources. Surveys are necessary; however, principals who operate according to the model of stewardship won't have to wait for the results from surveys to tap the school's vital signs. When the principals have a partnership with their stakeholders, the lines of communication stay open and everyone is aware of what is going on with resources. *Stewardship's* author Block tells us that what truly matters in our lives is usually measured through conversation. In schools, the principals' ongoing dialogue with all the stakeholders is the most powerful source of data. In my earlier book, *The Principal's Edge,* I stressed the skill of probing as one of the chief tools used by wise principals when they govern.

In an earlier chapter, I complained that too much school time (a major resource itself) is devoted to preparing students to do well in standardized tests that may not help their learning. I cautioned that the time would be better spent helping the students to improve their ability to learn for understanding. When the district office is assured that a principal is acting like a steward-sharing power with the other stakeholders—they tend to trust the principal and the other stakeholders more. They believe the teachers will seriously evaluate each student's progress in learning for understanding. This will cut down the district office's over-reliance on standardized tests. The majority of good teachers know very well which students are "getting" the material, and going beneath the surface so they can fully grasp its significance. Good teachers do their own diagnostic probing and spend more time coaching students in their specific needs; they will produce more learning for understanding and justify the resources consumed.

On the Resource Allocation Model (Fig. 3), under Evaluation, there are three questions that must be answered. What are the outcomes? How effective were allocations? What are the implications? Instead of the principals answering these pertinent questions alone, all the stakeholders should hold themselves accountable for answering them. Schools will be ready to make a giant shift toward improving learning for understanding when all the stakeholders, including the students, take more responsibility for improving outcomes by a better use of all resources.

In Stewardship All Stakeholders Are Responsible for Resources

In both Block's book *Stewardship* and Domain13 from *Principals For Our Changing Schools*, the proper use of a school's resources becomes one of the chief means of educating both the students and the staff. In a sense, the medium is the message. When the principal, staff, and students share the same vision of the school and agree to work toward its realization by using all resources to that end, we have a true Learning Organization.

In a Learning Organization there is true creative commitment. I have seen families in which this was true. The hardworking parents sacrifice to put the oldest sibling through college (scarce resources in the house were used sparingly), and then each of the siblings help the others along the education path. When the parents are old, the successful sons and daughters pull together to make sure their parents are well taken care of in their old age.

I have had firsthand experience of a Learning Organization at a large university in which all the stakeholders were deeply committed to the vision. What signalized this institute was the conviction shared by the stakeholders that they were associates (partners) whose input was taken seriously in the creation of the vision, the design of the programs, and their daily operation. This particular Learning Organization is still alive, flourishing, and exciting. It celebrated its 25th anniversary this year.

I saw how the creative intelligence of the stakeholders could find ways to feed the 5000 with a few loaves and fishes. In this Learning Organization, the professors (chosen by the institute council) not only lectured and answered questions each morning, they also attended each other's classes and participated in panels in which the students could question the three professors simultaneously. This is a wise use of resources and a good model for any Learning Organization. Every Steward Principal is capable of creating such a Learning Organization. The stakeholders will be more than accountable; they will be totally committed.

It is ironic that we should be trying to get schools to act like stewardships. The earliest "schools" were run by the students, who would pay the professors to lecture. If the professors were disappointing—didn't teach well—they were not renewed. Tenure was unheard of in these informal gatherings of the Greek peripatetics or the medieval professors at Paris and Bologna. The students seeking to learn were willing to pay teachers who could help them accomplish the task. Notice the knife cuts both ways. With a group of students who really want to learn, it is much easier for a professor to teach well. In a middle school in which the students really want to learn and the teachers are anxious to teach well and learn at the same time, the principal will have no trouble managing resources. Universities today are run like huge corporations in which the student-consumers have little or no say in the governance. If that is true in higher education, what about K-12? State departments, county commissioners, school boards, and Central Offices argue pointlessly about buildings, busing, and budgets, while the teachers and students at the site are wasting their most precious resource—their time— because they are getting conflicting signals about scheduling, testing, and instruction from the top.

Block repeats again and again the idea that stewardship means choosing service over self-interest. We can only change organizations for the better when the stakeholders change their own mind-sets in the direction of service. In order to change schools, the stakeholders from top to bottom must choose between service and self-interest. Both are attractive. The fire of self-interest has been burning around us for the last decade or two. We find it hard to get leaders in whom we can have faith.

Superintendents move every three years. Perhaps we ought to start by asking ourselves how much we choose service over self-interest ourselves. How many school board members really seek the position so they can improve learning in the school? If you could answer honestly, "The majority do," then we would have better schools by next Wednesday. Ask parents if they really care about the quality of education not only for their own child but others as well. If you could honestly say, "Most of them care more for the quality of education in general than for pushing their own child forward," then we would have great schools by next Tuesday. If teachers cared more about the quality of instruction in the school and if students cared more about their own learning and contributing to their community of learners we would have better schools next Monday. If the principals get bitten by the "cause" of improved learning in their schools, we will have great schools late Sunday afternoon. Notice in every case it is putting first things first (learning and instruction), acting more from altruism and less from self-interest, acting as a responsible partner who is accountable for resources, being committed to the "cause," and cooperating with a steward principal. It can only be done with Steward Principals creating Learning Organizations.

A SENSE OF COMMUNITY CREATES SERVICE-ORIENTED USE OF RESOURCES

Most K–12 schools in my experience are run from Central Office where the district, county, and state mandates are faxed and distributed. The really important decisions are still top-down. This will continue to be true as long as curriculum, standardized testing, and budgets are not in the hands of the site managers. It is difficult to get stakeholders to buy into a "cause" if they don't feel that they are a part of an empowered community.

We are at a juncture in this country in which education can go one of two ways. The new voucher and contract-for-profit school movements will win at the cost of leaving public schools floundering worse than they were. They will have to keep their open-door policy in which all children are accepted, while the voucher-subsidized private schools will be free to control enrollment, dismiss troublemakers at will, avoid the high costs of special education, and be exempt from governmental regulation. It isn't a level playing field. Or we can follow the advice of pioneer educator John Dewey, who said, "Unless local communal life can be restored, the public cannot adequately resolve its most urgent problem: to find and identify itself." Schools can flourish only if and when the local community finds and identifies itself. If the public schools splinter, we will have lost our chance to build true community and America will continue to disunite.

Sergiovanni in *Building Community In Schools* makes it clear that improving teaching, developing sensible curriculum, creating new forms of governance (e.g. site-based management), providing more authentic assessment, empowering teachers and parents, and increasing professionalism must rest on a foundation of community building. The only way to get people to choose service over self-interest is through participation in community. It is in a community that we usually find the "cause" for which we are ready to sacrifice our own good for the common good. When there was local community, the public school served as an aid to parents in transmitting this sense of community. Now the public school remains one of the last neighborhood organizations that might not only profit from improved community building, but play a part in it.

Think, for example, what happened to the farmers and the live-in servants with the passage of time. Before World War I these two occupations composed the single highest group of workers in the United States. After that war, they entered the factories and began to make more money than they had ever seen. They moved into the cities. Many moved into the middle class (without live-in servants). A few made it to the upper middle class. They scattered into suburban neighborhoods in which the common denominator was no longer ethnic, nor value-based, but the cost of the house. The automobile and the highway system allowed development of the exurbs as well as the suburbs, and the rest is history.

It is absurd to think that we can recapture the community of a small farming village today, but it is imperative that we discover ways to bring people of different cultures, colors, crafts, concerns, and commitments together in community. The success of schooling depends on it; perhaps the neighborhood school may be the locus for forming neighborhood communities. Within five minutes walking distance of my home there are two public schools: an elementary school and a middle school. I have been in the middle school often because it is used for voting. The elementary school that is a few steps closer is foreign territory to me. I have never set foot in it. Why shouldn't I feel some sense of responsibility for both these schools? They are the only buildings in my immediate neighborhood that I support with my tax money, except for a fire station and a post office. I am very interested in improving education and I have something I could offer these schools. The fire station and the branch post office seem to do well without my help, but I bet I could be helpful to some of the young students and their teachers in my two neighborhood schools. I have been thinking of organizing a group of the neighbors living on the streets that border both schools and asking them to come with me to ask the two principals how we could be of service.

Having profited from good public education myself, I feel I have a debt to pay. I know I could read stories to the young students in our neighborhood elementary school. I could give them a few thousand ball point pens, many reams of paper, crayons, and coloring pencils that seem to multiply in our desk drawers. I know I could let the kids that walk past my house know that I am there for them if they need help. In the middle school, I could tell them what it takes to become a psychologist and the kinds of work psychologists do. Having worked in a prison, I could tell them that I never met an inmate who really loved his father nor many who finished high school. I'm serious about starting this neighborhood club dedicated to helping the common schools in our neighborhood do their jobs easier and better. I'll bet some of my neighbors will join with me in this venture. One thing I can promise: every neighbor who joins with my wife and myself in visiting the schools will rejoice to see how many good teachers we have and how many students are really anxious to learn. It will certainly make them more sympathetic when the next school bond is being debated. I think it is so unfair for the media and the public to lambaste public education without having first-hand knowledge of what goes on in their schools. It not only takes a village to bring up a child, it takes a lot more "candle lighters" and a whole lot fewer "darkness cursers."

Historically, the public school served as a "bridge" between two social groupings—the family and the work world (society). The family and neighborhood used to be made up of people who were intimate, private, and exclusively living together. Many of us came from neighborhoods that housed aunts, uncles, cousins, grandparents, as well as close family friends with the honorific title of "aunt" and "uncle." This family-neighborly social grouping was characterized by a feeling of belonging and personal security, trust, intimacy, and loyalty. The German word *Gemeinschaft* captures it. The other society was associated with the world of work, commerce, and its marketplace relationships. This second is epitomized by the German term, *Gesellschaft*. This group is held together not by kinship or intimacy but rather by contractual guarantees of performance. It was known to be impersonal and temporary. It existed only during the period of the contract, whereas your relations with your family, friends, and neighbors were assumed to be on-going.

With the advent of the industrial revolution, our grandparents left the farm and live-in service moving to cities and later to suburbs where the closeness of kinship and intimacy was lost in the hustle and bustle of anonymous living. Now the schools started to be governed by school boards whose members were not infrequently the owners of the mills and factories. It was only logical that these successful businessmen should stress the role the school played in preparing people for the world of work. The bureaucratized school, with its teachers' unions and businessmen school boards, no longer served the role of helping parents to raise their children. Schools focused on preparing workers. Now some question whether public schools are capable of preparing students to step into the post-industrial, post-modern information age. The information age requires knowledge and skill used in an atmosphere of trust, loyalty, and security. The school must be a nurturing community both inside and outside the building, or the students won't have sufficient trust to drop their defenses and risk learning. This school community must help them share across cultural and ethnic lines, so they can feel that they belong. The first item on our agenda in school reform has to be the forming of a school community which bonds the many disparate communities from which students come.

Through procurement, monitoring, and allocation of school resources, the Steward Principal, teachers, parents and other stakeholders can begin to share, the way a family does. It would be so
much easier to form such a sharing school community if the
geographical neighbors of the public school took an interest in
the students and the school, giving an example of what a healthy
neighborhood community can bring.

Only about 25 percent of families have school-age children.
Unless the 75 percent majority with no school-age children
reaches out to help bring community to public schools, we may
be missing our last chance to have the common school that
Jefferson fought so hard to build. With good stewards in the
schools, good stewards in the neighborhood, good stewards in
the business community recognizing that the most precious resource we share is our children—all can help public schools do
what only they can do: teach children to accept differences and
rejoice in similarities.

The school alone cannot take full responsibility for modeling community and giving children the experience of feeling
they belong and are both wanted and respected. As long as the
key decisions are made close to the smell of the chalk, the Steward Principal, teachers, parents, and children will have the assurance that they are members of a true learning community.
The neighbors, business community, and civic groups will see
that they play their role in making this school community
possible.

Children can feel what I felt as a child: the neighbors worked
with the parents and teachers to look out for us school children.
All adults in the neighborhood felt a responsibility for us. Teachers, merchants, and policemen all looked out for us. Because we
were young, inexperienced, and vulnerable, adults felt obliged
to protect us. They smiled at us. It is possible once again for
children to feel this sense of safety and acceptance. School communities flourish with Steward Principals, servant-leaders, and
servant-followers, but it really does take a village to bring up a
child or to build a learning community.

SUMMATION

When we started to discuss the role of the steward principal
and the management of scarce resources, we opened up a

Pandora's box. The definition offered by La Cost and her team was a great beginning. We learned that the budget is key because it encompasses the financial crystallization of an organization's intentions.

Next, we discussed the steward as a servant-leader, stressing the fact that this type of leadership will carry the day in schools of the future. An illustration of the present handling of the school supply closet gave us a chance to outline the Resource Allocation Model in Figure 3. The handling of resources strongly reflects the Steward Principal's intentions. It is important for the principal to involve all stakeholders in the process of planning for resources. Even the earliest steps of procurement and apportionments should involve all who will use the resources. This is a great way of encouraging responsible behavior among all stakeholders. We stressed the idea of partnership as a means of managing and allocating resources. We must learn to think of estimating future needs, taking into account statistical fluctuations. This demands the ability to guesstimate. The responsibility for all resources should be spread among all the stakeholders if the school is to be a Learning Organization. The more site-management is implemented, the more the stakeholders will need this type of empowerment. Ultimately, the school must listen to the intentions of the community when it comes to the handling of resources. We tried to demonstrate at the end of this chapter that only when we can have a true community (*Gemeinschaft*) held together by feelings of kinship and intimacy will we be able to utilize the school's resources in a fully responsible way. Instead of relegating the management of resources to a secondary level of importance, we pointed out that the way a Steward Principal manages scarce resources may be the clearest indicator of his or her leadership style. When the principal acts as a servant-leader empowering the stakeholders as partners, not only are supplies well managed, but morale is high.

Finally, we turned the question upside down and asked, "If the students are the school's most important resource, how can the Steward Principal and the other school stakeholders make sure that the students can learn by experiencing true community?" Our answer: the school alone cannot form a true learning community. It needs the contributions of parents, neighbors, the business community, civic and church groups to make this happen. It takes a village made up of many communities actively supporting students in a neighborhood school to build a learning community. Of course the children are worth it. They are our best resource and the Steward Principal is one who can bring all these resources together to build the learning community.

QUESTIONS FOR REFLECTION

1. Why is it that Steward Principals seem to have a knack for distributing scare resources in ways that don't alienate the stakeholders? How do they do it?

2. The budget for the school is a key because it encompasses the financial crystallization of the organization's intentions. It really means putting our money where our heart is. Why?

3. Is Robert Greenleaf too idealistic when he talks about "Servant-Leaders"? Have you ever known any?

4. How did Ann, the new principal, solve the problem of squirrels in the supply room?

5. The first principle of Stewardship is to maximize the number of choices for those closest to the actual work. What does that mean when applied to allocating scare resources?

6. What did you learn from the Resource Allocation Model? Is it realistic and practical enough to help you?

7. Steward Principals include all stakeholders in Resource Planning. Why is that such a good idea?

8. How are Procurement and Apportionment alike and how are they different?

9. The alternative to patriarchy or parenting is partnership. Why does the Steward Principal play the role of servant-leader in handling supplies, allowing the stakeholders to be partners?

10. Block repeats again and again the idea that Stewardship means choosing service over self-interest. How is this exemplified in the life of a Steward Principal?

11. The only way to get people to choose service over self-interest is through participation in community. Can this be illustrated in the handling of scarce supplies?

12. Does it really take a village to bring up a child?

5

THE STEWARD PRINCIPAL MOTIVATES ALL STAKEHOLDERS

*A teacher who can arouse a feeling for one single good
action, for one single good poem, accomplishes more than he
who fills our memory with rows on rows of natural objects,
classified with name and form.—Goethe*

Of all the duties of the school principal, the most important
and at the same time the most difficult one is the task of motivating all the stakeholders: teachers, other staff, students, parents, and others. Goodlad says you can tell a good principal if
he or she is quick to praise the stakeholders. I have puzzled over
this statement for a long time. The best explanation I can offer is
that the good principal likes and praises his or her staff because
all or most of them seem to exert themselves, putting out more
effort to improve their performances as a means of achieving
the shared goals of the school. *The best principals are good motivators.* The accomplishments of well-motivated stakeholders will
be their greatest reward.

Most people work hard because they like doing what they
are doing and seeing it succeed. The fact that others praise their
joint accomplishments doesn't hurt at all, but they work consci-
entiously because they like to do what they are doing. Steward

Principals know they are successful motivators when the stakeholders are learning better and at the same time enjoying the learning process. The Steward Principal knows the best advice is their own good example—the example of a committed life. He or she teaches values by making good choices in their presence. The stakeholders see what the principal does and are positively influenced by it.

IS IT ACCURATE TO SAY PRINCIPALS MOTIVATE STAKEHOLDERS?

While giving a talk recently to Future Leaders (a group being groomed to be principals), I discussed the concept of motivation. One of the teachers said she doubted that any person could motivate another. Her idea was that all motivation is self-motivation. The more I thought about it, the more I knew she was at least partially correct, but I was also partially correct and wanted to defend my statement, "Principals have a duty to motivate all stakeholders toward educational excellence." Granted, the stakeholders must ultimately move themselves into action, but it seems to me that others can make this action more or less difficult by their modeling and interventions.

My own father attended night school for almost 20 years while I was attending elementary, high school, and college. He truly motivated me by his example. I was moved to study the way he did—voluntarily and consistently. My mother's life-long pursuit of learning inspired me to want to look up words, to improve my vocabulary, and to increase my perceptual and communication skills. Neither of my parents had more than an eighth-grade formal education, but they certainly motivated me to pursue life-long learning. Did they really motivate me? I think so. How else can I explain my continuing to study and going to classes at 76 years of age? I didn't really give a satisfactory answer to the young principal-to-be who kept insisting on the primacy of self-motivation, but I did read for her the definition of motivating others from Domain 14 in *Principals For Our Changing Schools*, prepared by team leader Cynthia D. McCauley and her group of fellow North Carolinians.

"**Motivating Others:** Creating conditions that enhance staff's desire and willingness to focus energy on achieving educational excellence; planning and encouraging participation; facilitating teamwork and collegiality; treating staff as professionals; providing intellectual stimulation; supporting innovation; recognizing and rewarding effective performance; providing feedback; coaching and guidance; providing needed resources; serving as a role model." (26)

In the discussion that followed, we came to a general agreement that a good principal somehow did make it easier for the stakeholders to motivate themselves toward educational excellence. This is the message of our present chapter.

An old friend of mine who makes his living as an accountant is fond of saying. "What gets measured and hence rewarded gets priority and gets done." He and I often argue the point. I tend to side with the famous management consultant Edwards Deming, who preached against extrinsic motivation and in favor of intrinsic. He loved to say it's a worker's pride in his or her work that makes the difference. It is the manager who works hardest at removing barriers to the workers' pride in their workmanship who is the best motivator. If Deming were speaking to principals, he would give this advice, "A stakeholder who feels important to the job will make every effort to be on the job and pay keen attention to the job. Those stakeholders will feel important to the job if they can take pride in their work, knowing that they are making a real contribution to student learning. They will feel good if they have been able to influence the system, so learning will be enhanced. When principals make it possible for stakeholders to have more control over their workday (choices and discretion), have clearer ideas of what is expected of them, have the necessary resources, feel potected from those who meddle, these Steward Principals will be effective motivators. The stakeholders will work harder because they see the work and themselves as important and realize that their contribution is significant."

Deming was a bear for removing the blame for poor performance from individual workers and placing it on the system.

He believed the system kept workers from doing things correctly and taking pride in their work. As principals you realize that much of your job of motivating stakeholders comes down to removing barriers to pride in their work. There are many barriers imbedded in our local and state educational systems:

♦ children come to school unprepared to learn, too many students are behavior problems

♦ too many programs are initiated from above without much thought

♦ too many good programs are started and then left to die on the vine for lack of funding

♦ teachers are kept to rigid schedules and given little time to plan and almost no room for discretion

♦ the standardized tests take precedence over individual coaching

♦ curricular demands—often unrealistic—discourage both teachers and students

♦ there is seldom enough time or resources

♦ parents can override the teachers' decisions

Obviously a lone principal can't remove all these barriers, but principals can make it known to the policy makers that outcomes will improve greatly if they work hard to remove some of these barriers from the system.

Deming felt that the exclusive reliance on extrinsic motivators (teacher of the year, principal of the year, monetary rewards, parking spaces for winners of contests, etc.) severely limited an organization's ability to excel. Of course he intended that we pay workers fairly and provide equitable benefits, but he felt too much emphasis on the external rewards did little to liberate stakeholders so they could perform at their best. These extrinsic rewards keep principals from learning how to get people to want to do what needs to be done, from learning to lead. When people are working toward their own personal best, they use the words "challenging, rewarding, and exciting" to describe the tasks they do. People truly enjoy such experiences; there is something about the work that is intrinsically valuable. No wonder Goodlad said that principals who judged their stakeholders to be above average ran the most satisfactory schools and were judged by the stakeholders to be trustworthy leaders. They were able to free their stakeholders from barriers and make it possible for them to find real satisfaction in the performance of their daily work. The stakeholders could experience the satisfaction of knowing that if they increased their own efforts and learned to improve their performance, the outcomes would improve and the work itself would be rewarding beyond their dreams.

THE STEWARD PRINCIPAL AS A MODEL IN MOTIVATION

What about your own motivation as a principal? You have the greatest joy when you perform at your best and are able to serve people well. To be really effective, you must experience the work of a principal as enjoyable and challenging. You must feel that your work calls upon you to use all your skills and talents to the fullest. You must feel motivated yourself in order to be a model for your stakeholders. When you help the stakeholders by removing obstacles yourself or interceding with policy makers to remove obstacles, you are acting as a model. In fact, you are exercising your skills as motivator. You know how much you like to solve problems. When as a Steward Principal you find opportunities for the stakeholders to solve their problems, make discoveries, explore new ground, reach difficult goals, or figure out how to deal with external threats, you are not only removing the barriers to pride in workmanship and offering them a chance to feel real satisfaction in their accomplishments, you are acting as a model in motivation.

As a Steward Principal, you are acting the role of model motivator when you constantly help stakeholders use more effort to improve their skills and knowledge so they can perform at peak levels and make a significant difference in their performance. As a good model in motivation, you know the strengths and weaknesses of each of the school's stakeholders; so you can offer challenges that are feasible and not frightening to any of them. Too strong a challenge, and the stakeholders become anxious and less effective; too little, and they are bored. With the proper amount of challenge, stakeholders flourish. Your key to structuring activities for maximum intrinsic motivation among stakeholders is much the same as that of a teacher motivating a student to learn. The key is finding the proper balance between opportunities for action (learning) and a student's skill level or aptitude. The Steward Principal is called a principal because he or she is the model (as principal teacher) for removing obstacles to learning for all the stakeholders.

Twice a year when I have the opportunity to talk to groups of superintendents, I tell them their job as models of motivation is to remove the barriers and obstacles that interfere with principals experiencing pride in their work. When superintendents allow principals the freedom to solve their own problems the principals can take pride in their work. Just think how much more enjoyable your job as principal would be if you could use your talents to help teachers teach better and students learn better, rather than spending your time and effort caught up in bureaucratic squabbles, excessively demanding paper work, and the idiosyncratic vicissitudes of school boards. School boards that spin like weathervanes in a storm can send out enough conflicting signals to kill motivation in all stakeholders. As school boards, superintendents, Central Office staffs, principals, assistant principals and teachers act more like models in motivation rather than control agents, the students will take more responsibility for their own learning and the results will be rewarding to all.

Stakeholders will respond freely to principals who walk the way they talk and are trusted servants. Students will respond in the same way to teachers and parents if they act like servant-leaders. When students see their parents and teachers acting like servant-leaders (this does not preclude setting limits and exerting disciplinary action), they will freely give them their allegiance and show great improvement. "*Talis rex, qualis grex*" is a great Latin phrase that roughly translates, "the followers (flock) will take on the characteristics of the king or leader." If, today, we see too little initiative, self discipline, and high aspirations in our students, it may well reflect an attitude on the part of too many of our political leaders who grossly underestimate the improvement in public education over the last two decades. By every measure, public education is doing a better job today than it did in the recent past. The more our leaders are willing to trust principals and teachers, the more the improvement will increase. Steward Principals have been able to overcome great obstacles to bring about a closing of the gap between minority and majority test scores, the greatly lessened "drop-out rates," and higher school attendance records across the board. Students are taking school more seriously. Now we must discourage political leaders from using "public school bashing" as a means of getting elected.

This same phrase *"Talis rex, qualis grex"* may seem topsy-turvy at first glance when applied to principals, but it deserves some reflection. Although the principal is not at the top of the policy-making hierarchy, he or she is truly the leader in the school. In my experience, schools take on the characteristics of the principal. The chief duty of principals is to motivate stakeholders to exert greater efforts to improve their performance so their actions will improve school outcomes and implement the shared vision. If that is true, then the principal as the servant-leader should exert his or her efforts as any servant would: to help stakeholders want to work harder, want to improve their skills and knowledge, want to accomplish greater things, want to serve others more fully, and want to accomplish the shared vision for the school. The principal acting as servant-leader tries to remove the barriers to pride in workmanship, improve the resources, help the stakeholders improve their competence, and make the work easier in every way possible so the actual workers—students and teachers—can together experience the joy of a job well done. When students and teachers are learning together, you know that the school has an excellent principal (servant-leader) who has made this collegial approach possible. It is impossible to exaggerate the importance of the principal's role as motivator. All great principals are models in motivation. It is crucial.

Greenleaf tells us that the servant-leader is servant first. It begins with the natural feeling that one wants to serve. I can't think of a better example of this than my wife. She has been dedicated to the service of others all her life. She is always looking to see what others need and want, trying to respond to their needs even before the person puts them into words. As a result, she has been chosen for leadership roles during much of her life. She accepted these posts simply so she could serve better. In these roles she was always servant first, leader second. She never had a need for power, prestige, or possessions for herself. She was sharply different from other leaders I have known who were leaders first and servants second. These were not bad people, and in many cases they did an adequate job of organizing people and getting things done, but they were not true servant-leaders. Some leaders never attempt to be servants. They are born autocrats, and most of them are eminently forgettable. The true servant-leaders, like my wife, who took care that other people's highest priority needs were being served, are never forgotten.

The best test, yet one that is difficult to administer, asks, "Do those served grow as persons? Do they, while being served, become healthier, wiser, freer, more autonomous, more likely themselves to become servants?" If so, their leader is definitely a servant-leader. My wife is not the only servant-leader I look up to and respect. I have met countless public school principals who are true servant-leaders. Recently, I met with thirteen of them in Winston-Salem. They were each chosen as principal of the year for North Carolina. I studied them over a long weekend. They possessed all the attributes of servant-leaders. I can guarantee you the stakeholders in their schools are healthier, wiser, freer, and more autonomous because they have had these servant-leaders as their principals.

HOW CAN PRINCIPALS MOTIVATE STAKEHOLDERS BETTER?

We might summarize what we said above in this way: the Steward Principal tries to make the jobs that the other stakeholders do more meaningful and self-fulfilling. You can be sure that Steward Principals who model good motivation and act like servant-leaders, moving obstacles out of the way for the stakeholders, will be sadly missed when they move on. The Irish say it best, "After the chieftain falls, the fighting seldom continues."

When we talk about motivation, we sometimes limit the meaning to a pep talk or cheerleading. Yet it is possible to be a great motivator without being a charismatic leader. When principals act as servant-leaders, spending their time and energy trying to make stakeholders' jobs more "user friendly," they will earn the trust and allegiance of their stakeholders. With this willingness to work on behalf of the stakeholders, the principals naturally speak favorably about their associates. Their stakeholders trust them and work hard to improve their knowledge and skills in order to accomplish the shared vision more effectively.

In Domain 14, we find a diagram entitled, "Job Characteristic Model of Work Motivation." I found Figure 4 most helpful. The team led by Cynthia D. McCauley uses this diagram to explain the job characteristics of work motivation. There are three critical psychological states that must be considered in designing a "user-friendly" job.

EXPERIENCE MEANINGFULNESS OF WORK

Three men were working together using pickaxes to breakup the hardpan on a piece of land in a little known French town called Chartres. As they took a break in their work, a small boy asked the first laborer what he was doing. He replied, "Little man, I am using a pickax to break up some very hard packed earth." A few minutes later, the lad asked a second worker what he was doing. He said, "I am helping to dig a deep foundation so others can come along afterwards and build some huge building." When he came to the last worker, the little boy was surprised to hear a totally different kind of answer. This man said, "My son, I am building a cathedral here in this small town. It will take hundreds of men like me to build it, and it won't be finished for generations, but when it is, people from all over Europe will come here to worship and marvel. Then people, even those from far over the seas, will know of the town of Chartres." I heard that story over fifty years ago and never forgot it. I'll bet the first man tired early each day. It is fatiguing to break up hardpan. The second man had more energy, but not as much as the third. He was energized by his vision. With vision comes real motivation, and this becomes the air beneath our wings.

We know from many sources that people are more highly motivated when they experience their work as meaningful and worthwhile. When principals can help stakeholders realize that

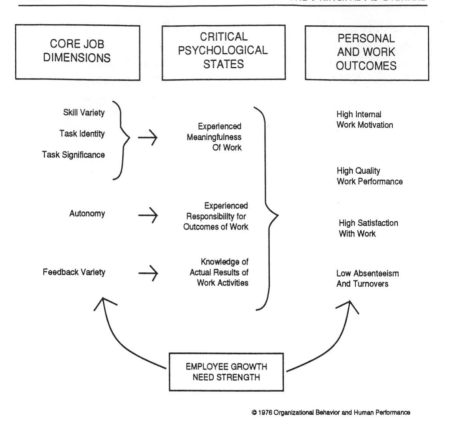

| CORE JOB DIMENSIONS | CRITICAL PSYCHOLOGICAL STATES | PERSONAL AND WORK OUTCOMES |

Skill Variety

Task Identity

Task Significance

Experienced Meaningfulness Of Work

Autonomy

Experienced Responsibility for Outcomes of Work

Feedback Variety

Knowledge of Actual Results of Work Activities

High Internal Work Motivation

High Quality Work Performance

High Satisfaction With Work

Low Absenteeism And Turnovers

EMPLOYEE GROWTH NEED STRENGTH

© 1976 Organizational Behavior and Human Performance

Figure 4. Job Characteristic Model of Work Motivation

they are engaged in meaningful and challenging work, they are motivated to make greater efforts, improve their skills, and rejoice in the outcomes. Unfortunately, all too many workers find little or no meaning in the work they do. They feel that they could be replaced by a robot. Incidentally, the word "robot" comes from the Czech word *robotnik* which means a serf or slave. When teachers and students find no meaning in their work they tire early, feeling deep sadness and discouragement. Outcomes suffer. Steward Principals invest a lot of time and effort making it clear to stakeholders how important their work is. To be meaningful, a piece of work has to have wide and deep significance. What we do has to make a real difference. In the United States,

Germany, Japan and other technically advanced countries, robots now replace workers who did spot welding, metal cutting, and car assembly and painting on assembly lines. These persons are now free to do more meaningful work. Of course they have to be trained and motivated to use their critical thinking skills on more meaningful and demanding tasks.

It is my conviction that the work of a school principal is among the most meaningful and demanding types of work in our society today. No one except parents play so significant a role in the formation of our children. Principals should constantly awaken their own appreciation of the meaningfulness of their work. This will help the other stakeholders do the same. Any policy changes that make the principal's work more meaningless (capable of being done by a robot) is counter-productive.

EXPERIENCE RESPONSIBILITY FOR OUTCOMES OF WORK

It really shouldn't be hard for teachers to realize how important a role they play in the learning of students, but it is. Why? It is daunting and frightening to realize how much raw power teachers wield. After all, the teacher influences what a child learns, the way he or she learns, and the joy or pain he or she experiences. However, teachers are quick to tell you how much the other influences in society affect these same school outcomes. Teachers can point to many cases where advantaged children flourish while disadvantaged ones flounder. All this is true. Children in school carry varying burdens. For some the burden is light as a feather, for others it is backbreaking. Teachers can only do so much. The public or the Central Office is unfair when it expects that in the few hours in which a teacher has the students, he or she can counterbalance massive outside influences from the family and society.

The teacher should not be held responsible for whether all children learn an equal amount, pick up the same skills at the same rate, and learn to care about learning to the same degree. That is unrealistic. What the teacher does have responsibility for is making sure that children from diverse social conditions with differing genetic endowments are given equal opportunities to experience the joy of learning, to appreciate that they can learn, and have some successes every day. At the end of the year all students should feel more self-esteem because they have worked hard to learn something and were able to reach a level of mastery that impressed the teacher as well as themselves. They should have a higher appreciation of their own worth and importance, and that of others. This is not too much to ask. Good teachers do it.

Teachers rightly complain that the rigid system often makes such teaching (coaching) difficult if not impossible. Both unrealistic curricular expectations and the tyranny of standardized testing often interfere with the objectives listed above. Class size and excessive competition demanded by the system and parents often put teachers at a great disadvantage as they try to do what they know ought to be done. There is no better way to kill teacher motivation than to make individualized teaching and coaching—the one thing they can do well and feel accountable for—impossible to accomplish.

Teachers can only feel joy in their accomplishments if they have the opportunity to really make a difference in the learning outcomes of their individual students. Standardized testing is often the only accepted measure of student outcomes. Teachers know that these tests cannot measure the real learning which can take place in a child who is coached well. No doubt, we need standards. Perhaps we should agree on the standards first, then find a variety of means to evaluate the students' performances one by one against these standards. It seems we got the wagon in front of the horse. We should set standards first, evaluation second, and make both contingent on the time the student needs to meet the standards. This change alone would greatly motivate students and teachers.

Time constraints also rob American school teachers of job satisfaction. Japan, France, and Germany devote twice as much time to basic core subjects as we do. Moreover, the rigid time schedules within which U.S. teachers work (an average of 51-minute periods regardless of the difficulty of the subject matter and the needs of the students), the impossible curricular demands that can't be met by a majority of students in the time allotted, the lack of time allowed for teachers to work one-on-one with students, and the shortage of planning time to work together, make it most difficult for teachers to continue to work at a high level of motivation. Adding more time isn't the answer if we continue to use the added time in the same way we have in the past. We need to find better ways of teaching and learning.

What can a principal do to help teachers gain responsibility for work outcomes? The principal has to work hard to change the system. Teachers will have to be given more autonomy. At the same time, they need to have more training in teaching students with different learning styles, cultural backgrounds, levels of skill, motivation, familial support, etc. They also need time each school day to be away from the students so they can plan new learning experiences, consult with their colleagues, and design cooperative teaching experiences.

Most teachers would love to be more responsible and accountable for learning outcomes, but they really are hamstrung. The principal's job is to remove these barriers so teachers can take pride in their work. Teachers survive only because of small victories and their genuine love and devotion to the children. They know we should be doing better; in many cases they even know how to do better. In all too many cases, they are caught in systems that are designed to make it impossible for teachers to teach and children to learn. No wonder principals worry about the turnover and the burnout of teachers. Deming was right. The fault more often than not lies in the systems, which herd youngsters together for purposes of learning, when the only thing they have in common is their chronological age. The tests are used to police the teachers rather than to help students learn better. The curriculum remains a cafeteria of disconnected pieces of knowledge with no overall themes to make connections. It is often a mile wide and a quarter-inch deep.

What is remarkable is the number of teachers who work effectively even under these handicapping conditions, yet still feel responsible for the learning of each child. They do this because they are motivated by good principals, parents, and students who give them positive feedback. These great teachers are motivated by the satisfaction that comes from a job well done, the feeling of pride of accomplishment. It is great to see someone learning and knowing you have helped in the process. It feels good to be responsible. At 15 years of age, what we clamored for most was to be given responsibility.

HAVE KNOWLEDGE OF ACTUAL RESULTS OF WORK ACTIVITIES

To maintain motivation, individuals need to know how they are performing and how their performance can be improved. Normally, we get this understanding from feedback and reflective practice. Teachers and students especially need feedback because the outcomes of learning are not always immediately apparent. Here is where we make a huge mistake. We often rely on standardized testing as the sole means of giving this feedback. The problem is that most standardized tests give teachers and students the wrong kind of feedback. Our need to reduce all knowledge to facts, all skills to rote functions, to quantify everything as if qualitative evaluation was worthless, leads us to construct more standardized tests. The results from these tests send a clear but negative message to teachers and students. Such messages are not helpful in motivating teachers and students. The unwise use of time and standardized tests often make it impossible for principals and teachers to get knowledge of the actual results of their work activities.

Steward Principals with years of experience know a simple truth. The best teachers love to have you visit their classes. Your presence and obvious pleasure are a great positive reinforcement of the teacher's good work. Your suggestions for improvement are gladly accepted by most. On the other hand, ineffective teachers dread your classroom visits. They are usually unwilling or unable to accept and profit from suggestions for improvement. Principals soon find excuses for not visiting these classrooms. Their dream is that these ineffective teachers will get better training, or be transferred, or terminated. Nothing kills stakeholders' motivation more than situations in which the principal is powerless to correct the damage done daily to the students by teachers who are ineffective. Often the principal motivates stakeholders most when he or she is successful in getting rid of an ineffective teacher. Leadership demands the fortitude to take a stand.

The federal government, when it contributes money to states and to local educational agencies for students in special programs, demands that each student have an Individual Educational Plan. As mentioned earlier, ideally we should have an

IEP for each student. The IEP should contain a cumulative file containing samples of the student's work, indicating the progress he or she is making in mastering the essentials of a basic education. The file would contain anecdotes, samples of the student's work, subjective evaluations by various observers and statements from the students themselves. Each student with his or her respective parent(s) should have the opportunity to go over the IEP monthly with the teacher, and every four months with the principal or assistant principal, to ascertain how the planned educational experiences for the previous period fared and to plan new experiences for the next period. Some diagnostic testing would be necessary in order to make clear what the student's strengths and weaknesses are.

If principals had other means of getting and giving feedback besides the results of standardized tests and classroom visits, it might lead to an improved learning situation for students. The principal could sit with the teachers and go over an IEP to find out why a student was having trouble in one area while showing real progress in another. Granted, parents need to be educated so they no longer demand quantitative feedback and ranking on a monthly basis, and granted, we would have to loosen curricular and testing demands. Also, we would have to make school calendars and schedules much more flexible, and tailor teaching methods to the learning needs of the student. We would have to allow teachers time to do one-on-one work and more time for training. However, the results in improved learning would more than compensate for these changes in the system.

In some private schools, where there is a ratio of one teacher to 10 to 15 students, teachers know results and are motivated. They are highly motivated by this knowledge of results. Teachers teach better, coaching individual students and giving and getting feedback. They can do it because they are freed of the constraints under which most public school teachers work. To motivate teachers, parents, and students, let them experience the delight of knowing that their added effort, growing personal knowledge, and skills have improved the Learning Organization.

To improve motivation, the principal learns to use a variety of feedback sources and avoids relying solely on the results of standardized tests. By removing barriers from the teachers and students, the principal will rejoice in greatly improved learning outcomes. When the tide comes in, all ships rise. The level of motivation in the school rises across the board.

MOTIVATION HELPS INITIATE AND SUSTAIN DESIRED BEHAVIOR

What knowledge and skill does a principal need in order to effectively motivate a staff to achieve personal, professional, and educational excellence? The same knowledge and skill that will motivate parents and students. The five essential clusters outlined in Domain 14, *Principals For Our Changing Schools,* should prove helpful for effective Steward Principals.

ENHANCING THE MEANINGFULNESS OF WORK

The first step involves making sure that the work of each of the stakeholders is challenging. Research in psychology points out that people work best under an amount of stress that challenges them without overwhelming them. When a group of telephone executives working under heavy stress were studied, the results gave us a fascinating picture. The executives who not only survived but flourished under the challenging conditions were characterized by three things. They were more **committed** to the various parts of their lives. They felt a great sense of **control** over the things that happened in their lives and finally, they experienced **challenge** in a more positive light. Whether a principal is trying to motivate a teacher, secretary, custodian, student, parent or assistant principal, it is important to enlist the **commitment** of the stakeholder to the shared vision, offer him or her manageable **challenges** that stretch their present skills and capacities without overwhelming them. If they can stay within themselves and avoid panic (feeling out of **control**), they will grow from the experience. There is a great sense of accomplishment and pride in their work when stakeholders perform above their usual level. The principal can only offer challenges that stretch people without breaking them if he or she knows each stakeholder well enough to make a valid judgment on how little or much challenge he or she is capable of handling. The principal knows that stakeholders can learn to stretch themselves, to become more confident so they can tolerate greater challenges without fearing loss of control. The more the stakeholders become committed to the shared vision and confident in their ability to tolerate stress and handle challenges, the more they grow. From encountering challenges and mastering the skills needed to meet them successfully, the person grows in ability and self-esteem.

Besides providing challenges to the stakeholders, the Steward Principal encourages teamwork and collegiality. In my experience, the principals who are most successful in enhancing the meaningfulness of the stakeholders' work allow time for teacher interactions so they can work together and be supportive of each other as they face the challenges. Moreover, the principal who continually emphasizes the significance of the work at hand by word and example is most successful in getting the stakeholders to accept difficult challenges and work as a team to surmount obstacles to the attainment of the shared vision.

ENHANCING RESPONSIBILITY FOR WORK OUTCOMES

The authors offer three useful suggestions: take a participative approach to decision-making; allow teachers more discretion; and finally, encourage teachers to develop close relationships with parents.

The key to motivation is creating an environment in which all stakeholders feel they are included in the group. What makes a Learning Organization successful is the relationships. These are at the heart of any cooperative work. What causes schools to fail is their bureaucratic structure. Bureaucratic organizations tend to practice exclusion instead of inclusion. They build their relationships around contractual agreements and exclude too many people from both their processes and the sharing of good results. In my experience, bureaucracies care less about attaining good results than they do about finding scapegoats, and thus avoiding blame. Most workers in a bureaucracy never get the opportunity to design the system. The structure of the bureaucratic system operates through fear rather than the desire for challenge in the pursuit of excellence.

Max DePree's explanation of the need for inclusiveness in

any organization in his book *Leadership Is An Art* has great relevance for every school organization; I would highly recommend it to principals.

If we think of motivation as merely a means of improving results (products, profits, etc.), it somewhat cheapens the concept. I would rather think of motivation as dealing with people in a way that makes them feel an essential part of a group that cares about their growth, job satisfaction, and well-being.

We must sincerely believe that every person brings a unique offering to the group and deserves to be included in all the group is, has, and does. *This means that we have to believe in the intrinsic value of diversity.* The secret of success for any Learning Organization is respect for diversity and recognition of what it contributes to the whole. It takes a lot of courage to do this, because we are under great pressure from many sources—not the least of which is advertising—to believe we have an endless appetite for anything as long as it breathes an "air of exclusiveness." If we yield too easily to the temptation of selfishness, the cure is found in inclusiveness. If exclusiveness breeds selfishness, the antidote is inclusiveness. Changing "Not in my neighborhood" to "Yes, in my neighborhood" is the way a school or nation becomes inclusive and a real community-based Learning Organization.

The concept of "people first", accepting diversity and opening our group to all regardless of race, color, religion, or culture requires better communication skills. Members of homogeneous groups tend to get careless about expressing themselves: they can take so much for granted. But in communicating with diverse people, we have to be aware and alert, constantly editing what we say in the light of others' sensitivities. People know infallibly whether or not they are included. Look back to your own experience: you knew when you were accepted and included, when you felt needed, involved, and cared about as a person. In these circumstances, you felt you received fair wages and benefits. You were given the opportunity to do your very best. Your leaders gave you these opportunities to perform before you gave proof of task-relevant maturity. You felt you understood the whole process. You shared in productivity, gains, profits, ownership, appreciation, seniority, bonus, etc. When a majority of the stakeholders in a school feel this sense of inclusiveness, a skilled motivator-principal is directing a true Learning Organization school.

Of course inclusiveness is a two-way street. It requires something from everyone. Those who want to be included must respond actively. A principal who tries to accept diversity and be inclusive has a right to expect that the stakeholders will pull their weight, rejecting exclusiveness.

According to DePree, if you are a leader, you have a right to expect that your stakeholders will be faithful. As you are faithful to them, they must be faithful to you and each other. Being faithful or loyal is more important than being successful. This is what we mean by being spiritual: committed to transcendent values. If one is successful at the cost of being unfaithful, that person doesn't deserve to be included. If we are unfaithful to what we believe in, we are failures no matter how much the public applauds our apparent successes.

In a true Learning Organization, all members realize that reaching their potential is more important than reaching group goals. There is no way to be inclusive without becoming vulnerable. The very act of being inclusive means we drop our defenses and lay ourselves open to betrayal. It is the opposite of a bureaucracy, where we keep our defenses up and choose to be the first rat off the sinking ship. If you as a principal are vulnerable to your fellow stakeholders, they have the obligation to strive to be open and honest with you. When we belong, we must of necessity become intimate in the sense of being real and sincere. DePree says being an insider is not a spectator sport. It means being fully and personally accountable. It means we give up superficiality and become genuine in our relationships.

When you look around the neighborhood or the world, you can't help but see that people seem to be backing away from each other into exclusivity. Instead of becoming more inclusive, we are splintering into clans, tribes, and ethnic groups that claim they can make it on their own in an exclusive fashion.

They say this even as everything points out that we humans, animals, and plants are in this together. If the ozone hole gets much bigger, we will all find ourselves in serious trouble. If, as is predicted, there are a thousand nations on this globe in the 21st century instead of the hundreds we now have, how will we be able to communicate and cooperate, while telecommunication, travel, weaponry, and nuclear power technologies conspire to shrink the globe into a tribal village?

If public schools teach one thing, it ought to be the necessity of being *inclusive and accepting of diversity with all its rich gifts.* It should help us learn to communicate and negotiate without the use of violence. A Steward Principal who motivates others well will learn that lesson in his or her school everyday. Our cultural heritage as Americans is based on this type of inclusiveness. *E pluribus unum.*

If we humans kill off enough species by pollution or enough languages and cultures by ethnic cleansing, there won't be much diversity left. Then this thin film of planetary life (including our own), which flourished precisely because of diversity will suffer and may die. *Biophilia* in the words of Edward O. Wilson, is "the innately emotional affiliation of human beings to other living organisms." We are hard-wired by our evolutionary history to have affinity for life in all forms. Diversity and inclusiveness should be the first lesson learned in any school. If not, "The last one out turn off the lights."

The third cluster of knowledge and skill necessary for a Steward Principal who is a good motivator involves making sure that all the stakeholders receive feedback. There is no lasting motivation without knowledge of results.

PROVIDING KNOWLEDGE OF RESULTS

Under the heading of Providing Knowledge of Results, the authors of Domain 14 stress providing personal feedback and maintaining feedback systems. When I see feedback mentioned in connection with motivation, I am reminded of the first serious experiment I carried out as a young psychologist. I used measures of reaction time and varied the amount of feedback the subjects received. My hypothesis was that subjects who were given immediate knowledge of their results (feedback) would perform significantly better than subjects who were not so informed. The results of my Master's thesis clearly indicated that when subjects were given immediate knowledge of their results (feedback), they performed 25 percent better than the control group who lacked such feedback.

I often think that golf is a popular game precisely because the feedback is so immediate. Whenever I overhear a foursome finishing a round of golf, they seem to be having a lively conversation about the game's results. One says, "I never saw you hook a ball as badly as you did on the 12th. You were lucky you came out with a six." Not to be outdone, another golfer can't resist saying, "You should talk about luck! If your chip on the ninth didn't hit that tree limb, you would have had at least a seven or eight."

It strikes me strange that forty-year-old golfers who get excited about the immediate feedback from their game don't realize that schools deprive their sons and daughters of this pleasure. They often have to wait weeks and even months to get feedback from their school tests. If you play a round with the club pro, you expect to get some coaching and feedback along the way. Students would learn better if teachers coached and gave immediate feedback like golf pros. Providing knowledge of results makes all learning easier. Incidentally, teachers fare better when they have a principal who gives them positive feedback. Well-motivated people are like volunteers: they give more than they get. Most good people make a living at what they get and make a life by what they give.

SHAPING EFFORT-PERFORMANCE EXPECTATIONS

When discussing the fourth cluster of knowledge and skill demanded of a motivating principal, shaping effort-performance expectations, the authors in Domain 14 highlight the importance of the principal serving as a role model. Only a principal who is shaping his or her own effort-performance expectations at a high level can expect the stakeholders to go that extra mile. We discussed this above, but I would like to add one point. If the whole purpose of schooling is to help students love to learn, one of the areas in which a principal should serve as a model is in the actual learning itself. A "learning principal" (one who is consistently trying to improve his or her knowledge and skills) motivates teachers to learn, and "learning teachers" are fine models for "learning students." When I think about a Learning Organization, I envision a group of people working together with one purpose: to help all stakeholders become more proficient at learning. Frederick Perls, the famous psychoanalyst, gave this memorable definition of real learning.

> Learning requires living with a tolerable level of discomfort. If you are not a bit uncomfortable, you aren't learning, you're practicing, relearning, coasting.

I see a motivating principal as one who *comforts* the afflicted but is just as serious about *afflicting* the comfortable. In fact, that has been my motto for over 50 years. When I get too comfortable I realize that I may be just "practicing, relearning, coasting," and I reach out for a challenge that will necessitate my learning some new knowledge and skill. This always requires living with a tolerable level of discomfort. I like to look in the mirror and ask myself, "Is what you are doing or about to do getting you closer to your objectives?" That is self-motivation.

Under the same heading of shaping effort-performance, the authors encourage principals to enhance individual productivity. When we set work and self-development goals, the attaining of these goals most certainly entails work, but it doesn't feel like work. Work is more fun than amusements if we enter it willingly and gain satisfaction from doing it well. Our productivity takes on real excitement when we work cooperatively with peers who see the same vision and are driven to make it a reality.

SHAPING PERFORMANCE-OUTCOME EXPECTATIONS

Finally, when discussing the shaping of performance-outcome expectations, the authors of Domain 14 stress two things: being aware of valued rewards, and linking rewards to performance. They tell us that effective principals make it a point to know exactly what it is that each of the stakeholders find rewarding. We all have similar needs, but we differ greatly in our wants. In a large school with 100 or more teachers, it is essential that the principal, assistant principals, department heads, and/ or lead teachers spend quality time with the teachers learning what each teacher finds rewarding. When a principal has a good working relationship with the stakeholders, he or she has firsthand knowledge of what means the most to them. This knowledge should determine what the reward will be in each case. Someone once joked that money isn't the only important thing in this world, but it sure comes in way ahead of whatever comes in second. That is not a very good joke, and it isn't accurate when speaking about motivating educators. Granted that teachers rightly wish they were better compensated, most of them would gladly settle for rewards with a longer shelf life than money. The fact that they are in education proves that.

My widowed grandmother helped support a large family by running a sewing machine in a small factory that produced fine ladies' garments. When she died in her late 80's, among her meager treasures was a note written by her boss 55 years before. He apparently left it pinned to her machine one evening. It simply said, "Mrs. O'Connor, I appreciate the care you put into your work and the consistent way you work each day. You deserve to be commended." It was dated and signed by the owner, Mr. Warner.

Rewards are effective only if they fit the personality of the recipient. If Mr. Warner had given my grandmother a dollar (a huge sum in those days), it would have been appreciated and enjoyed but it would not have lasted as long or have been read as often as that simple note. Worse still, I wouldn't have known what a great worker my kindly old grandmother was. After her funeral I read her tattered note from Mr. Warner with tears of gratitude in my eyes.

Finally, the authors insist that principals should link rewards to performance. I think the story about my grandmother illustrates this well. When personal praise and public recognition are given in appreciation for a job well done, the recognition and appreciation should be clearly linked to work accomplished. Principals who celebrate and express pride in the accomplishments of their schools are good motivators. Rewards need not be competitive; when a school has had a banner year, all the stakeholders deserve to celebrate what their cooperative work has accomplished.

SUMMATION

When asked the question, "Can principals really motivate stakeholders?" we had to answer in the affirmative. In fact, we had to admit that one of the prime roles of the Steward Principal in forming and maintaining a Learning Organization is that of motivator. We found the definition of motivation offered by Cynthia McCauley and her team to be most informative and helpful. We then concluded that principals motivate others well only if they are themselves well-motivated. We acknowledged that one of the greatest difficulties principals face is that they are expected to motivate their own stakeholders while they themselves receive little or no positive motivation. The principal's life can be a lonely one.

We developed the idea of a servant-leader to show how a Steward Principal motivates the stakeholders by removing obstacles that interfere with the stakeholders' enjoyment of their work. Steward Principals are servant-leaders.

We followed the lead of Deming, who claims that much of the poor performance and lack of motivation in an organization is the result of problems in the bureaucratic system itself.

Next we pointed out some ways that principals can be better motivators of their fellow stakeholders. Principals motivate best when they enhance the meaningfulness of work, stress responsibility for work outcomes, provide knowledge of results, shape effort-performance expectations, and shape performance-outcome expectations.

We joined with Max DePree, who insists that when the stakeholders feel included in the designing of the system, they take a proprietary interest and go the extra mile. We stressed the need to include all stakeholders in the decision making and to celebrate the enriching diversity among the members.

Finally, we concluded that the only authority deserving of allegiance is that which is freely and knowingly granted by the stakeholders to their principals in response to and in proportion to the principals' clearly evident servant stature. The Steward Principal who serves the needs of the stakeholders most effectively motivates the stakeholders to do their best work and take pride in what they do.

QUESTIONS FOR REFLECTION

1. Goodlad says you can pick out good principals very easily. They are the ones who are quick to praise their stakeholders and give most credit for the success of the school to them. Do you agree? If so, why so; if not, why not?

2. Most people who work hard say they do it simply because they like what they are doing. They enjoy seeing how their labor with others leads to observable results. Is that what motivates principals?

3. In one sense, no one can motivate another, we can only move ourselves; but principals who remove obstacles to stakeholders' good feelings about their work are true motivators. Do you agree? If so, why so; if not, why not?

4. Cynthia D. McCauley and her team in Domain 14 define motivation as creating conditions that enhance staff's desire and willingness to focus energy on achieving educational excellence. How do Steward Principals accomplish this?

5. As a principal what do you do to enhance conditions in your school which further both students and teachers to work hard for educational excellence?

6. Why is it that principals who act like servant-leaders or Stewards seem to be the most successful motivators?

7. What does it mean that a principal's own behavior is often a great motivator to the stakeholders?

8. Why is it that both teachers and students are motivated best when they experience the meaningfulness of the work they are engaged in?

9. People seem to work harder when they experience responsibility for the outcomes of their work. Why?

10. Why do good teachers enjoy visits by the principal to their classrooms?

11. What does DePree mean when he says that leaders have a right to expect that their stakeholders will be faithful?

12. A Steward Principal is one who comforts the afflicted and also afflicts the comfortable. Is that a good way to look at motivation?

6

THE STEWARD PRINCIPAL IS SENSITIVE

"As leaders learn to be more sensitive, they sharpen their perceptive skills and begin to develop better moral reasoning."

In his *Leadership is an Art*, Max DePree points out that, "To be a leader means, especially, having the opportunity to make a meaningful difference in the lives of those who permit leaders to lead." (27) The most significant factor in determining a principal's effectiveness in forming and maintaining a Learning Organization is the quality of his or her interpersonal encounters with each stakeholder. Studies make it clear that principals spend up to 80 percent of their working time engaged in conversation with stakeholders. The remainder of the time is spent on things that "go bang in the night" and a little bit of planning. When principals become more adept at handling interpersonal relations, they avoid one of their biggest time-wasters—time spent correcting misunderstandings. Misunderstandings arise either because the principal has been less than sensitive in an earlier conversation, or the stakeholder lacked sufficient sensitivity to "read" the principal correctly. Most principals spend a lot of time smoothing ruffled feathers and soothing hurt feelings. Greater sensitivity on both sides could have avoided these mishaps.

Skills learned in sensitivity training pay large dividends in all labor-intensive organizations, including K–12 education.

When Steward Principals are skilled enough to recognize and handle the great diversity among the stakeholders, they take into account their varying priorities, values, and relationships. This is especially true when the principal is leading a multicultural school. In this chapter we will focus on the sensitivities needed in one-on-one communications, as well as those in dealing with groups.

WHY SO MUCH EMPHASIS ON INTERPERSONAL SENSITIVITY?

I met Matthew Kurtz during a workshop on sensitivity training. In my session I was explaining the idea that principals can only succeed at interpersonal relations if they are sufficiently sensitive, and they can only be sensitive to others if they learn to be sensitive to themselves. Put simply, their *interpersonal* skills are imbedded in their *intrapersonal* skills. Our limited sensitivities to others are founded in our inability to feel our own feelings. For example, if I hear that a teacher lost her father, I have to go inside myself and dredge up the feelings I experienced when my dad died in order to begin to understand her feelings of loss. To be empathetic with others demands a keen perception of our own inner psychic life. After the session, as I started to walk toward the door, I noticed that Matthew remained seated after all had left the auditorium. When I walked up to him I couldn't help but see the pain in his eyes. He wasn't crying but his eyes reflected sadness and bewilderment.

With 45 years of clinical experience, it wasn't difficult for me to see that he was suffering through a serious life crisis. I wondered if anything I said had triggered his present state. As I slowed to make a social remark, he asked if he could see me for a few minutes. We were having box lunches so I suggested that we each grab a box and find a place where we could eat and talk.

Here with some omissions is the story that Matthew told me. He had been sent to this workshop on sensitivity by his superintendent. Matthew, a previous "teacher of the year" in his district and recognized as one of the best science teachers in the state, had been appointed an assistant principal. After one year in that job, he was praised for his work of organizing the school for the principal. As a result of this success, he was el-evated to a principal's job at a nearby middle school. A year and a half into this new job, he had been called in by the new super-intendent and told bluntly that his interpersonal skills were so deficient that he would be demoted unless he made major changes in the way he dealt with stakeholders. Matthew was devastated. He had no idea that there were any problems with the way he was carrying out his duties as principal. No stake-holders had come to Matthew to complain. He thought he was well-liked and respected. This was almost more than he could handle. His world had come tumbling down.

Matthew told me his superintendent had sent him to this workshop on sensitivity with these instructions: "Learn how to be sensitive to people or you will no longer be a principal." I asked Matthew if he thought the superintendent was sending him here as a punishment. "Yes," he replied, "I don't believe people can be taught to be sensitive in a weekend workshop. I must have been insensitive for most of my life, but I wasn't aware of it. I surely never thought my lack of sensitivity interfered with my work. How did I get to be "teacher of the year" if I am so insensitive? Lack of sensitivity didn't seem to hurt my work as a science teacher. I didn't play "buddy" with the students but I did teach a well-prepared science class, correct their homework and tests, and get the results back to them on time, and I was fair. I was willing to give extra time to any student who ap-proached me and asked for help. As assistant principal, I didn't have to handle student discipline problems or squabbles between teachers. The principal was glad to handle those chores, pro-vided I would devote my time to getting classes, buses, teach-ers, and activities scheduled efficiently. He had no head for organizing. I spent most of my time setting up the computers and organizing school activities. Everyone seemed happy with the results. I found chaos and replaced it with order. The princi-pal said nothing about my lack of sensitivity."

Lunch was over and I knew we had a lot of unfinished busi-ness. Since I was giving a class right after lunch in which I would be covering material on sensitivity, I suggested Matthew attend my class, and we arranged to get together that evening after the other classes were finished. I couldn't help thinking how cruel it was to send Matthew into a job for which he was poorly prepared. True, he was a good science teacher and great organizer, but now he was a principal confronted by all kinds of intricate interpersonal problems that would not yield to his detached scientific approach. Matthew was beginning to realize that the Steward Principal needs to have a grasp on the theoretical aspects of interpersonal relations, as well as supervised practice in applying the knowledge and skill. Matthew, like many principals, had received little or no preparation in graduate school for dealing sensitively with stakeholders.

SENSITIVITY DEFINED

That afternoon I shared with the class the definition crafted by Ivan Muse and his team, contained in Domain 15 of *Principals For Our Changing Schools,* hoping Matthew would begin to get a glimmer of what the superintendent meant when he told him he lacked sensitivity. I have some doubt about the superintendent's own sensitivity. Both Matthew and his superintendent could profit from studying this definition.

> **"Sensitivity:** Perceiving the needs and concerns of others; working with others in emotionally stressful situations or in conflict; managing conflict; obtaining feedback; recognizing multi-cultural differences; relating to people of varying backgrounds." (28)

When principals are sensitive, they demonstrate consideration toward the feelings, attitudes, needs, and intentions of others, and sense what others feel about themselves and their place in the world. Was Matthew Kurtz insensitive in his dealings with stakeholders? Evidently, the superintendent had received many complaints from a large number of teachers, parents, and students, so it is probably safe to conclude that Matthew, gifted as he was in other ways, was lacking in sensitivity. A Steward Principal who lacks technical skills cannot completely make up for this lack by increased interpersonal skills, but these skills go a long way. The more frequent case is one like Matthew's, in which the principal has some fine technical skills but is seriously lacking in sensitivity skills. Many colleges and universities that prepare educational leaders are beginning to introduce sensitivity training. Site management, no matter what else it demands of a principal, certainly will demand his or her developed sensitivity in dealing with stakeholders.

SIX STEPS IN DEVELOPING SENSITIVITY

Sensitivity training as a professional tool started with the National Training Laboratory for group development in Bethel, Maine. This group introduced sensitivity training groups in the 1940s. Their bold psychological approach often frightened corporate leaders. Some CEOs were afraid the brutally confrontational training was getting their executives into too deep psychological waters. I remember I had some serious misgivings myself at the time. I was afraid that some of the less than adequately trained trainers were unleashing demons in the participants, which they were not equipped to handle. In some cases, my fears were justified. However, looking back, the good the training groups accomplished outweighed their failures. The idea of training people to be more sensitive in dealing with others was in its infancy, but there were clear objectives, which are just as valid today. If Matthew is to become more skilled at interpersonal relations, he will have to meet these objectives.

In Domain 15, Ivan Muse and his team state these objectives clearly. I paraphrase and apply them in this manner.

Step # 1: To understand better one's behavior, its impact on others, and the ways in which one's behavior is interpreted by others; (Matthew had no idea that over the last 18 months, the stakeholders in his school were complaining to others about his lack of sensitivity. He didn't know himself well, nor did he realize the impact his actions were having on others.)

Step # 2: To understand better the behavior of others and to more accurately interpret verbal and nonverbal cues in order to become more aware of and sensitive to the thoughts and feelings of others; (Matthew seemed unable or unwilling to understand the behavior of his stakeholders, so he missed verbal and nonverbal cues, which precluded his discerning their thoughts and feelings.)

Step # 3: To understand better group and inter-group processes, especially those that facilitate and inhibit group functioning; (Matthew could handle the schedules and organize, but he didn't perceive the nuanced responses that would come from different cultural groups. There were subtle inter-group frictions that he missed.)

Step # 4: To improve diagnostic skills in interpersonal and inter-group situations by accomplishing the first three objectives; (How could Matthew improve his diagnostic skills in interpersonal situations? He was oblivious of the complexity of these relations and had never been taught to question or diagnose his feelings and communications, and those of his stakeholders. In this area Matthew was socially naive.)

Step # 5: To put learning into practice so that real-life interventions will succeed in increasing stakeholders' effectiveness, satisfaction, or output; (Our hope is that Matthew, with some coaching, can learn in the future to be more sensitive. To accomplish this, he will need time with a good mentor who will help him through role-playing and other techniques to improve both his intra- as well as inter-personal skills.)

Step # 6: To analyze better one's interpersonal behavior and to learn how to help oneself, and those with whom one interacts, achieve more satisfying, rewarding and effective relationships. (No matter how gifted a principal is in these sensitivity skills, he or she needs to continue improving in sensitivity. I think that Matthew's improved sensitivity skills will not only improve his work as a principal, it will make him a better husband, father, neighbor, etc. It is a win-win situation.)

These six objectives set forth almost 30 years ago are even more crucial today. Fewer and fewer of us are learning sensitivity at home. All the complaints about mounting violence in and out of school indicates just how far we have slipped in civility.

Civility is founded on interpersonal skills. This is not a new gimmick foisted on educational leaders. It is a rather old idea: do unto others as you would have them do unto you. We no longer can take it for granted that children come to school civilized nor even that teachers and principals are as adept at interpersonal skills as they once were. Sensitivity training is an idea whose time has come. Moreover, we should only hire teachers and principals who can demonstrate sensitivity in interpersonal relations. For instance, Assessment Centers for principals are placing more emphasis on sensitivity.

SENSITIVITY MEANS ACCURATELY PREDICTING RESPONSES

Ivan Muse and his team have done a great service in explaining the process by which sensitive people predict what will occur in a social situation. Learning to predict accurately is a lifelong task. It certainly can't be accomplished in a weekend workshop, nor by reading a chapter of a book. Learning how to get along well with other people is one of our most basic human tasks . If you look at Figure 5, which outlines this process, you will see at the top left, External Factors and in the center, Internal Factors.

EXTERNAL FACTORS

If we start with box #1, "Sensing by Perceiver," we see that the level at which Matthew is perceiving is influenced by some External Factors. Which of these factors do you think come into play, given the scenario I shared with you? Matthew has played three *roles* in the schools: science teacher, assistant principal, and principal. Do the roles he has played have anything to do with his present predicament? Put another way, can a person's lack of interpersonal skills be hidden more in one role than in another? We can ask the same questions about *goals*. The goals for managing a classroom are different from the goals of an assistant principal, who has broader duties. Matthew seemed to have been sheltered in his role as assistant principal. Finally we arrive at the role of principal—being a principal is a job in which none of one's shortcomings remain hidden. Many principals are

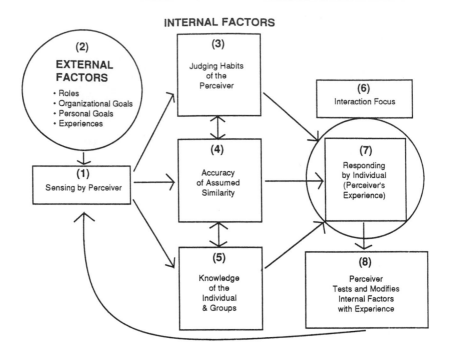

Figure 5. How Perceiver Predicts Effects of Social Interaction

caught daily in human situations that demand consummate interpersonal skills. You can't run away as a principal.

For the last External Factor, "Experiences," we ask this question: What kind of a family did Matthew come from? When I worked with Matthew later, I learned he came from a family that helped him believe in himself enough to pursue a college degree successfully. His family was intact, orderly, and painstakingly honest. They gave him support, but were very careful not to baby him. I could see that Matthew was a gentleman, so it was no surprise to find that his family was civilized, cultivated, and even genteel.

Matthew made one thing clear, his family didn't talk about or demonstrate feelings. From what he said, the family stayed fairly remote from each other. Neither were they great joiners. It was only through their membership in the local Methodist Church that they had contact with any people other than family members. These contacts were brief and formal.

Mathew could not remember any fights in the home. Unpleasant confrontations were avoided almost entirely. Matthew left home carrying with him the idea that most people made too much of their personal problems, and they would be better off if they swept emotional reactions under the rug where they would do less damage. Matthew was married to a young lady from church who as a lab technician found it easy to work alone. So far, their marriage appeared to be relatively satisfactory to both partners. They were presently trying to decide whether to have children. Be your own psychologist; certainly there isn't anything seriously wrong with Matthew. He appears to be a rather well-adjusted, healthy, intelligent human being. But what he learned in the family relative to getting on with people contradicted what he needed in the role of principal.

As a principal it is impossible to keep emotions under the rug. Not all people are remote and aloof; some are very "touchy feely." Some resent cool treatment and an aloof response. In even the best schools, there is a lot of fighting over one thing or another. Running a school comes down to building a team, and it is impossible to build a team without sharing something of your feelings with the members. Matthew might be one of the better members on that team as long as he could hide his lack of sensitivity. He couldn't be the leader of the team, because his insensitivity would become apparent, and it did. In spite of his real gifts, his inadequacy in interpersonal relations held him back. Although the superintendent may not have exhibited great interpersonal skills himself when he so advised Matthew, nevertheless he was correct. Matthew needed remedial work in sensitivity. He could profit from studying the internal factors offered by Muse and his team.

INTERNAL FACTORS

1. Judging Habits of the Perceiver. In box #3 in Figure 5 we find the first Internal Factor: "Judging Habits of the Perceiver." There is no question that judging habits of individuals greatly influences the way they perceive other individuals or groups. A clear example of this would be the way the KKK perceived people of color and the Black Panthers perceived whites. Another example would be the way Ted, a friend of mine, perceived obese people. He judged them harshly, believing they have flawed characters. He was a thin, high-strung, "type A" person, who had never had to struggle with a weight problem. Consequently, he judged fat people as weak-willed and self-indulgent. Though he didn't walk around verbalizing these assumptions, his behavior (body language) gave him away. Obese people never felt that he accepted them, and they were right. This judging habit hurt his effectiveness in dealing with people.

Judgment can be "level" and "spread." My friend Ted is a low-level judger of people, because he tends to be rather harsh in his judgment of himself and everyone else. However, once he gives his unconditioned approval to a person, that person becomes a "saint." There are only a couple of "saints" in his life, and they can do no wrong. On the other hand, when he judges someone to be a "sinner," from then on that person can do no right. Most low-level judgers have high expectations of themselves and others, and they are quick to put others down. They tend to be rather harsh in judging fellow humans, and for that reason they find it hard to trust them.

Take the example of a principal who views most teachers as mediocre. According to Goodlad's research, such principals—low-level judgers—are seldom found leading first-rate schools. As aforementioned, principals who tend to widely praise their staffs—high-level judgers—are more apt to be respected leaders themselves.

Many high-level judgers can have high standards for themselves and others, yet tend to be tolerant and optimistic. They believe in the perfectibility of their fellow humans. They say, "Failure is not sin, low aim is." These high-level judgers believe that if they raise the bar a little at a time, many—if not most—of their stakeholders will learn to jump higher. High level judgers tend to be better motivators.

The second term "spread," is the tendency of perceivers to rate others within a narrow or a wide range. Suppose I asked you as a principal to rate the teachers in your school on this scale: *superior, good, average, below average, poor*. After each teacher's name on the list, give one of these ratings. Now look at your ratings and see if they are all contained within two categories—for example: good and poor, or superior and average. This would indicate that you tend to judge on a narrow band. If,

on the other hand, you rated some of your teachers in all five
categories then you would be a broad judger. This is a good test
of one's sensitivity. The more people are able to differentiate
among different individuals and situations, the better chance
they have to be sensitive. For you as principals, it is certainly
worthwhile to learn to be high and broad level judgers. Improving in this area will be the first step toward becoming a more
sensitive perceiver.

Some principals act like gun slingers making off-the-hip judgments like fast-drawing Wyatt Earps. They are prone to be low,
narrow judgers who dump people into one or the other bin rather
quickly without taking time to get sufficient information before
they judge. Ted acts that way sometimes, and I suspect Matthew does too. Unfortunately, once these quick-draw judgments
are formed, they tend to solidify and become resistant to change.
Matthew as much as admitted that he made premature judgments and allowed them to get fixed in concrete. For instance,
within a month he took a dislike to an overweight teacher named
Helen who would weep when she came to his office. It seemed
the slightest thing bent her out of shape. He judged her to be
inadequate and without character. After 17 more months of observing her, Matthew—now getting some coaching in interpersonal skills—is beginning to see Helen for what she is: the loving
heart of the faculty. The teachers treat her like a beloved aunt
and the students love her. They seek her advice before going to
see the school counselor. Matthew learned in time that Helen
was an overweight, tearful treasure.

Matthew seems to be learning to doubt his own infallibility—a prerequisite for greater sensitivity. Ted seems more convinced of his own infallibility each day. I see him riding blindly
toward personal disaster. In the not-too-distant future, Ted may
be taken down at high noon in the OK Corral. You live by the
gun, you die by the gun. Ted is an insensitive man who is setting himself up for trouble. Mathew is slowly becoming more
sensitive and learning to joyfully accept diversity.

2. Accuracy of Assumed Similarity. As humans we have
the tendency to assume that other people share our thoughts,
feelings, and behavior. This has positive and negative implications. We can communicate with other humans precisely because

of this comity. When it is diminished, communication becomes impossible and violence usually takes over. If we assume too much common ground, we never learn to understand and communicate our own unique feelings, thoughts, and behaviors, because we mistakenly believe there is no need for it. After all, if everyone is just like me, they won't need any explanation of my thoughts, feelings, and behaviors. On the other side, if we don't feel a person or group has anything in common with us, we are tempted to dislike them and avoid communicating with them. It is too bothersome to have to explain everything you think, feel, or do. The secret is to avoid the extremes: believing that others are exactly like us or believing they are totally different from us. Insensitive persons take it for granted that others think, feel, and behave the way they do, or that others are so dissimilar, it isn't worth the bother to try to understand or communicate with them. Sensitive people assume some similarity with every other human person, but not complete similarity. Using the similarity that exists as a foundation, they can learn to understand others and accept them, relating to them in a loving and respectful way.

Matthew got in trouble because he thought he didn't need to explain himself to his stakeholders. Assuming that everyone thought, felt, and behaved like him, he felt they should understand why he closed the door to his office and worked on his computer during the hours when the teachers were free to see him. His response to such a complaint, had it been made to him, would have been, "All they had to do was knock. They knew I was in the office." Incidentally, the previous principal had an open-door policy. After the last bus left, he was available for an hour or more for the faculty. Teachers thought that Matthew's closed door meant he was hiding so he wouldn't have to deal with their problems. Worse still, they assumed he didn't care about them or their problems.

Experienced principals know that listening is the secret. When the stakeholders feel comfortable communicating with the principal, they open up. When they confide, the sensitive principal learns more about them. Only when Matthew learned to overlook Helen's weight and tears did he listen to her message and discover that he and she had much more in common than he had thought. He learned what we all must, to respect differences, appreciate similarities, and make connections.

3. Knowledge of the Individuals and Groups. When we talk of the principal's sensitivity, we mean to include his or her sensitivity to individuals and to groups. Matthew and Helen typify an individual relationship that floundered for reasons given above. Some principals have serious trouble communicating with certain groups. There are two types of knowledge that affect sensitivity: knowledge about groups (stereotyping) and knowledge about individuals (differentiating among individuals within a group). Stereotyping is worth addressing first.

Let us suppose that I am a WASP (White Anglo-Saxon Protestant) high school principal interviewing to fill the empty position of English teacher in my school. I am told by the secretary that Eamon Kelly, the Irishman, is next on the list for an interview. Before Eamon enters the room, I have a movie flash in front of my eyes, my Irish stereotype. Having noticed the unusual first name and the Irish surname, I begin the interview with a large number of assumptions or hypotheses. He is probably red-haired, freckle-faced and strongly built. He is probably a Catholic, married with a houseful of kids. I know that the Irish are great fighters, drinkers, and story-tellers. So I anticipate a lively interchange, but I will have to make allowances for the fact that the Irish exaggerate, are emotionally explosive, and extremely tricky. I must keep my guard up because he will try to charm me and get away with things. "Forewarned is forearmed," my tight stereotype has prepared me. I am set for the interview. Luckily, I know what the Irish are like. Eamon will be like all the others.

In walks Eamon Kelly and I allow myself a tiny mental pat on the back. I am right; he fits my preconceived picture. Sure enough, he is red-haired and freckled-faced. I pride myself on my knowledge of people. I am relieved because I now have the upper hand. I have him pegged. I really don't need to listen too diligently because I already know so much about him. My experience with the Irish warns me to be careful. They tend to be independent and disloyal to the boss. I'll be polite but get rid of him in a few minutes. I can dismiss him without much of a hearing, telling him we have found a local candidate we think will fill the bill. "Don't call me, I'll call you if something else comes open." I get rid of Eamon quickly without listening, so I will never know what might have been had I bucked my stereotype and listened to his story. Now I will never know the full truth. That is the way prejudices are preserved in place.

On the other hand, if I had chosen to put my stereotype on the back burner and listened to Kelly I would have learned that my hypothesis was full of holes. In reality Eamon was an Australian with excellent academic credentials who was a trailing spouse. His wife had received an appointment to Duke Medical School, where she was going to teach Epidemiology. Kelly was a Methodist with no children and an outstanding international soccer player. He wanted to teach English in an American high school where he could coach and develop a winning soccer program.

My stereotype implodes like a huge soap bubble breaking. If only I had chosen to listen to Eamon Kelly instead of relying on my Irish stereotype, I would have found a treasure. How often is this the case? No one knows the full damage that stereotyping does, because no one can know what might have been if we hadn't prejudiced ourselves with these rigid pictures. This type of cultural insensitivity is contemptible for two reasons. It is unfair to the subject, who isn't even given a hearing because of a prejudicial stereotype. It is equally as bad for society. How many excellent persons are passed over who might have made a huge contribution? A prejudiced principal who misses out on hiring an Eamon Kelly hurts his school irreparably but no one even knows about it. How must members of minorities feel when they know they are being stereotyped?

Stereotypes interfere with sensitivity, because the perceiver fails to recognize a person's unique attributes or categorizes that person according to a set of false preconceived group characteristics. Eamon's Irishness precludes his being seen as a unique individual. The more we exaggerate the homogeneity of a group, the more it prejudices us. Incidentally, another indirect but accurate measure of prejudice is the extent to which we overestimate the number belonging to certain groups. People who are prejudiced against Jews offer ridiculously high estimates of the number of Jews in their locality. People who are prejudiced against Blacks, Hispanics, or Asians overestimate in the same way. You can test yourself on this dimension of prejudice.

A Crack in the Bell Curve. A recent *New York Times* best seller was *The Bell Curve* co-authored by two fine scholars, the late Richard J. Herrnstein and Charles Murray. This research work studied the distribution of measured intelligence scores among groups. From my reading and the reviews, this is a balanced scholarly work that will make a fine contribution to our learning. There is only one problem. A section of this great work can be misunderstood by people who themselves are prejudiced. Reactions to the book have ranged from accepting the book as "gospel" and using some of its findings to justify prejudices, or to thoughtlessly branding the whole book as racist and claiming that it is not a scholarly work. Here we see prejudice working on both sides.

Among the ideas that have harmed mankind, one of the most durable and destructive is that the human species is divided into biological units called races, and some races are innately superior to others. This idea leads to deep prejudices, and we see its tentacles in public education. There is no question about the facts. Blacks and Hispanics score lower on psychometric tests purporting to measure intelligence. Whites score higher, and Asians score even higher. Does that mean that Blacks and Hispanics are less intelligent than Whites and Asians? It is tempting to think that way. Murray says it doesn't mean that any particular Black or Hispanic child is necessarily less intelligent than any White or Asian one. He agrees that the variations within the races are greater than between the races. That means that the smartest Black is further removed from the least smart Black than the groups of Blacks and Whites are separate from each other. It simply means you can find huge numbers of Blacks who are much smarter than the vast majority of Whites or Asians. Unfortunately, too many of these extremely gifted Blacks are being by-passed because of prejudices that can easily flow from a superficial reading of *The Bell Curve*. This is not the fault of the authors, but one wishes they had done more to counteract what they should have seen as possible misconceptions arising from their conclusions. If people conclude that it is wrong to spend money on races whose performance on IQ tests is traditionally inferior to those of other races, they are caught in a logical fallacy and are making decisions with no evidence.

The serious use of intelligence testing is a relatively recent innovation. It is less than a century since we seriously tried to measure raw human intelligence. Unfortunately, psychometry—the measurement of mental faculties like intelligence—has a long and checkered history. There are two major difficulties with the idea of measuring intelligence. First, we don't know enough about intelligence to really understand how it can be measured accurately. Second, with all the research we now have on intelligence testing, the best we can do with it is to separate subjects into three groups. One group of individuals does poorly on these tests, another group does fairly well, and a third group does very well. How much of this is due to genes, how much to memes (culture and training), and how much to the subjects' own motivation is still a mystery. We can't even discern between achievement and aptitude in many cases. We certainly are in no position to compare races on the basis of these inaccurate measurements. Yet all too many minorities have been handicapped by the misuse of such test results.

I am convinced that racism is one of the reasons we are not making the progress we should in public school education. For this reason it is worth our taking time to understand the subtle but powerful effect that standardized testing, especially intelligence testing, has in fostering such racism. In *The Bell Curve* we learn that northern European Jews score much higher than Sephardic Jews. Further, we learn that Nordics tend to score higher than people from countries bordering the Mediterranean. We learn that enlistees in World War I had an average mental age of 13. We shouldn't dismiss these "findings" out of hand, but we should ask deeper questions about their significance. Could there be a third or fourth factor that might explain these differences without it meaning that one group is less intelligent than another? Do the tests measure a native ability, or are they culturally biased? Is the somewhat new and shaky field of psychometry supported by findings in biology and genetics? Many say it is not. Racism always wants the quick and simple answer.

The human species arose 300,000 years ago, the equivalent of the day before yesterday in evolutionary history. That means that any differences among the races must have emerged since then. Superficial adaptations like skin color can evolve very quickly, in a matter of several thousand years, whereas changes in brain structure and capacity take far longer. The natural sciences are beginning to point out a serious gap between cultural advances and brain structure evolution. Our brains are structured much like they were in the skulls of early members of the group Homo Sapiens. In contrast, our cultures have evolved into greater complexities at a blinding rate of speed. To sum up, innate differences in intelligence among the races have simply not had enough time to evolve. In the not-too-distant future, scholars will laugh indulgently at our naive attempts to prove that Nordics are smarter than Mediterraneans, northern Jews are smarter than Sephardics, Asians smarter than Whites, and Whites smarter than Blacks and Hispanics.

A perhaps more devastating argument is that genetic diversity among the races is miniscule. Molecular biologists can now examine genes in different geographical populations. What they have found is that the overwhelming majority of the variations observed—more than 85 percent—are among individuals in the same race. Only a tiny residue distinguishes the "so-called" races. We humans are so much more alike than we are different, it makes little sense to talk about intellectual advantages of one group over another.

We live in a world that is growing smaller and at a time when only a global community can save us. Yet all around us, ethnic groups and cultures are declaring war on their ancient enemies, retreating from contact with the world community and teaching their children to be myopic and chauvinistic. How will we preserve our global habitat and assure its well-being for our children? How will we save the earth from devastation unless we stop playing these dangerous racial and ethnic games? When I say racism is killing public education, I mean racism on both sides. Unfortunately, none of the races can claim that they are tolerant and anti-racist as long as even a minority of their members make their mark in life by putting down the other race. Being white doesn't make one a racist; one is a racist if one is unfair, uninformed, unsanctified, and unwilling to share God's gifts. There are professional racists of all cultures and colors in our country who use their alleged defense of their race as a means of furthering their own selfish needs. They are doing harm to their own race and other races as well. A major goal of US public education is the elimination of racism. Unfortunately, school children are often its victims. We certainly don't want racial slurs to ride on the back of intelligence testing. It is safe to say that all members of all races have more than enough intellectual potential to perform at least 50 percent better than they do now. If schools could be a partner in bringing this about, it might cut down on some of the racism that is engulfing us.

Sensitive principals and teachers who work hard daily to break down racial barriers are doing a great service to the country. This isn't the first time that some Americans have felt it their vocation to persecute minorities. After the Civil War, Lincoln was confronted by a huge group of bigots who formed a political party aptly titled the "Know-Nothings." Lincoln said at the time, "Our progress in degeneracy appears to me to be pretty rapid. As a nation we began by declaring that 'all men are created equal.' We now probably read it 'all men are created equal except Negroes.' When the Know-Nothings get control, it will read 'all men are created equal, except Negroes, and foreigners, and Catholics.'" They may not carry the same name, but today there are many groups of bigots like the "Know-Nothings" who are pushing racial and cultural hatred in this country. In the middle of the next century, we may wake up and find that the public schools were the most effective agency in our society for reducing prejudice. It will be sensitive Steward Principals and teachers who lead the way.

Maybe the Horatio Alger myth was too Pollyanna-ish; it was certainly too individualistic, but it still speaks to the American dream. The present tendency to think of intelligence in genetic terms that handicaps certain groups is altogether too pessimistic. Sensitive principals constantly remember that the people of different races overlap in ability to such a great degree, the differences in their academic achievements are much more likely attributable to cultural rather than to genetic causes. All children ought to be learning more and better—and they will, if we believe they can.

4. Interaction Focus. Among the Internal Factors, we have included discussions on sensing by the perceiver; the judging habits of the perceiver; the accuracy of assumed similarity; and finally, we spent time on the perceiver's knowledge of the individual and groups. It would seem fairly obvious that a principal who has a deep knowledge and understanding of individuals and groups is capable of being more sensitive in dealing with both.

In dealing with others, we are forever making hypotheses about how others will respond to our actions. For example, suppose I am introduced to the Queen of England and I hypothesize that she will reach out and give me a big hug. If I perceive, judge, and assume this based on my lack of knowledge about royalty, I will probably embarrass myself and others by reaching out to hug her, only to find her withdrawing rapidly and the British secret service whisking me away rather abruptly. One does not touch royalty. I should have known that and simply bowed my head. Most human interactions with strangers or even with intimates are based on a series of hypotheses. Based on our judging habits, assumed similarities, external factors, and knowledge of the individuals, we make hypotheses about the way we think others will react.

Interaction focus is the critical stage in which the perceiver decides which approach to take in an interaction. I was wrong in my interaction with the Queen of England. Now suppose in another circumstance I am going to meet an old friend of mine. We grew up together, went to high school, and spent most of our free time together. We have been in touch over the years, but haven't seen each other in five years. I make the hypothesis that when we meet, he will smile, come close to me, shake my hand and give me a big hug. With that assumption in mind I decide to do the same. We have a wonderful meeting. He grabs my hand and reaches his arm around my back and hugs me; I do the same to him. We are laughing and obviously rejoicing in our long-awaited reunion. Unlike my fiasco with the Queen, I am confirmed in my hypothesis and, incidentally he is confirmed in his. This is what sensitivity is all about.

Even when my dear friend and I sit down in the airport restaurant to have a cup of coffee, the sensitivity we share directs our conversation. I ask about his wife, who has a heart condition. He inquires about my wife, and says he hopes he'll get a chance to see her while he is in town. I remind him that we are having a little dinner party for him the next night so he can meet some of our friends and then he will have a chance to visit with Mary. Sensitivity is dynamic: preceding the interaction, occurring during it, and following it. I am sensitive to what he is saying. I see that he looks tired and tell him I won't keep him up too long tonight but will pick him up the next day at whatever hour he wants to get started so we can look around the city.

Sensitivity doesn't guarantee that all interactions will be ideal. However, it ensures that the perceiver will attempt to "read" individuals and situational factors as accurately as possible before deciding on the most appropriate course of action. Celebrities often become insensitive people because their "handlers" control situations and make it unnecessary for the celebrity to hone and polish his or her sensitivity. Many of the rich and famous pay the inestimable price—the loss of their sensitivity.

Since principals interact with countless individuals and groups each working day, it isn't hard to surmise that those who are sensitive and make excellent hypotheses concerning interactions with others are much more successful than those who are awkward and careless in relating with the stakeholders. Some think this sensitivity may be the greatest of all the gifts a principal needs.

When a sensitive principal heads up a school the teachers and staff seem to be at ease. The whole atmosphere of the school is friendly and comfortable. But the sure tip-off is the way the students react. A Steward Principal who is skilled in interpersonal relations creates a faculty who is striving to be more sensitive. When students interact with teachers and other staff and find them sensitive and receptive to their unique selves, they seem to flourish. Students who attend this type school are learning not just academic skills but also the skills of human living. Today, we cannot take it for granted that polite, civil, sensitive, kind, and considerate relations are learned in the home, church, or neighborhood. The school that helps in this is a marvel to behold.

5. Response of the Individual. Sensitivity primarily is expressed when two individuals interact face to face but it is also present in our telephone conversations, letters, memos, etc. When a student enters the principal's office he or she often assumes that a punishment is imminent. Is it any wonder they adopt a rather defensive stance? I know a principal in Pennsylvania who worries about this stereotyping of student-principal interactions. He has regular ten-minute meetings with individual students all through the year. He reassures them that they are not in his office for punishment, but rather for a personal chat so he can get to know them better and learn how he can help them get more from their schooling. He has told me that a wonderful transformation takes place when the students understand that they are important to the principal as persons. Most of them quickly drop their defenses and talk freely about themselves and the school. They leave happy and a few are able to say something like this, "Thank you, Mr. Kennedy, I really liked talking to you." My friend the principal is very sensitive. He has learned over the years how to put a middle-school student at ease. Incidentally, he also knows much more about his school than most principals.

6. Perceiver's Reaction to Interactions. When Charlie Kennedy began to function as a principal, he wasn't as sensitive as he is now. He was a "type A" personality who gave the impression that he didn't have time to waste on small talk. He was all business. It took him about seven years and one heart attack to realize that he was actually wasting time by his brusque and curt manner of dealing with stakeholders. Many teachers felt he didn't like them and as a consequence were reluctant to approach him. The students said he was a "bear" and not a Teddy. They avoided him like the plague. Charlie was totally insensitive to this set of reactions he was causing. He enjoyed working alone in his office. Unfortunately, he was getting further and further out of touch with the school.

The heart attack didn't kill him; in fact, it seems to have done him some good. As Nietzsche says, "What doesn't kill you, can help you a lot." When he went back to his job after recovering, he was much less driven, angry, impatient, and impersonal. He had been touched by the outpouring of kindness he received from the stakeholders during his illness. Perhaps as important, he had looked into the abyss of death and now saw the world in a different light.

Charlie told me that the secret lay in his beginning to reflect on what was happening in his interactions with the stakeholders. After the teacher or student left his office, he would reflect for five minutes on the interaction. He was learning to assess the level of sensitivity he had exhibited. After he observed and tested the responses of the teacher or student, he ruminated about his own responses recalling his personal set of judging habits. He evaluated whether his efforts at communication had been sensitive, and if he had grasped the feelings of the other person. On reflection, he began to be able to see when he had trampled on the feelings of others. As his judgment became more accurate, he was able to become confident in using the proper approach with individuals and quick enough to sense changes in their responses as the interview proceeded. At last, he could pick up subtle clues and respond appropriately. Charlie Kennedy still makes mistakes at times, but I know from firsthand experience that the teachers, parents, and students feel great affection for him and praise him as a kind and sensitive servant-leader. It wouldn't be fair if I didn't let you in on a secret. His wife helped him more than anyone to change the tempo after his illness. She had preached for years that he wasn't sensitive to people's feelings. Now Charlie is slower, but amazingly he gets much more accomplished. He doesn't try to do everything himself. He is a team builder. He says, "TEAM means *Together Everyone Accomplishes More.*" With empowered and enabled stakeholders, the school is doing just splendidly. Charlie says he had a paradigmatic mind shift, discovering that the more dispensable he thought himself to be, the more indispensable the stakeholders thought he was. "It's a puzzlement," he says. He became a servant-leader, and it showed.

We have looked briefly at the external factors and the seven internal factors that demonstrate the process by which a perceiver predicts (hypothesizes) what will occur in a social interaction with another person. We can see that Charlie has become much more skillful in predicting the responses of others, so he can regulate the way he interacts with them. In the old days he had a set way of acting (one size fits all), by which he treated everyone as if they would react the same way he would. He wasn't sensitive, so he couldn't understand why so many of his stakeholders were so thin-skinned and sensitive. He didn't cry. He was puzzled why some of his teachers left his office crying. He didn't remember slights and couldn't believe that people would hold against him things he said months before. Charlie didn't know much about himself and even less about others. He just didn't get it. In order to grow in the skill of sensitive inter-personal relations, he needed first to improve his intra-personal skills. He couldn't be sensitive to others until he learned to be sensitive to himself.

NO SELF-KNOWLEDGE, NO SENSITIVITY

As we go through the nine Domains of Knowledge and Skill, I have one fear that someone will imagine that these knowledges and skills are easy to come by. They are certainly within the reach of all of us, but to achieve them we have to undergo some seri-ous life changes. Insensitive people don't become sensitive by attending a two-day workshop on sensitivity. Charlie's heart attack propelled him to give up his preconceived ideas about personal relations. All insensitive principals may not have to go through the firing-crisis that Matthew went through, or the heart attack suffered by Charlie, but they do have to go through some life-changing experiences in which they change their way of looking into themselves and outwardly at others. They need to get some critical feedback from the "significant others" in their lives. In a word, they must begin to listen and change; neither is easy.

In our program at PEP, we have a unit in which the principal is asked to give the names of seven persons with whom he or she works. These people are requested to write to the PEP fac-ulty member a candid and detailed appraisal of the principal, noting his or her strong and weak points as a leader. The re-spondent is assured that the principal will not see what they write. The PEP faculty member reads over all the assessments and coordinates them before sharing them with the candidate.

The candidate never knows who said what. It is a life-changing experience for many principals. Having gone through the same process myself many years ago, I can tell you what happens. As you hear and then later read these comments about yourself, you are both delighted and humbled. You are delighted that so many of your people noted good qualities you didn't even know showed. You are humbled and somewhat hurt by the comments on your weaknesses. However, if you are a person with any skill for self-appraisal, you are not surprised by any of the negative comments. In fact, you have to acknowledge their accuracy. What hurts is the realization that these people who work with you are so aware of your limitations. It is a sobering experience—and a necessary one.

I have sat with principals who were deeply hurt by the feedback they received. A few were deeply scarred. It is agonizing for a man or woman in a position of power to realize that their human weaknesses or lack of knowledge and skill are seen by others as interfering with their work. Most of us have to be a little hurt to be willing to make a serious change in our lives. It is shattering to find that one is 40 pounds overweight, but it is worse to continue to deny it.

The common notion the old Greek philosophers shared was that a person needs to know himself or herself, to see oneself as others see one. Socrates, Plato, Aristotle, and countless others stressed the need for self-knowledge. It has always puzzled me that we make so little of this in modern education. We are much more apt to talk about winning friends and influencing people than we are about self-knowledge. We are certain that students need to learn how to get along with others, so we stress interpersonal skills. Unfortunately, we leave out the prerequisite for interpersonal skills, which is self-knowledge or intrapersonal skills. If we don't know the way around our own hearts and memories, and aren't in touch with our own feelings, we will be ill-equipped to deal sensitively with others. Principals who have honed their intrapersonal skills will be much better prepared for the interpersonal encounters that make up the substance of their daily routine.

KING LEAR'S PLEA,
"WHO IS IT WILL TELL ME WHO I AM?"

Poor King Lear reached old age without even an approximation of an answer to the most significant question posed to each of us by the community of life. In his 70s, he still didn't know who he was. Of course he was the king, but as a person he certainly didn't have much self-knowledge. Consequently, he was gullible and his tricky daughters, Goneril and Regan, could manipulate him with their falsehoods. Worse still, his lack of self-knowledge led him into a rage in which he misread the deeper, unselfish love of his daughter Cordelia.

When I teach principals, I often ask the difficult question, "What would you like your own child to learn in school ?" My assumption is that what principals think is important for their own children is precisely what we should try to teach all children. I get a variety of answers, all of them having some merit, but the answer I like most is this one: "I would like my daughter to learn early in life who she is and how she fits into her world. I chose this because I think everything else flows from it. If she knows who she is and what she is for, she will know that she is the decision-maker in her life, and she is about making a world in which it is easier to live, love, and learn. She will know what she has to learn to get along with others without compromising her principles. She will be a lifelong learner who strives to gain the skills and knowledge necessary for making a world that will be friendly to her children and their children. She will extend it to include all children, all persons, all living creatures in the community of life. She will learn to be a 'leaver' rather than a 'taker'. 'Takers' are people who have taken the rule of the world into their own hands. On the other hand, 'leavers' are those who leave the rule of the world in the hands of God—the spirit of all living beings."

I'll admit I don't get this answer too often, but I believe that is what most principals really want for their children. If the principal's daughter is successful at self-knowledge, she will be able to relate well with others. If she relates well with others, she can work cooperatively with them and learn the further skills and knowledge necessary to make a world in which it is easier to live, love, and learn. It really doesn't make a big difference whether she does this as a doctor, lawyer, teacher, farmer, priest, dancer, bus driver, insurance salesperson, computer programmer, or candlestick maker.

When discussing the theory of multiple intelligence in his book *Frames of Mind,* Howard Gardner offers seven intellectual competencies, the last two of which he refers to as the Personal Intelligences. He calls them interpersonal and intrapersonal intellectual competencies. To explain them more fully, he introduces two giants in the history of psychology, William James and Sigmund Freud as champions of the two kinds of Personal Intelligence that taken together give us a sense of self. As you remember, Freud was a pessimistic European intellectual who focused on the development of the individual psyche, the battles within the individual's immediate family, the struggle for independence, the manifold anxieties and defenses that are a part of the human condition. For the famous Austrian, founder of psychoanalysis, the key to health was self-knowledge and a willingness to confront the inevitable pains and uncertainties of human existence.

William James, the Harvard professor, was a quite different type of person. Although he had great respect for Freud and his work, he had a different world view. William James was more optimistic and outgoing. He focused less on biological (or genetic) constraints on behavior and more on the possibilities of change and growth in a person. He stressed the importance of relationships with other people as a means of growing and learning more about oneself. He often said a man has as many social selves as there are people who recognize him and carry an image of him in their minds. In the United States, the ideas of James had a wider hearing than those of Freud. Consequently, we Americans have grown up with more emphasis on the development of interpersonal intelligence. In Arthur Miller's great play *Death of a Salesman*, Willy Loman, the chief protagonist, is a classic example of a man who thought being liked by others would carry the day. He lacked self-knowledge and when age made it impossible for him to cover the territory and make sales, he became despondent and committed suicide. It is important to balance Freud and James. A person needs to know himself or herself, and this can only happen if we use both our inter- and intra-personal intellectual competencies. I stress the need for intra-personal intelligence only because so much emphasis seems to be placed on the getting along with others. That side should not be denigrated, but it alone is insufficient if we are to have a fully developed personality. As we enter the new millennium, we will need to teach ourselves and our children how to be more intro-spective if they are to develop their intrapersonal intelligence. We and they need time and place to be alone, silent, and reflec-tive. To King Lear's question, "Who will tell me who I am?", we answer: To find out who you are is the purpose of your life pil-grimage—you must walk with others but you must also walk alone. No one can tell you who you are; you must discover it for yourself. Servant-leader principals seem to know themselves better than most. Maybe that is why they are so sensitive and make such good Steward Principals.

PRINCIPAL, KNOW THYSELF

A principal needs both personal intelligences. In my experi-ence, Steward Principals spend 80 percent of their time using interpersonal skills. They are by definition "people persons" who must almost constantly interact with stakeholders. So they cer-tainly need highly developed interpersonal skills. But what many miss is the fact that Steward Principals spend 20 percent of their time learning more about what is going on inside themselves. They have sensitivity toward their own inner selves as well as sensitivity to others. I can't resist including an anecdote that has come down through the ages. When the James brothers, Will-iam and Henry, were celebrities, it was said that William wrote psychology with the flair of a novelist, and Henry wrote novels with the heavy dullness of a scientific paper in psychology. In any case both of them had highly developed personal intelli-gences. Good counselors or therapists are noted for their skill in handling introspection as well as interpersonal communication. They are able both to read their own subtle feelings and extrapo-late from them in dialoguing with others. Many older people are revered because they are able to draw upon their wealth of experience in order to advise members of the community. Other seniors age like Archie Bunker with little or no added skill in personal intelligence. Intolerant bigots, fanatics, zealots, and despots are examples of people who lack basic personal intelligence. They may have power, but they are barbarians loose in a civilized world—bulls in china shops. We see examples of these types among our politicians, government, and business leaders. Less and less do we see them among principals.

Principals with good intrapersonal skills seem to handle the interpersonal very well. They have the ability to notice and make distinctions among other individuals, in particular, among their moods, temperaments, motivations, and intentions. In our examples, neither Matthew nor Charlie were able to do this. Principals skilled in interpersonal intelligence can read the intentions and desires of many individuals and can act upon this knowledge. You all know principals who seem to be able to get the most disparate groups together and lead them into consensus. I have seen it in skilled parents and teachers as well. It is a great gift, one worth a lifetime of cultivation.

But can we develop our personal intelligences? For instance, can a principal like Matthew or Charlie get some help in improving their inter- and intrapersonal skills? If we take intrapersonal intelligence as an example, how would one learn this skill and knowledge better? Much of psychotherapy is aimed precisely at helping people to know themselves and others better to improve their abilities to live productive lives. The alcoholic, the drug user, the wife beater, the frightened neurotic are all suffering from some lack of development in their inter- and intrapersonal intelligences.

The study of good literature and art are two of the best ways to improve one's ability to know self. Stories are the way generations have taught their young to know themselves and others. When principals become so busy they have no time for novels, movies, plays, operas, museums, concerts, etc., they are starving their inner life. Meditation is another way to improve one's self-knowledge. When we pray, we open doors to learning more about ourselves and our vocations. We sing hymns together, and these get us in touch with our feelings. If we paint pictures, make crafts, play an instrument, write poems, read mysteries, and attend good plays, we are nurturing our spirit and learning more about ourselves.

If you watch Dustin Hoffman play Willy Loman in the movie version of *Death of a Salesman*, you will learn a great deal about your own feelings. What a shame that so few people try their hand at writing poetry. T.S. Eliot once said, "in developing the language, enriching the meaning of words, the poet is making possible a much wider range of emotion and perception for other men, because he gives them the speech in which more can be expressed." Read some of Robert Frost's poems like" Mending Walls" where the old stick-in-the-mud farmer keeps repeating, "Good fences make good neighbors." Or read Frost's "The Death of the Hired Man," and you will find two interesting definitions of "home". The husband says,

Home is the place where, when you have to go there.
They have to take you in."
His wife replies,"I should have called it,
Something you haven't to deserve."

I apply these quotes to school. A sensitive principal suspends very few students because he or she knows that the school is the only home for some kids.

In this short discussion, we would be remiss if we didn't mention two other ways to improve our intra-personal intelligence. Writing a daily journal is a marvelous way to deepen our knowledge of our own feelings. Perhaps the best way to deepen our self-knowledge is to love someone so trustingly that you feel free to talk over with them your deepest feelings. It is assumed that the significant other will love you in return and be able to use you as a mirror in which to see him or herself. Developing two personal intelligences together is like washing hands—one washes the other. We need time alone to be silent, reflect, and meditate, and we need intimate time with the loved one to share our deepest feelings.

Having taught school for over 50 years, I found that many of my self-deceptions were pointed out to me by my students. They were mirrors into which I could see myself with my strengths and weaknesses. It is almost impossible to trick students over a long period of time. They instinctively know whether you genuinely love or just tolerate them. Teaching is a way to develop both our personal intelligences. Principals who have been successful in the classroom bring a wealth of experience (inter- and intrapersonal) to their new office. Even with that they need to continually work to improve their skills in self-knowledge and the knowledge of others. No other duty should take precedence over this one.

THEORY X, THEORY Y, AND THE JUDGING HABITS OF THE PRINCIPAL

When principals take over a schoo,l they bring with them a set of assumptions about the stakeholders. Some insensitive principals—I trust not too many—bring to the job a set of Theory X assumptions.

1) All stakeholders inherently dislike work and will avoid it whenever possible.

2) Stakeholders must be directed and coerced to put forth adequate effort toward the achievement of organizational objectives.

3) Stakeholders prefer to be directed and to avoid responsibility.

I wish I had never met a principal who felt that way. Unfortunately I have met a few. Moreover, I have encountered some school boards, state directors, Central Office personnel, superintendents, assistant and associate superintendents who shared these assumptions. The assumptions seem so crude on first reading that you wonder how they could be taken seriously, but when you begin to see how much school administration consists in monitoring, "snoopervising," micro-managing, and over-regulating, it is difficult to deny that there must be some top brass who espouse these Theory X tenets. It is absolutely impossible for educators who espouse Theory X to be truly sensitive in their dealings with the stakeholders. How can you be sensitive to people whom you have prejudged to be lazy, careless, and irresponsible? The answer is ,"You can't." Principals who are prejudiced in this way cannot act in a sensitive manner with stakeholders.

The Theory Y approach is just the opposite. D. M. McGregor, who first offered the contrasting Theory X and Theory Y views of human nature in his book, *The Human Side of Enterprise* (29), claims that administrators who espouse the Y approach bring the following set of assumptions to their work:

1) Physical and mental effort in work is as natural as play or rest.

2) People will exercise self-direction and self-control in the service of objectives to which they are committed.

3) Commitment to objectives is a function of the rewards associated with their achievement and the most significant rewards (satisfaction of ego and self-actualization needs) can be products of efforts directed toward organizational objectives. In other words, our work toward the school objectives can be satisfying and fulfilling and help us to become all that we are capable of becoming.

4) People not only accept but also seek responsibility.

5) Imagination, ingenuity, and creativity in solving organizational problems is widely, not narrowly, distributed in the population.

We could reform public education in a short time if all the players involved were able to shift into a Theory Y set of assumptions. Imagine if superintendents and central office personnel followed the Theory Y assumptions in their dealings with principals. Suppose principals did the same in dealing with teachers and students. Suppose teachers did the same when dealing with students and parents, while students and parents followed Theory Y assumptions in relating with principals and teachers. Then all I could wish for would be that politicians and the media might follow Theory Y when writing and talking about schools and educators.

Sensitive principals assume that most people under the proper circumstances are self-motivated (a fact well-documented in research). Of course, this in no way precludes exceptions. There are lazy, careless, and irresponsible people, but they are the minority and many of them could change if the "system" that helps create and sustain them offered some challenges and encouragement. Self-motivation is also characteristic of young people. If we reinforce their need for achievement and show signs of accepting their efforts and outcomes, they can often amaze us with their drive and ambition.

Responsibility for motivating others mirrors the hierarchy of power and authority. Within the school context, teachers motivate students and principals motivate teachers. In addition, the higher a person is in the organization, the more credit he or she is given for being self-motivated and self-directed. The servant-leader is just assumed to be both self-motivated and self-directed. McGregor in 1960 and Deming in 1990 both said that when people lower in the hierarchy of an organization avoid responsibility or lack ambition, these deficits may be the consequence of limited opportunity and experience, not an inherent human characteristic. When we point the finger of blame at the system rather than at the stakeholder in any organization, we are going to be right more often than wrong.

Many years ago when I was in my teens I worked in a sweatshop. We worked on piecework. You were paid by the number of automobile tail lights you assembled. It took some time to get the hang of it, but in a couple of weeks you could pick up speed and turn out more work. Some of the older men and women for whom this work was their sole support (I still lived at home with my parents) worked at a very fast pace, but I noticed that they would look at the clock often and keep close watch on how many they completed in an hour. They could make up to 67 cents an hour if they assembled 100 tail lights in that time. I was only making about 24 cents an hour at my rate. They explained to me why they watched the clock and their production so closely. A month earlier you could make 67 cents for assembling 85 pieces in an hour. What happened? Some "rate buster" started to go faster and faster and the bosses increased the production level necessary to make the old wage. Now you had to do 100 an hour to make the 67 cents. Ask yourself: Was the system at fault? Or was it a case of lazy, careless, irresponsible workers?

Could you find parallels in the school business? Why do we

have teachers who teach only for the tests and couldn't care less whether the youngsters are learning to understand and appreciate connections between the subjects? The teacher is acting like a slave driver who cares little for what happens to the slaves as long as they cut the cotton quota. On the other hand, we have to ask ourselves: Why do some otherwise good teachers act so insensitively? Could it be that the system that rates each classroom teacher solely on the test results their students garner, which publishes a profile of the school and classrooms, and which punishes schools and teachers whose pupils do poorly on the end-of-course standardized tests, may be perpetrating a poor system? The school board, the superintendent, district office personnel and the principal have the obligation to treat the teachers with sensitivity if they want the teachers to be as sensitive as they should be to the students. This we know for sure: there will be little long-lasting learning in a classroom in which the teacher is insensitive to the students. However, many very highly motivated and very sensitive teachers either leave school work or stay and become insensitive because the whole bureaucratic system itself is in need of sensitizing.

A sensitive principal can help all the stakeholders to realize that a Learning Organization is possible only when there is team learning, and team learning is possible only when the stakeholders have sufficient inter- and intrapersonal knowledge and skill to act sensitively with self and others.

A true Steward Principal is able to get stakeholders to want to do something that the principal is convinced ought to be done, that she has thrown herself 100 percent into accomplishing it. When the stakeholders catch the fire of the principal, they buy into the Shared Vision; improve their Personal Mastery; join in the Team Learning in pursuit of the vision; break down Mental Models that interfere; and begin to do the type of Systemic Thinking that makes success possible. These are the five dimensions of a Learning Organization. I developed these ideas, suggested by Senge, more fully in an earlier book, *The Principal's Edge* (30), Through all this process, the Steward Principal, acting like a servant-leader, is able to maintain sensitive relationships with all the stakeholders so they can work together with a minimum of friction.

SUMMATION

We opened the chapter with the story of Matthew Kurtz, a principal who lacked sensitivity, and then moved on to a definition of sensitivity taken from *Principals For Our Changing Schools*. There followed a discussion of the Six Steps for Developing Greater Sensitivity. To understand Sensitivity better we looked at the external and internal factors involved when we predict the responses of others. Assuming that the more sensitive a person is, the more successful he or she will be at predicting the behavior of others, we offered suggestions on how to do it better. We distinguished between knowledge of groups as opposed to individuals, which led us to a discussion of prejudice. We used the best seller *The Bell Curve* as an example of how an otherwise good scientific study can sometimes apply its data in a manner which can contribute to prejudice and insensitivity.

We made the assumption that a principal's growing knowledge and skill in dealing sensitively with stakeholders could never outrun his or her growing knowledge of self. We claimed No Self-Knowledge, No Sensitivity.

It was helpful to look at Howard Gardner's Theory of Multiple Intelligence to understand the connection between a principal's inter- and intrapersonal intellectual competencies. We offered suggestions on how a principal could improve his or her intrapersonal intellectual competencies. In addition, we discussed McGregor's Theory X and Theory Y assumptions about stakeholders, and tried to show that the more sensitive principals will find it helpful to follow the Theory Y approach in dealing with the stakeholders. Finally, we pointed out that a system can be insensitive as well as a person or group of persons. We found some examples in the field of education in which the bureaucratic system itself makes it difficult for the stakeholders to act in a sensitive manner. Both McGregor and Deming reinforce the idea that systemic insensitivity is often at the root of interpersonal insensitivity.

QUESTIONS FOR REFLECTION

1. Why is it that we can only be sensitive to others if we learn to be sensitive to ourselves?

2. In Domain 15 Ivan Muse and his team define sensitivity in this manner: "Perceiving the needs and concerns of others; working with others in emotionally stressful situations or in conflict; managing conflict; obtaining feedback; recognizing multi-cultural differences; relating to people of varying backgrounds." As a principal what are your strong and weak points in the area of sensitivity?

3. Looking at the six steps in developing sensitivity, which steps have been easiest for you? Which steps are still hard for you?

4. Why is it that principals noted for their sensitivity seem to have a sixth sense when it comes to predicting the responses of others?

5. When you reflect on Matthew's personal and social history, what do you find that might account for his difficulites in carrying out the role of principal?

6. Can a principal be insensitive to stakeholders and yet be unaware of this inadequacy? Why? What should be done?

7. Why do some principals act like gun slingers making off the hip judgments of obese people? Did Ted know he was hypercritical?

8. Why must we first acknowledge our own fallibility and lack of perfection before we can begin to be tolerant of others?

9. Explain how the principal's stereotype of Eamon Kelly kept him from ever knowing him. What is so bad about stereotyping?

10. How could a good scientific book like *The Bell Curve* leave itself open to much criticism?

11. How did Charlie Kennedy learn to improve his sensitivity? Is there another way?

12. Who can tell King Lear who he really is?

7

THE STEWARD PRINCIPAL KNOWS THE POWER OF THE SPOKEN WORD AND UNSPOKEN GESTURE

Speech finely framed, delights the ear.—2 Maccabees 15:39

In the ever-evolving role of the public school principal, skill in oral and nonverbal expression is becoming highly sought after. The principal today is per force a communicator, not just in the school building but in the broader community. The principal speaks for the school in many different ways. In this chapter, I would like you to enter into an agreement with me. We won't talk about specific situations in which experienced principals must be effective communicators; rather, we will discuss how we would help prepare a teacher recently appointed to the principalship for the communication demands that will be laid upon him or her. As a principal, I want you to reflect on what you wish you had known about communication before you took on the responsibilities. This will help you decide what to do in preparing someone else for the job. If you are a newly appointed principal ready to take over a school next August, this chapter will help you learn what knowledge and skills you need in order to become an effective principal communicator.

GOOD COMMUNICATION BY THE PRINCIPAL IS THE KEY TO EFFECTIVE SCHOOL OPERATIONS

The first thing I would say to the newly appointed principal is that the demands of the principalship are heavy indeed, but there is one skill that can lighten the load. Good communication skills can make things run much more smoothly. If you already have good communication skills or are willing to work hard to improve your skill, you can make up for many other skill and knowledge areas in which you lack proficiency. Why is this so? Because principals spend somewhere between 60% and 90% of their workday communicating with all the stakeholders: teachers, parents, staff, students, Central Office personnel, state department personnel, salespeople, reporters, neighbors, city officials, county officials (fire, police, health, welfare, building inspectors, etc.).

Most of a principal's wasted time is the result of poor communication in the first place. Recently, I had to put up some molding around the walls of a room in our house. I am not a trained carpenter, and I found it difficult to use the miter box and cut the strips on a bias. The sawing wasn't hard, but figuring out beforehand how the ends should be cut so they would fit together was a difficult task. As I made many mistakes and had to repeat the work, I was reminded of an admonition my uncle Ernie made while trying to teach me carpentry. He constantly repeated this advice, "Measure three times, saw once." Last week in doing my room, I measured once and sawed three times. I wasted a lot of time and a lot of wood. It is much the same in communications. If the new principal learns to measure three times (find out what effect his or her message will have on the receivers), then say it once, there will be fewer misunderstandings and much time will be saved. Many times miscommunication ruffles the feathers of some stakeholders and it takes months, even years to get back on an even playing field with them. So to the new principal I say, take time in preparing even the two-minute interchanges that are the stuff of most principals' days. *Once you are appointed principal, even your chance remarks are noted and often given an importance you never intended.* Every newly elected president of the United States (governor, mayor, school superintendent) has had to learn the hard way that authority figures are taken very seriously. They are quoted and misquoted regularly. Authority figures have to be very careful about how they banter and joke. Veteran principals can give hundreds of examples of how they were surprised when an old friend who knew them as a teacher took offense at something said as a newly minted principal. It was often something said countless times with no misgiving when they were just teachers together. Think carefully before speaking; however, if you get too paranoid, you will lose your spontaneity—an important part of your leadership. So what to do? We will try to help new principals to gain in knowledge and skill in this domain—Oral and Nonverbal Expression.

COMMUNICATION DEFINED: ITS BEGINNING AND END?

In preparing the new principal to be a more effective communicator, our first problem is to limit what we mean by communication. Some of the definitions I have come upon are omnibus definitions that include everything human under the rubric of communication.

Since we are following the excellent outline of *Principals For Our Changing Schools*, it seems wise to offer the definition presented in Domain 16 by Ivan Muse and his development team.

> "**Oral and Nonverbal Expression:** Making oral presentations that are clear and easy to understand; clarifying and restating questions; responding, reviewing, and summarizing for groups; using appropriate communicative aids; being aware of cultural and gender-based norms; adapting for audiences." (31)

THE PRINCIPAL'S MOST COMMON COMMUNICATIONS

When you were a teacher you did most of your communication in your classroom. The style of this communication was determined to a large degree by your teaching methods. Teaching is a form of communication and most principals were selected primarily because they were good teachers or communicators. However, teaching in a classroom is something most principals have to forego. Many principals wish they could go back to being classroom teachers after they run into the buzz saw of the principalship. The *interactional communication* that took place in the give and take of classroom discussion could be fun for both the students and the teacher. It was also both profitable and enjoyable when you used it with fellow teachers. You talked for a couple of minutes when on corridor patrol or in the coffee room. You had communication contact with the teachers with whom you worked, and so you could read from the same sheet of music. Now as a principal, the interactional communication gives way to *transactional communication* or communication with a purpose. The new principal continues to do some interactional communication, but now it is not as casual and incidental. Stakeholders initiate communication with the principal for well thought out reasons.

The new principal is placed in a different role in the transactional communication, which occurs when a stakeholder requests a few moments of the principal's time. The most common remark principals hear from teachers and staff is, "I don't want to bother you, but do you have a minute or two? I have something I need to run by you." Does that sound familiar to you veteran principals?

Principals are greeted with this request many times each hour. It may lead either to more time wasting or more effective use of the principal's scarce time. It all depends on how the new principal responds to these requests.

TRANSACTIONAL COMMUNICATION

This is not something extra. It is the stuff of principals' communication. Successful Steward Principals learn to use five-minute interchanges with great skill. They realize that keeping the lines of communication open on a one-to-one basis is essential in a Learning Organization.

Transactional communication occurs as a simultaneous sharing event; that is, when people share in the creation and interpretation of messages. As the sender communicates with the receiver, the receiver provides "feedback" that causes the sender to reply or share another message. School principals typically engage in this type of communication when the initiator is the stakeholder. However, it can be initiated by the principal as well. Used skillfully, this type of communication is what makes successful principals.

When, on a cold December afternoon, you receive your 36th request from a teacher for a few minutes of your time, you may wish you were back in the classroom or on a cruise ship passing leisurely through the Panama Canal, but you have no choice but to respond.

In *Principals For Our Changing Schools*, Ivan Muse and his development team offer us a great process model. We can use this in helping the new principal to prepare for the communication demands outlined above. The Communication Process Model (Figure 6) depicts nine elements that when understood correctly can give a principal great help in learning how to use **transactional communication** in an effective manner.

Like most communication models, this one offered in *Principals For Our Changing Schools* is comprised of a message to be sent by the sender, the encoding of the message by the sender, the transmission of the message through a channel, the decoding of the message by the receiver, and the reception of the message by the receiver.

Add to these three more elements that can have a major bearing on the quality of the message: feedback, potential barriers, and the environment in which the message is sent and received. Now we have a good grid to place over our communications when we analyze them.

AN EXAMPLE OF A TRANSACTIONAL COMMUNICATION

It is late on a hot August afternoon, the second day of school, and only the second day the new principal Marcia Loughlin has been in charge with all the students, staff, and teachers present. Mike Taylor, the physical ed teacher who has been in the school only a year, approaches the principal with a request. "I don't want to bother you, but do you have a minute or two? I have something I would like to run by you."

The smiling principal responds graciously and asks if they can talk where they are—out in the parking lot—or would the teacher prefer to go to the principal's office where they can have

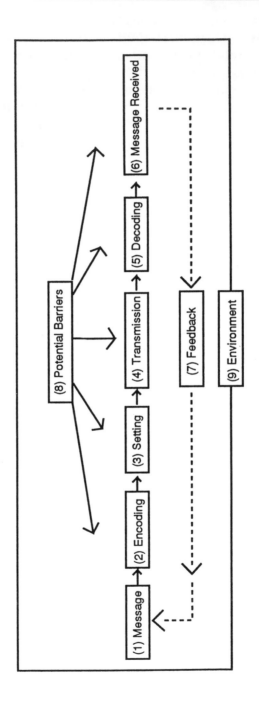

Figure 6. Communication Process Model

more privacy? Parents are still driving up and shouting greetings to the teachers and principal. Mike thinks it would be better to go back to the office. There has been no message up to this point, but Marcia has wisely removed some barriers and made an effort to ensure that the environment would be a safe and friendly one.

They go across the school yard and enter the outside door to the principal's office. At this point Mike is much better prepared for the communication than is the principal. Why? Because Mike has considered the matter and decided that the message he wanted to send to the principal was important enough to make the request, and that privacy was needed for the transaction. Mike knows what he wants to say, why he wants to say it to the principal, and what response he hopes he will get from Marcia, the new principal.

Seated in the principal's office, Mike says, "I have a big request that I hate to ask of you on the second day of school, but it can't wait. I don't have much time to delay. Last Saturday night I did something really stupid. I went to a party held at a friend's house and drank too much. They wanted to drive me home, but I insisted I was able to drive myself. To make a long story short, I got stopped by a Highway Patrol officer for driving erratically. He gave me a breathalyzer test, and I flunked it. I blew .10, so my license was lifted by the judge and I have to attend AA meetings and do 100 hours of community service during the next six months. This is embarrassing for me to tell you, and I know it won't make you think very highly of me, but I am in a pickle. I can't drive to and from school

because of the suspended license, and I can't teach my 12 o'clock gym class because I have to be at an AA meeting that won't get out until 1:15. I can't go to the later meeting, because I am coaching track, and that takes up the afternoon. Could you help me out of this mess? I will do anything you want as long as it doesn't interfere with what the court ordered."

This is the *message*. How would you rate it ? You as the new principal can see the sender's nonverbal cues (manner of dress, facial and verbal expressions, bodily posture, etc.). Is the message clear, concise, uncluttered by many parallel issues? Does it appear that the sender has thought out the message well beforehand?

Now we move to *encoding*, which is the ability to put thoughts into words or actions. It takes place in the sender's mind as soon as he decides to transmit a message. Mike had to organize the message in words, facial expressions, and body movements; I am sure he practiced it at home and probably tried it out on his wife. This encoding is key to the success of the transaction, because the meaning of the message could be distorted by the unrepentant attitude of the sender, the inaccurate and clumsy words chosen, etc.

Now how does Marcia, the new principal, function in her role as co-communicator? She is listening in a nonjudgmental manner and trying to ensure that the already embarrassed teacher will be able to get through this ordeal with as little pain as possible. Confession may be good for the soul, but it can be painful when you have to admit to your boss that you have acted in an inappropriate manner.

We move on to the *setting*. There is a time and place for everything, and the setting was controlled by the sender because Marcia was sensitive enough to ask him where he would like to have the conversation. The principal maintains eye contact, avoiding sly glances at her watch; she seats Mike in a comfortable chair with no furniture barriers between him and her. She gives him her undivided attention. Is she sending any messages even at this point in the transactional communication? Her positive, accepting, sensitive handling of the session speaks volumes. She is a good communicator. In her mind, Marcia has an outline that she is filling out as she listens. The outline has three parts: topic, discussion, outcome. Before Mike leaves the office, Marcia must be sure that she understands the message (topic). She takes an active part in the communication (discussion or dialogue), so she will be sure that she does grasp the message, and finally, she must be as certain as she can be that both she and Mike clearly understand and agree upon the outcome of the session.

When we talk about *transmission* of a message from the sender to the receiver, we acknowledge that if the message is to be communicated effectively, it must be well organized and clear. Marcia is satisfied that Mike has made a good transmission of the message. He is not "blowing smoke" or giving misinformation. Marcia notes a congruency among the content, the choice of words, the facial expressions, and the bodily posture. As far as she can judge, Mike looks like he is telling the story in an honest manner. When Marcia sends back her message, she wants to be sure she is expressing herself in a similar manner.

The new principal has had no trouble *decoding* the message. No filter has blocked her decoding. Sometimes the child, spouse, or parent of an alcoholic will have problems communicating with people who abuse alcohol. Our principal has no such filter. Although she is definitely opposed to driving while under the influence, she has not prejudged the teacher and put him into the role of one who needs punishment. She wasn't shocked by what she was hearing, even though the results of it will certainly make her job more difficult.

Filters are only one of the potential barriers that interfere with communication. The barriers can also consist of:

♦ Paying more attention to the speaker's mannerisms of speech than to the substance.

♦ Appearing to pay attention but allowing the mind to tune out.

♦ Allowing all kinds of distractions to divert our attention.

♦ Overreacting to certain words or phrases, thus losing the forest for the trees.

♦ Allowing an initial lack of interest in the subject to prevent one from paying close attention.

♦ Allowing our own prejudice against the sender to interfere with our reception of the message.

Now we come to a time when the principal who has been actively listening must indicate that she has received the message. The sender will be watching very carefully all the signs of facial expression, bodily posture, tone of voice, etc. Only the principal can make it clear that the *message is received*. As Mike was painfully transmitting his message, the receiver was deciphering it (decoding) and now must indicate to the sender that it has been received.

Remember when you had the misfortune of banging the family car into the garage door? You came into the house and confessed your crime. You watched your father's every cue to see how badly he was taking it. It was only when he indicated that he had received the message that you could take a breath. He understood that you had done real damage to the front left fender. It would cost money. The car could be driven, but it looked awful and would need immediate repairs. How you prayed that the feedback from your father would not be too severe.

Now the principal must give *feedback*. It isn't sufficient to say the message has been received and understood. The principal must respond fully. Actually, she has been responding from the beginning, but now she responds to the full message. Feedback is nothing more or less than sending a message back to the original sender that will further the dialogue and make it possible to bring the transactional communication to a successful end.

In order to bring this example to a close, we will make up a message as encoded and transmitted by the principal. Marcia says, "First of all, I want to express my sorrow that you find yourself in this situation. I want you to know we think highly of you as a teacher, and speaking for myself I can assure you we will try to do whatever we can to help you get through the ordeal. As to your practical questions, Bill McCarthy comes in from Centerville and arrives at school early. Would you be adverse to asking him to drive you until your suspension is over? He goes within a block of your house every morning. In the afternoon, I am around here until after you finish track practice, so I would be glad to drive you home after school. There is one problem, I can't always leave promptly at five o'clock. You may have to wait around for me, unless you can get another ride.

"The noon class is a little trickier, but I may be able to pull a switch. We are scheduled to get an intern in PE second semester. The intern is supposed to start at Middlebrook this semester. If I can switch with Frank Edmonds, the principal at Middlebrook, we might be able to get the intern to come here this semester. You could coach and supervise the intern at times agreeable to both of you. With the intern coming, you would be covered for the noon class. Luckily, your AA meeting is held in a church within a short walk of the school. It should work out."

I realize not all problems are so easily solved, but this is an illustration of a transactional communication in which the principal did a masterful job. I am certain that principals who can handle their transactional communications in an efficient and kind way will be considered good communicators. When most people say, "You are a good communicator," they really mean "you are a good listener." There is another side to communication that we will take up presently, but much of the communication handled by a principal resembles the example above. The good Steward Principal communicator has more than an adequate IQ; he or she has a good EQ—or Emotional Quotient. Standout principals in my experience are characterized by high emotional intelligence. They are able to read their own feelings and those of others, and stick to their own goals and promises no matter how tough the opposition. They are also able to move others to open their minds and change their behavior. This kind of emotional intelligence contributes greatly to their ability to communicate humanely. In my opinion, this communication skill will help principals lead their stakeholders into forming a true Learning Organization.

Recently, while lecturing to school superintendents, I referred often to Daniel Goleman's book *Emotional Intelligence* which I found most helpful. The superintendents requested that I direct them in a series of seminars following the key chapters in Goleman's book. They were most taken by his Chapter 16 (32). We have had two seminars to date and will have four more. The superintendents are deeply interested in this development of what Howard Gardner calls the Personal Intelligences.

In our example above, it became apparent that Marcia would be an excellent communicator because of her high emotional intelligence. The key to this emotional intelligence is her capacity to be self-aware. Put simply, without good intrapersonal intelligence (self-knowledge), it is impossible to have good interpersonal intelligence—the indispensable ingredient in communications. There is a crucial difference between being caught up in a feeling and becoming aware that you are being swept away by it. Marcia had enough awareness of her own feelings to be able to empathize with Mike in his present situation. Self-awareness builds on self-observation. Self-awareness means being aware both of our moods and our thoughts about our moods. Good communicators fall into foul moods as all people do, but what differentiates them is their ability to be aware of their mood and to get out of them so they don't botch up interpersonal relations or communication.

As a brand-new principal, Marcia probably had some real fear and trepidation about handling her first serious personnel problem. Fortunately, she was aware of this mood of anxiety and was able to put it aside to give full attention to Mike's problem. All Steward Principals learn to do this so they can become servant-leaders, willing to put aside their own anxieties in order to be of service to the stakeholders. They are invariably good communicators.

THE STEWARD PRINCIPAL EFFECTIVELY DELIVERS AN UNINTERRUPTED SPEECH

In an age of 7- and 15-second sound bytes, we have few noted orators. Few of today's political candidates could even remotely be considered an orator. On the other hand, every one of them has the capacity to deliver an adequate, uninterrupted speech—one that keeps people's attention and communicates the message.

In this section, I want to discuss some of the ways principals can prepare themselves to give 15- or 20-minute speeches that are effective and persuasive. There are three reasons why all principals should be competent, even polished speakers. First, public education is being sold short by many of our erstwhile friends. Politicians, especially the fiscally conservative type, are out to cut taxes first and educate children second. There is room for much school improvement, but the sad thing is that we do not sufficiently communicate our successes to the public. Someone like a principal, who knows the true situation in the schools, will have to speak for them in the public forum. It has to be from the grass roots. It can't be solved by state or federal leaders. Even speakers from Central Office or the state Department of Education don't have the credentials a school principal has when it comes to talking about present day school practices. No one knows a school better than a principal. We need to have principals out in the public explaining what we are trying to do, how we have succeeded, and where we can improve.

The second reason I think principals need to do more public speaking is because the ability to give an interesting, coherent, clear, and concise 15- or 20-minute talk is the mark of a well-educated person. Every student who graduates from high school should be able to compose and deliver a polished 10- or 15-minute speech.

If you want to show people what your school is trying to do to educate their children, give them a sample by presenting a talk that they will find informative, interesting, entertaining, and persuasive. There are very few principals who couldn't do just that if they put their minds to it, studied basic public speaking, practiced, got feedback and had the courage to jump into the fray.

The third reason I would like to see all principals improve in their speaking ability is to model for teachers, who also must be able to give a good talk to adults. If teachers and principals find creative ways to avoid speaking in public, how will the students ever hone their skills with the spoken word? A person who can give a clear, concise, interesting, and informative talk has a tremendous advantage in this period of history in which we allow others to do the writing and speaking for us. There may be too many engineers on the market today, but there will never be too many engineers who speak effectively about what they do. This is true of doctors, lawyers, butchers, bakers, and candlestick makers, and is especially true of educators. We are suffering from a terrible drought—very few of our citizens can or want to speak in public. That fact itself may be a serious indictment of our recent public school education. The schools aren't requiring students to write and speak. Once it was routine for every student to learn to speak well, then only the debating team, and now there are few debating teams and oratory is on holiday.

Where have all the orators gone? When I was in college 60 years ago, I faithfully read a monthly magazine called *Vital Speeches*. Each issue contained 15 or more speeches by politicians, scientists, preachers, adventurers, etc. They were marvelously crafted and made for fascinating reading. Unfortunately, today we are in a post-oratorical society that seems to be willing to accept 30-second spot announcements, and has little patience with well-prepared pieces of polished speech making. The loss is great, because many of the complex issues we should be dealing with can't be encapsulated in short sound bytes.

THAT'S JUST RHETORIC

We often hear the remark "That's just rhetoric." It is often spoken in a derogatory manner as if to say what was spoken was not substantial, not to be taken seriously, lacking in credibility, just showy fluff. It's a shame that rhetoric has been put down the way it has been. Believe me, Steward Principals who are successful in getting stakeholders to commit to a vision put much time and effort into improving the rhetorical skills.

To be an effective speaker, the principal should consider how best to get the audience to listen to his or her word pictures of the "vision." Today, with all the competing media messages slickly delivered, the principal (like classroom teachers) has to work hard to gain and keep the full attention of the audience. It isn't sufficient to merely speak grammatically and logically: one has to do more. We have to use rhetoric. To get stakeholders to commit to a common vision, the principal must be able to move not just the stakeholders' minds but also their hearts. We are learning more today about the important role emotions play in our thinking and judging. Rhetoric touches the whole person and gets him or her motivated to act according to some desirable goal. Rhetoric is the key to effective leadership and stewardship.

WHAT IS RHETORIC?

In ancient Greece, there were three arts concerned with excellence in the use of language: grammar, logic, and rhetoric. The Greeks taught that the speaker who wanted to express thought and feeling well had to develop skill in all three. Today, we have some speakers who use grammar well or at least correctly. Others use logic fairly well, but almost none who make use of rhetoric—the art of persuasion—with any proficiency.

Watch the talk shows on TV, and you will see examples of poor grammar, faulty logic, and screaming instead of rhetoric. Watch the politicians as they use or misuse statistics in seven-second bytes, or use misinformation to blacken their opponents' reputations and confuse the audience. This is not rhetoric, it is sophistry—a misuse of rhetoric. Many principals and teachers today are suspicious of the very word "rhetoric" and well they might be. Even the early Greeks and Romans spawned groups of sophists who began to use the skills of rhetoric as tricks to deceive rather than as means to illuminate the mind and move the heart. If I read the signs of the times correctly, the changes about to break forth in public education will demand that principals become orators who skillfully craft not only the substance of their message (vision) but the style in which they express it. Without such skilled public school communicators who can tell the true story, the public will be duped by charlatans who use smoke and mirrors to convince the public that we can do with less public schooling, arts programs, libraries, museums, etc.

As a principal, you find yourself almost constantly trying to persuade stakeholders not only to listen to what you have to say but also to agree with you, and think and act accordingly. As Steward Principals you are "persuaders." To persuade means to advise thoroughly. I don't believe you can advise thoroughly without the skillful use of rhetoric. *You are not only trying to persuade stakeholders to do something, but to believe that it is the better thing to do.*

The strong group of teachers who control the English department at Lincoln High School is persuaded that block scheduling will interfere with their way of doing things. Consequently, they use their considerable power to dissuade other teachers from going along with the introduction of seminars. Their main objection is that seminars will make it necessary for them to accept block scheduling and force them to give up lecturing. They can't conceive of lecturing through a 90-minute period. Yet they don't feel comfortable in a classroom in which the students are interacting with the teacher and each other. Yet, this is precisely what you as a Steward Principal envision. The "establishment" of English teachers feels it cannot give up control of the 50-minute hour and certainly cannot switch to the role of seminar. Your job as Steward Principal is to use whatever skills you can muster to convince these teachers that seminars will help the student and meet more learning styles, and that a steady diet of lecturing is often counter-productive.

This is not a far-fetched example. How do you go about persuading these English teachers to change? *You use rhetoric.*

The Greeks have words for the three instruments of rhetoric: *ethos*, *pathos*, and *logos*. In order to persuade the English teachers to accept the changes discussed above, you will have to use these three main tools.

Ethos. *Ethos* signifies a person's character. Establishing one's character is the first step in any attempt at persuasive speaking or writing. If you have earned the reputation of a Steward Principal, this will help. The Steward Principal is perceived by the stakeholders as one who is deeply accountable for the purposes of the school without acting to define purpose for others, control others, or take care of others. You as the persuader must reinforce the idea that as a Steward Principal you are not acting as a dictator who enforces change, but rather as a persuader who tries to help people see that they too are accountable for the purposes of the school, and must consequently ask, "What is best for the learning of the students?"

Under *ethos*, you must prove in your speech and writing that you are the kind of leader who knows what you are talking about and can be trusted for your honesty and good judgment. You must appear likeable to them as well as trustworthy. Many of you will wince as you read this. You may ask, "how can I get up in front of the faculty and tell them I am a person who knows what she is doing, and that I have the best interest of the students at heart? Wouldn't that be obnoxiously proud and arrogant?" No. If we are to learn to persuade, we must rediscover the art of rhetoric. When you stand up to speak or when you draft a document, initially you must spend a lot of time establishing your credentials. Why should you be listened to and taken seriously?

For the sake of argument, suppose you had been principal of a year-round school for three years before you took over duties at Lincoln High. In the *ethos* part of your presentation, you might call on your successful experience in changing school curriculum and scheduling to create a year-round school. You could give examples of the teachers who at first found the new ways difficult but eventually were able to see that the changes were beneficial for students, parents and teachers as well. Although *ethos* must be handled in the beginning, it should also be interspersed throughout the talk. In it you are talking about yourself and giving reasons why the audience should listen to you and believe what you are saying.

In my last 12 years teaching principals, I have come to the conclusion that principals find it rather difficult to talk about themselves in a way that highlights their experience and accomplishments. For that reason, it may strike you that my advice about using *ethos* in your talks and writings is a little too much like being a braggart. Believe me, schools will not be reformed until principals, who are the most experienced hands-on educators, begin to speak more authoritatively about what should and should not be done in school renewal.

Another part of *ethos* concerns itself with rendering your audience or readers benevolent. Simply put, get them comfortable with you as a person and to your message.

We are a generation that has been nearly entertained to death. The principal must offer some inducements to have the hearers or readers give their attention freely. One of the things I always did when I was speaking around the country was to arrive at the place I was speaking a day early, so I could familiarize myself with the town or city. In my talk, I would choose my illustrations with an eye to using their local department stores, colleges, churches, theatres, bus routes, etc. as subjects. Nothing renders an audience more benevolent than a speaker's efforts to familiarize himself or herself with the local scene. The speaker who knows the main avenues—Broadway and Seventh Ave. intersect at Times Square in Manhattan, for instance—will appeal to New Yorkers as someone who might know something else of importance. The speaker becomes credible when he or she is attuned to the audience and their environment.

A delightful example of this use of *ethos* appears in Shakespeare's play, *Julius Caesar*. Caesar was assassinated by Brutus, his erstwhile friend. The citizens of Rome are gathered

in the forum around Caesar's dead body, grieving for their mur-
dered leader, and they want an accounting. Brutus, one of the
conspirators, mounts the rostrum and says the following.

> "Romans, countrymen, and lovers, hear me for my cause,
> and be silent that you may hear: believe me for mine
> honor, and have respect to mine honor, that you may
> believe:... If there be any in this assembly, any dear friend
> of Caesar's, to him I say, that Brutus' love to Caesar was
> no less than his. If then that friend demand why Brutus
> rose against Caesar, this is my answer: Not that I loved
> Caesar less, but that I loved Rome more. Had you rather
> Caesar was living and die all slaves, than that Caesar
> were dead, to live all free men?"

This use of *ethos* was effective with the mob. They seemed to
accept Brutus' explanation for his part in the conspiracy and
murder of Caesar. Brutus is satisfied that he has won over the
populace, so he allows Marc Anthony to speak after him. Notice
how Marc Anthony uses *ethos* even more skillfully than Brutus.

> "Friends, Romans, countrymen, lend me your ears: . . . .
> Come I to speak in Caesar's funeral. He was my friend,
> faithful and just to me: but Brutus says he was ambi-
> tious; and Brutus is an honorable man. He hath brought
> many captives home to Rome, whose ransoms did the
> general coffers fill: Did this in Caesar seem ambitious?
> When the poor have cried, Caesar hath wept: Ambition
> should be made of sterner stuff. Yet Brutus says he was
> ambitious; and Brutus is an honorable man . . . . I thrice
> presented him a kingly crown, which he did thrice refuse:
> was this ambitious? Yet Brutus says he was ambitious;
> and sure he is an honorable man . . . . You all did love
> Caesar once not without cause. What cause withholds
> you then to mourn for him?"

The short speech of Brutus' mainly illustrates the role of *ethos*.
So does the somewhat longer opening portion of Anthony's

address, but Anthony goes on with the purpose of avenging Caesar's death, and to do this he resorts to *pathos* and *logos*. *Pathos* is the motivating factor then *logos*, the marshalling of reasons comes last.

Pathos. *"Si vis me flere, primum est tibi flendum."* When I was nineteen, I learned this Latin phrase and it has been with me ever since. Roughly translated, it says: "If you want me to cry, you have to first cry yourself." Notice how Shakespeare has both Brutus and Marc Anthony use emotional language in their speeches. Even the short excerpts I shared with you are loaded with words that touch the heart, not just the brain.

Good speakers or good writers always take into account the fact that humans are not merely rational machines, they are also greatly influenced by their feelings. We can often see more through a tear drop than through a telescope.

When you speak as a principal to a group of parents, you will only move them if you aim at their feeling processes as well as their logical ones. I'll never forget a principal called Mario. I witnessed him as he was trying to persuade a group of parents to consider the possibility of a middle school going year-round in the coming year. The more he offered statistics to prove that year-round schooling was a growing national trend, the less the parents listened. When he said it would save money by cutting down the number of schools needed, they became belligerent.

The parents who were opposed to the idea had one argument in common: "If we send our children to a year-round school, it will interfere with our vacation schedule." As I sat there listening, I was overwhelmed by the lack of sense in the objection. What is a week's or two-week's vacation schedule change compared to a year of improved educational opportunities for a child? Mario was getting more and more frustrated. Finally, one of the teachers whose 10-year-old daughter was in the audience asked her to speak to the problem. The young girl, who had just finished her fourth grade in a year-round school, went directly to the emotions. She stood up and said, "We are having better vacations now that I go to the year-round school. We were able to go to Disneyland last February, and it was wonderful to be able to go into all the exhibits without waiting in long lines.

Besides, I found that the inter-session in school is just what I needed to get some electives, like astronomy, which I never thought I could study in regular school. My brother used his inter-session to get some help in math and was able to get back on track in less than a month. We both love the year-round school and hope you will have a year-round middle school ready so we can attend it."

You could hear a pin drop. The youngster had supplied the element of *pathos* as well as *logos*. The parents who were complaining about changes in their vacation schedule began to admit that the companies they worked for might be happy to have some of the employees take spring, fall and winter vacations instead of having all employees out in July and August.

We are finally arriving again at a place where we can admit that emotions and feelings are not externals that interfere with reasoning and logic, but rather essential parts of the human processes. When you present an oral or written piece that aims at persuading others to your way of thinking and acting, you must include a plea to their emotional intelligence as well as their rational intelligence.

Brutus is foolish to let Marc Anthony speak after him. Anthony, using pathos, succeeds in changing the mood that Brutus had established. One citizen cries out: "Caesar has had great wrong"; another exclaims: "He would not take the crown; therefore, 'tis certain he was not ambitious." Finally, a citizen cries out, "There's not a nobler man in Rome than Marc Anthony." Anthony using the rheological tools of *ethos* and *pathos* has won over a crowd that previously was agreeing with Brutus. Mario, the principal who was trying to reach a hostile audience, was wise to let the 10-year-old girl speak about year-round schooling. She was able to hit all three: *ethos* because she was an innocent child speaking for students, *pathos* because she touched the feeling of her parents, her brother, and herself and through them the whole audience; and finally *logos* because she gave two substantive reasons for year-round schooling: the opportunities for strategically placed enrichment and remediation classes during the three intersessions.

As principals trying to persuade teachers, parents, students or others, you also have to learn the skills of *pathos* and *logos*.

Trained as most principals are in a non-classical tradition in which most of the emphasis is on the social sciences, it is not surprising that they often rise to speak armed with charts and statistics. (Incidentally, so do politicians and business managers.) The principals launch directly into a set of reasons why some program should be instituted or put to rest. What we learn from the old Greeks is very important. Don't move to the *logos* before you have taken the time to develop the *ethos* and *pathos*.

If an audience or group of readers are given a heavy serving of *logos* without attention to *ethos* and *pathos*, they may resist the argument. Unless you first establish your credibility as a spokesperson and show how important your topic is, the audience or readers will suffer from attention deficit.

Logos. *Logos*, the marshalling of reasons, comes last. Just as you shouldn't bring motivating passions (*pathos*) into the speech or article until you have first aroused favorable feelings toward your own person, so you are better off not resorting to reasons or arguments in favor of your position until you have first established an emotional mood that is receptive to them. Once the little girl spoke about how much she loved the year-round school, Mario, the principal, could move on and give reasons to persuade the parents to look more favorably at the year-round school.

Incidentally, a change in name can have quite an effect. Mario learned to refer to the year-round school as a "four-season school." That term was much more acceptable; it cut away the impression that children would be in school 365 days a year. Why not attend school during each of the four seasons and have time out of school in each of the beautiful seasons?

Reasons and arguments should be used to reinforce the drive of the passions, but reasons and arguments will have no force at all unless your listeners or readers are already disposed emotionally to move in the direction that your reasons and arguments try to justify. Persuading people isn't easy, but it is one of the main goals of a Steward Principal.

Just like the principal who was trying to introduce seminars into a high school curriculum, or Mario who was trying to persuade some hostile parents to look more favorably at the four-

season school, so Marc Anthony had his own agenda. He wanted
to get the citizens of Rome to mutiny against Brutus and the
other assassins. Marc Anthony offered some reasons why Caesar should not have died even in the earlier part of his speech
when he was developing *ethos* and *pathos*. Caesar wasn't ambitious or greedy. He cared more for the citizens than he did for
himself. But now, when he comes to the end of his speech, Anthony commingles *pathos* and *logos*. He succeeds in moving the
citizens of Rome to take up arms against Brutus, Cassius, and
the other traitors. He does this by slyly mentioning Caesar's will
and intimating that when the citizens learn of its provisions,
they will find themselves Caesar's beneficiaries.

> "But here's a parchment with seal of Caesar;
> I found it in his closet, 'tis his will:
> Let but the commons hear this testament—
> Which, pardon me, I do not mean to read—
> And they would go and kiss dead Caesar's wounds
> And dip their napkins in his sacred blood,
> Yea, beg a hair of him for memory,
> And, dying, mention it within their wills,
> Bequeathing it as a rich legacy
> Unto their issue."

The citizens beg Anthony to reveal the contents of Caesar's
will to them. But before he tells them that the will provides a
gift of seventy-five drachmas to every citizen, he launches into
a peroration that raises their passions to a fever pitch.

> ". . . This was the most unkindest cut of all;
> For when the noble Caesar saw Brutus stab,
> Ingratitude, more strong than traitors' arms,
> Quite vanquished him: then burst his mighty heart;
> And in his mantle muffling up his face,
> Even at the base of Pompey's statue,
> Which all the while ran blood, great Caesar fell.
> O, what a fall was there, my countrymen!
> Then I, and you, and all of us fell down,
> While bloody treason flourish'd over us."

The speech had its effect. Marc Anthony mixed *logos* with *pathos* and the citizens cry out for revenge against the assassins and their cohorts, calling them traitors and villains. They are no longer honorable men. "We'll mutiny," the citizens roar, and "We will burn the house of Brutus and go after the other conspirators." Then and only then does Marc Anthony clinch the matter by revealing how every citizen of Rome benefits from Caesar's will. That does it. The riot has been started and Marc Athony's rhetoric has turned the citizenry against the mutineers. History was changed that day. *Logos* always remains the winning trump in the communicator's hand. You have to have plausible reasons but you must make the most of them by the prior use of *ethos* and *pathos*.

Meanwhile, back at Mario's school, I actually saw many of the parents beginning to listen to the arguments for the four-season school. Some of them were even discussing ways they could accommodate their vacation schedule to this new school year. As a Steward Principal, at times you have to get stakeholders interested in ideas in which they have no interest. I have always believed the art of teaching involves getting students interested in areas that presently have little pull on their attention but which will play a part in their further development. The use of rhetoric is indispensable to a teacher or a principal and should, I think, play a much larger role in education.

I highly recommend that you study thoroughly Oral and Nonverbal Expression (Domain 16) in *Principals For Our Changing Schools*. (33) In this chapter, Ivan Muse and his committee have covered the essentials in this area, which is so important for all Steward Principals. I didn't develop their definition as much as I would have liked to because I wanted to highlight the importance of rhetoric. This venerable aid to oral and nonverbal expression is seldom presented in modern books. Rhetoric will fill in some of the places where principals need added help.

In my college years, and later at graduate school, I made it a practice to form small volunteer groups who would be willing to meet regularly to improve their skills at oral expression. The groups were not unlike informal Toastmaster clubs. The members would choose two speakers each week whose duty it was to prepare a 12- to 15-minute speech, deliver it to the group, and seek feedback from the members. In a semester each member would be able to write and deliver three or more talks. Even now, 50 years later, I meet former colleagues from these speech groups who tell me how profitable they were in their professional lives.

SUMMATION

I tried to prove the statement that good communication by the principal is the key to effective school operations. I realize that not everyone would place as high a priority on the principal's skill in oral and nonverbal expression as I do. It may be one of my idiosyncrasies, but I believe in any leadership position, the leader has to to be able to set a vision before the stakeholders in order to persuade them to commit to the vision. Great leaders have great visions and are able to communicate them in a way that touches people deeply. The stakeholders must be moved in head, heart, and hand.

With the passage of time, I have become even more convinced that principals need to be able to persuade in oral and written expression. In times like ours when school reform is in the air, the principal must show the leadership necessary to bring about positive change at the building level. It is for that reason that I have placed so much emphasis on this subject. If the school leaders who have the smell of the chalk in their nostrils don't speak up and write, the direction of schools will be determined by others, who with all the good will in the world, don't have a glimmer of what goes on in schools today or how they should be renewed and reformed. To do this, principals and other educators will need to speak and write more often and more effectively.

In the first part of the chapter we talked about one-on-one communication in which the principal, Marcia, was using her emotional intelligence and communication skills to handle a difficult personnel problem with one of the teachers. In the second part of the chapter, we spoke about the principal using communication skills in presenting a 10- or 15-minute uninterrupted speech (public speaking).

Accepting the definition of oral and nonverbal expression offered by Ivan Muse and his cohorts, we went on to develop the distinction between interactional and transactional communication.

We emphasized the importance of the Process Model in Domain 16 and developed briefly the nine elements that comprise it.

In the second half of the chapter, I tried to develop the classical idea of rhetoric, and how rules of rhetoric can be utilized to accomplish what the principal wants to accomplish in oral expression. I am perfectly aware that there is little classical rhetoric available today in our communications. We still look back to Churchill, Roosevelt, Jack Kennedy and Martin Luther King for polished rhetoric. Today, Mario Cuomo is one of the few orators we have. I am also aware that the use of rhetoric can be corrupted, turning it into sophistry. Nonetheless, in any Principals' Academy, a large block of time should be given to preparing the principals to use rhetoric as they perfect their skills in oral and nonverbal expression. To make the best use of their experience, ideals, and passion, they should improve their communication skills. I want principals to be seen and heard in the school renewal process. Inside the school they must persuade those English teachers to use flexible scheduling so seminars may be introduced. Outside the school, they must illuminate the public so they will support school renewal.

QUESTIONS FOR REFLECTION

1. Once you are appointed principal even your chance remarks are noted and often given an importance you never intended. You have to watch what you say but as a communicator you must not lose your spontaneity. How do you walk that tight rope?

2. Do you accept the definition of oral and nonverbal expression offered in Domain 16 by Muse and his team? Of the six components listed which one do you consider the most important? Which has least importance?

3. How are interactional communication and transactional communication alike and how are they different?

4. In the process model offered in Domain 16 we find: a) the message to be sent, b) the encoding of the message by the sender, c) the transmission of the message, d) the decoding of the message by the receiver, e) the reception of the message by the receiver. In which of these actions is misunderstanding most likely to occur? Why?

5. How did Marcia, the new principal, handle communication with the PE teacher who lost his license because of DWI?

6. Give some examples of filters which might have derailed the communication between them.

7. I tried to argue that the time has come for principals to become spokespersons for their schools. Am I correct that principals should be doing much more public speaking?

8. The principal who learns to handle rhetoric in an effective manner will reach many hearers and get them to think and act differently. Why do we shun rhetoric when it is so important in persuading people?

9. To persuade means to advise thoroughly in an effort to help someone make a good decision. A persuasive principal can do great things for a school. How can principals improve in their ability to persuade others?

10. How can a principal learn the magic of ethos, pathos, and logos? How can he or she incorporate them in public speaking?

11. Here is a good tip in rhetoric: don't move to the logos until you have taken time to develop ethos and pathos. Why does this make so much sense?

8

THE STEWARD PRINCIPAL: MASTER OF THE WRITTEN WORD

William Wordsworth said to Charles Lamb,
"I believe I could write like Shakespeare, if I had a mind to try it."
Lamb replied, "Yes, nothing is wanting but the mind."

When I was teaching a class of principals, I referred to an airline magazine I had recently taken from a plane. I opened the magazine and read to them an advertisement for business leaders (managers), offering them a book containing form letters for almost all occasions. It made the pitch that the managers would not have to dictate or write letters themselves. They could use these prepackaged forms, merely filling in the blanks with the proper names and places and specific information. I thought this advertisement would get a rise out of the principals. I imagined they would be astounded that business managers would need such help. I was wrong. The principals admitted, "We get similar ads in our education magazines all the time." At this point I had to sit down for a minute. I just couldn't believe what I was hearing. Companies could make money selling principals books offering form letters for all occasions. Did it mean that school principals were unable or unwilling to write their own letters? I was honestly flabbergasted. In my day, principals had the skills necessary to communicate both orally and in writing to people in all stations of life. The last thing in the world I would have expected was a principal who was at a loss for words of any kind. What had happened to the preparation of principals? I refrained from asking the principals if they bought and used these books containing "cookie cutter" letters for all occasions. I hope they didn't.

In any case, when we talk about the principal as steward, we assume that he or she can use words, written and oral, to communicate with all the stakeholders. If the principal's vision for the school is so important, the communication of this vision is equally important. I have never met a really successful principal who didn't have a clear vision and the communication skills necessary to articulate this vision for teachers, parents, and students.

In the previous chapter, we developed the idea that the Steward Principal must have real skills in oral and nonverbal communication. In this one, we will take a rather novel approach to mastery in the written word. We will develop the concept of writing as thinking on paper.

WRITING: AN ESSENTIAL IN THE PRINCIPALS' EXECUTIVE PROGRAM

Not all of our principals take kindly to the required courses in writing demanded by the Principals' Executive Program at the University of North Carolina. Not to mention courses called, "How to Read a Book," "How to Speak, How to Listen," and "The Great Conversation." It would appear on the surface that the faculty members have little respect for principals' prior preparation.

Periodically I get an earful from an irate principal. The following is an example.

Tony: Tell me Jack, why do we have to take courses in elementary things like how to read a book, how to speak and how to listen? I especially dislike that awful course in creative writing, in which we are embarrassed to tears by teaching assistants from the English Department, who seem to relish slashing our assignments with huge red marks. It makes you feel like you are an idiot. I know a lot of principals who avoid PEP precisely because they don't want to be "dissed" by having to write assignments like middle school students and then get them back all marked up with red lines. How do you justify these courses?

Jack: Tony, all I can say is, it's like hitting yourself in the head with a hammer. It feels great when you stop. Seriously,the faculty found even before *Principals For Our Changing Schools* was published, mastery of the written word was an essential skill needed by successful principals. It was clear from our early classes that some principals either had not had a good preparation in writing, or they neglected to practice the skill. The teaching assistants from the English Department can be sticklers at times, but they do know the rudiments of good writing, and they endeavor to help the principals improve in this area.

Tony: I still think there are a lot of areas—like the use of technology, school law, and handling disciplinary problems— that would be more practical for us.

Jack: The faculty is working hard to make sure you get some help in the areas you mentioned, but I really think it is more important than ever today that practicing principals have facility in written expression. In Domain 17, India J. Podsen, Director of the Principals' Center at Georgia State University, leads the team that drafted the chapter on Written Expression. They define written expression as "expressing ideas clearly in writing appropriately for different audiences such as students, teachers, and parents; preparing brief memoranda, letters, reports, and other job specific documents." (34) I agree with that and go one step further. Even if a principal could say that she has the ability to write documents clearly and at an appropriate level, she would still need more help. Personally, I use writing as a means of helping myself to think better and I acknowledge I still need a lot of editing help when I write for publication. True, the aim of writing is communication, but much more. The aim of writing is to help us understand our world, for only then can we write our ideas out making our understanding available to others and clarifying them for ourselves.Thinking in writing is a form of understanding—a way of shaping first thoughts. Understood in that way, I can justify my own lifelong pursuit of writing, so I will be able to make sense of my world. I draw that I may see, and I write that I may understand. Only secondarily do I write to communicate to others. Does that help, Tony?

Tony: I like the part about hitting yourself in the head with a hammer best. Maybe that is why they say knowledge makes a bloody entrance. I'll do it but I don't have to like it.

WHY WE CLAIM WRITTEN EXPRESSION IS SO IMPORTANT FOR STEWARD PRINCIPALS

We know from experience and studies confirm that the primary qualities business executives look for in evaluating successful executives are honesty, candor, good judgment, intelligence, imagination, and the ability to write clearly and concisely. If that can be said for all executives, it is certainly true for principals. The point I would like to make is that principals can improve in all these areas by repetition. The more often principals act honestly, candidly, wisely, intelligently, and imaginatively, the more fully these good habits are developed in them. Is there any reason why the same isn't true of writing clearly and concisely?

I am now going to ask you an embarrassing question. Do you avoid writing as often as you can by using the telephone or some other substitute ? I find it is becoming less and less common to receive personal letters. I get telephone calls all the time, when I really wish people would write. When I have a written document in front of me, I can reread it to see if I understand it fully. The document gives me a record of the time and place where I am supposed to show up. I have a map I can follow. I know the facts of the case so much better than through a quick telephone call.

Someone will object and say that the computer is bringing back writing via e-mail, but I don't think so. What I find is that the sentence structure on an e-mail message is much closer to that of a phone call. It is almost like the old Western Union Telegrams in which you tried to say the most with the least words. There are many who think the written word in books will soon be a thing of the past and we will go completely electronic. Even if that dire prediction is fulfilled (I doubt it will be in our lifetime or our children's lifetime) it is still most important that we all learn to rid ourselves of the misconceptions about writing.

Writing is first and foremost a symbolic activity of meaning-making. Principals more than any other professionals are working in a world in which meanings are changing rapidly. They must write in order to make sense of their personal and professional worlds. Even if no one ever reads what you write, you should write that you may understand—just as you should draw or take photos so that you may see. We have to get away from the idea that you have to be an artist in order to draw, and even more from the idea that you have to be a professional writer in order to write.

In a more mundane sense, all organizations must maintain good levels of communication to function successfully. In a school in transition (and what school is not?), communication must be clear, concise, and even interesting. A good principal tells stories on paper and in this way avoids the cold, dull, impersonal educational jargon that turns people off so quickly.

Whether you like it or not, as a Steward Principal you are a model in many ways, including showing teachers and students how rewarding and enjoyable writing can really be. I'll never forget how much it impressed me to learn that the assistant principal of my high school wrote "cowboy stories" for the pulp magazines. This wasn't considered high-brow literary work. He supplemented his meager salary writing western stories at two cents a word, but he was a hero to me. I found out the pen name he used and really enjoyed reading his wild west stories. I think he became a role model for me. He was saving to buy a house for his wife and family. The few dollars he made each month from writing made the difference. Though he wrote to make money, he couldn't help getting better as a writer by just doing it. "To write better, write often," he told me when after graduation I got up the nerve to tell him I read and liked his stories.

In Domain 17 on Written Expression, India J. Podsen, the Team Leader, makes a serious point.

"Despite the obvious link between good writing and effective school leadership, today's principal preparation programs pay little attention to written communication.

In fact, no university at the graduate level offers required or elective courses in the job-specific writing skills so crucial to principals. As a result, graduate students leave the university under the false assumption that they write well enough to turn any phrase their jobs might require. Most, in reality, enter their careers dependent upon what they learned in grades K–12 and in undergraduate English composition classes." (34)

At our Principals' Executive Program, we came to the same conclusion and decided to make sure that the principals had the opportunity to sharpen their writing skills under the tutelage of some very gifted English majors. Many principals tell us that their teacher assistances' coaching was most helpful and benefited them as much as anything else they studied in the program. They were pleasantly surprised to see how quickly they could improve their writing skills and gratified when some of their teachers commented on how much they enjoyed reading their memos, vision statements, and thinking papers.

THE WRITING PROCESS

In *Principals For Our Changing Schools*, Domain 17 (35) you will find an excellent model for preparing principals to write clearly and concisely. The team of authors in this domain tells us that writing is not a linear process; rather, it has four key stages, all of which are interconnected. It encourages principals to understand the process in order to improve their writing. Seeing how professional writers do it will help the principal to overcome some personal "writing blocks." The model demonstrates how writing is taught today in language arts classes. This will help the principal explain this new method to parents who may have some doubts. Today, we are encouraging students to write across the curriculum; all teachers—no matter what their subject area—are encouraged to include writing assignments in their classes. We are beginning to realize that even if subjects are taught independently, good thinkers don't keep one subject hermetically sealed off from another. It is in writing that they can see how ideas in Environmental Studies incorporate materials from

Meteorology, Geography, Physics, Biology, Food Science, Soil and Water Studies, etc.

The model in Domain 17 highlights five key stages in the writing process: Prewriting, Drafting, Revising, Editing and the Final Product. I recommend that you read the chapter, always keeping in mind that these stages are flexible and need not be followed in a slavish manner. Since this material is covered well in Domain 17, I would like to take a somewhat different route and develop more fully the idea of writing as *thinking on paper*. We'll start with prewriting, always emphasizing the aspect of writing as thinking.

PREWRITING

We learn in Domain 17 that before a writer can begin work on a final draft, he or she must go through a series of steps, known collectively as prewriting. During this phase, the writer generates ideas and gathers data. This can be done in a formal or an informal manner. This prewriting phase can include all or some of the following: brainstorming, mind-mapping, free writing, outlining, audiotaping, problem solving, force-field analyses, observations, discussions, and document reviews.

If the Central Office requests a report from you on some topic, e.g., absenteeism over the last full academic year, you know what to do. You have your secretary check the sources (documents) and give you the data so you can write an answer in the form of a memo to Central Office. You still have to draft the memo, revise the draft, edit the revision, and finally either type or get typed the final product. No wonder most of us find writing a chore. It would be so much easier to call Central Office and tell them that your school's absenteeism was down from 4.5% to 4.3% during the last academic year. No wonder Central Office sends you so many forms to fill out—anything to cut down on the amount of composing that has to be done.

We usually collect and organize data first, and then write the document. This is standard practice. We did it most of our lives and consequently, most of us found writing a chore. It is so tedious, confining, nit-picking, and repetitious. We were told that once we felt we had enough material, we could start to organize it. The material could be presented in any of a number of ways: chronologically, by topic area, or via formats that high-light cause and effect, problems, solutions, comparative advan-tages, needs-plan-benefits, etc.

One of my biggest *bêtes noires* was the "outline." I must have been sick the week they taught outlining. It always perplexed me. How could I outline a piece of writing when I had not thought it out sufficiently to know what should come first, sec-ond, and third? I had the strange idea that if I could just take some paper and start writing on a topic, I might think it through and discover something that would make sense to me. Having an outline ready before I started to write always struck me as putting the cart before the horse. It meant I had figured some-thing out to my satisfaction, and now I was going through the stage of communicating my well-thought-out conclusions to someone else. I never really believed my thoughts were good enough to share with others in writing. I wondered what would happen if I just started to write, and later discovered connec-tions and relationships among the ideas. Maybe this would help me think things through. I might find a line of thought—some-thing I liked in what I had jotted down in a rough, hurly-burly way. Then I could think about it, figure out the argument, draft it, revise it, edit it, and put it in final form.

This worked for me. For others who have a different learn-ing style, it is better for them to use the outline first. For me the outline in the beginning puts me in a box; for others it gives them the structure they need. It may be that our writing style is closely related to our learning style. If we take into consider-ation different learning styles, why not do the same with writ-ing styles?

It was the final form—the polished performance—that fright-ened me and kept me from writing more. I was humiliated back in fourth grade when the teacher asked me to spell "Mississippi" and I asked if she wanted the river or the state. Not too profi-cient in spelling and even less adept at grammar, I was like so many others of my peers—fearful of writing. Then about 30 years ago, I stumbled on the idea that writing is something you should do to help you think and make sense of a topic or issue. When I write as a means of helping me to think better, I don't have to worry about anyone else seeing my writing. It is private, so I don't have to be concerned about spelling, grammar or style. Writing then becomes a means of making sense of my world, and most of it never has to be outlined, drafted, revised, edited or wind up in a final product. It becomes more like talking. Most people like to talk or converse, since they usually don't have to pre-talk, draft, revise, edit, and polish their oral communications unless they are giving a formal speech.

Early in my life, I found talking with others in informal conversations helped me make sense of my world. Listening to others helped me think better. It made it possible for me to get some meaning and significance out of things that were happening around me that I only vaguely comprehended. I always found in the past that reading helped me think. But not until I was nearly 50 did I begin to see how jotting down ideas helped my thinking. Writing for our own amusement can teach us to think better and make more sense of our world. I am not sure whether it was the writing of Mortimer Adler, or John Dewey, or Gordon Allport with his notion of functional autonomy that caused me to realize what I had been missing. The good news is that I began to see writing for what it is: a tool for thinking things through and an aid for our memory.

Could there be a connection these days between the current flight from writing and the apparent lack of depth in peoples' thinking about major political and moral issues? The media, with its seven-second sound bytes, does little to help people think deeply. If, as most of us agree, we want a more fair and more system for delivering health care in this country, we should do a lot of reading about the various ways health care is delivered in Canada, Germany, England, France, Japan, etc. More than that, we would have to understand the peculiar play of competitive forces in this country in which all players in the game (hospitals, doctors, insurance companies, pharmaceutical companies, wealthy, middle class and poor recipients) want to protect their independence, profit level, share of the pie, costs, expenses etc. In order to understand such a complex problem, I would have to read a lot but also jot down ideas on paper to help me grasp the facts. Very few Americans took the time to analyze the problem in this way, allowing "carpetbaggers" to obfuscate the picture and frighten the citizens away from much needed reform of the health delivery system. Only by writing down my thoughts, then seeing how they can be refuted by people coming from different sets of values, can I really get to the bottom of such complex problems. If more Americans wrote to think, more Americans would learn to think, and we might make more enlightened decisions.

MOST BOOKS ON WRITING TELL ONLY HALF THE STORY

I have a shelf full of books on writing, and I have learned a lot from each of them, but the book that has done the most for me is entitled, *Thinking on Paper* by V.A. Howard and J.H. Barton (36). They sum up my position neatly, "1) Writing is a symbolic activity of meaning-making; 2) Writing for others is a staged performance; and 3) Writing is a tool of understanding as well as a communication" (37). The authors try to teach us how to refine, express, and actually generate ideas by understanding the processes of the mind. What I picked up 30 years ago from Dewey, Adler, and Allport on writing for thinking is confirmed and expanded in this little gem.

Thinking in writing is in fact a form of understanding—a way of shaping first thoughts. On the other hand, communicating in writing is mostly a matter of reshaping our thoughts on paper. The drafting, revising, editing, and putting into final form as noted in Domain 17 are devoted to the second aim of writing: communication. When writing to understand, we don't aim to communicate in a final product, so we need not draft, revise, edit, or type perfectly on the word processor. We are writing for ourselves—to help us make things meaningful, understandable, and sensible. We are writing primarily to make sense of our world. Yet if we do decide to write for publication, we can sharpen our thinking during every stage of the process—outline, draft, revision, editing, and typing. It isn't an either-or, it is both-and. My only regret is that people fail to utilize writing as a tool for thinking, because they think the only purpose for writing is as a means of communicating our ideas to others.

When my wife and I were trying to decide on whether we would move to Raleigh, North Carolina to take an attractive job offer, we each took a piece of paper and wrote on the top: *We will go to Raleigh and take the job offer.* Then we drew a line down the middle of the pages, labeled the half on the left "Reasons For" and the one on the right, "Reasons Against." Then we went our separate ways to work out a decision. We didn't want to have too much influence on each other. The first rule was to put down whatever came to our minds regardless of how silly or trivial the reason might seem. Later, we would give a weight to the reasons on either side, but for the present we wanted to get down in writing whatever we had already thought about as well as new ideas we discovered. It was not a silly exercise. We wrote to understand, to discover, to learn. After some hours, we sat together and compared our papers. We had each come up with around 35 reasons split between reasons *for* and *against*. It was immediately apparent that the reasons *for* were more plentiful than the reasons *against*. We then cooperated to give a weight to each of our 70 reasons. We gave a (5) for a major reason, a (3) for a moderately serious reason, and a (1) for what we agreed was a superficial reason.

If this strikes you as a lot of work to do to make a decision, try to realize what it meant for a married couple in their 50's to uproot and start a new life in a city 650 miles away. If more people used such an exercise, they might avoid making serious mistakes, and they would use their powers of judgment more effectively. How many older couples do you know, who retired, moved to a distant paradise, only to find they couldn't adjust to the new environment? Long-distance movers love this approach. For my wife and I, thinking on paper worked. Our reasons were remarkably similar with enough differences to make them interesting. Raleigh won handily and we have been grateful ever since. The writing exercise consumed about two hours of our time. We have lived happily in Raleigh 22 years.

WRITER'S BLOCK

If you have ever suffered from "writer's block," you will understand more fully what we mean by the age-old problem of "getting it down on paper." Writer's block is the result of our tendency to separate thinking from writing, on the one hand,

and on the other, making a single desperate attempt to "get it all right." Through the years I have suffered from this malady, and the only remedy I know is to wait until it passes. It is much like the common cold: if you take medicines it goes away in two weeks, and if you don't it lasts a fortnight. If you think of writing as having some well thought-out ideas and only needing to find the right words to express them, you are an apt subject for "writer's block." The truth is, we think in words, so if we have something well thought-out, we already have the words, and writing it down is a piece of cake. What we have to grasp in this old-but-new approach is that *articulation precedes communication*. So you can legitimately have "thinker's block" but not "writer's block." Thinking with a pencil in your hand and a paper in front of you on which you write words and/or draw figures helps you shape first thoughts. On the other hand, in writing for communication (a performance), one reshapes and refines these first thoughts.

How often have I found myself sitting in front of the computer trying to write a chapter of a book only to find no words coming forward. I was blocked. It is a panicky feeling, especially if you face a deadline. Now I know how to avoid that awful feeling. I don't start at the word processor, I sit down with a pad of paper and begin to think on paper. Thinking on paper opens up all kinds of ways of addressing a problem or situation. We learn that writing is an activity, something you do, not something that "happens" to you. I will try to present an example of this type of "thinking on paper" to help Steward Principals express in writing the fruits of their years of school experience. Principals need to be heard from more, and they will be taken seriously when they improve their ability to express their thoughts in writing.

WRITING FOR PUBLICATION

For example, if you decide to write an article for the local paper supporting a bond issue for public schools, you may estimate that you are going to need six hours to write this article. You project that you will need two hours for *generating*, two more for *composing*, and the last two for *expressing*. Get someone you trust to edit it and in an hour more you can polish it up for publication. Seven hours may seem like a lot of time, but a good article printed in the paper can reach many thoughtful persons and may be a big help in passing the school bond. Principals need to be heard from on subjects like this. They know more about the education of children K-12 than anyone else. Writing will not only help principals think better, but by disseminating their ideas in writing, they will help others to better understand the process of educating the young, and perhaps convince them that it is worthwhile to vote "yes" on the school bond issue.

GENERATING IDEAS

Once again Howard and Barton in *Thinking on Paper* offer us a clear and concise presentation.

> "Thinking in writing is the practice of writing things down as you go, as you think things through. This includes note taking, marginalia, shopping lists, personal reflections as in diary keeping, calculations and diagrams, questions, ideas jotted down in haste on scraps or envelopes, and so forth. Feelings and attitudes, values and wishes all figure prominently in such jottings. Indeed, thinking in writing is anything set down to help you remember, organize, relate, deduce, explain, question, or express any thinking on paper that aids your understanding of a topic at hand.

> No doubt you have plenty of practice at this, but you may not have seen it as a vital first step in a continuous process of generation, composition, and expression. Many people find writing difficult because they try to do all three at once in a desperate attempt to get their ideas out and down, logically organized and nicely presented in a single effort." (37)

Suppose, when asked to write the article, you decided, "I am not a good writer, I will get someone else to do it for me." Or you might have said, "I saw a great article in the New York Times by Al Shanker, in which he gave reasons for such a bond issue, and luckily I have a copy of it." Then you might grab a piece of paper and a pencil, and start to jot down Shanker's reasons and material from other sources. You could ask some students in your school to give their reasons. There are all kinds of arguments you could discover. How about this one: any investment in our children will pay back in big dividends when they are able to get demanding and high-paying jobs because they received a good education.

Now you do some thinking about what those who oppose a school bond are thinking. You jot down reasons against a school bond issue: singles who have no children in school, older couples whose kids have already finished school, and young married couples who don't have children might complain that they are paying for the education of other people's children. How can you answer objections? Write it all out in rough form.

Next, you start brainstorming on what good will come from a bond issue, and what harm will occur if they don't vote for the bond issue. You bring in the strongest arguments at the end and you draw on your personal experience as a teacher and principal. You jot down stories of young children who have profited greatly from their education and are now using their skills to fight cancer, maintain law and order, build our buildings, paint beautiful pictures, write wonderful songs and plays, etc. By this time you will have sheets of paper with many informal jottings and quotes. You will be conscious that *ethos*, *pathos*, and *logos* all have their place. You haven't worried a minute about spelling, punctuation, style, format, etc. You have thought on paper. This process we have been going through is called *generating*. My excellent editor won't be happy unless I admit that this stage can also be called "prewriting" if it is a step toward publication. My point is that this thinking on paper is a tool we should use, even when we have no intention of publishing. We are just trying to figure things out for ourselves. Notice that up to this point, we haven't even thought of composing or expressing the ideas. We are generating ideas—thinking on paper.

When you do this thinking on paper, there is only one restriction. Try to write in whole sentences whenever possible or at least in whole phrases. This is one of the best ways not only to preserve but to discover and to identify your thoughts. We hardly know what our thoughts are until we see them on paper.

FORGET ABOUT FINDING THE RIGHT WORD

If we could only learn to just put words on paper without worrying about having the exact words, we would find writing so much easier and helpful in improving our thinking. It was the feeling that we had to correctly formulate everything in advance that hindered us from using writing as the powerful tool of thinking. So write on and on until you feel a flow of ideas onto the page. Write until you feel you have much too much material. Up to this point, we are more interested in quantity than quality.

Ask yourself a series of questions. How do I feel about writing a piece on school bonds for the local paper? How difficult is it? What should I read? (Be careful here or you will think you have to read everything written on the subject before you start to write.) Whom should I consult? Who is my audience? Since you are a principal, you can be sure that everyone in your school will hear about it and read copies of it. What are your strengths and weaknesses? If you have been in the school system for many years, you could make the point that we now pay relatively less money to educate children than we did 25 years ago. Now comes a very important question: "How can I best present the issue of school bonds?" Many find it easy to follow the old journalistic format: who, what, how, when, and where.

Continue jotting down ideas and you will discover new relations, perspectives, and formulations. You may be pleased to see you have come up with some neat ideas that are well phrased. Write until you find yourself repeating yourself and going in circles. You now have all the material you need. This is the time to take a break from *generating*—overnight if you have the time. Having devoted the first third (two hours) of your allotted time to *generating*, you next will *compose* for another third (two hours). The last third of your time will be devoted to *expressing* the ideas.

COMPOSING

I found out that composition really is the skill of leaving out the right things and arranging the rest in a way that will instruct, inform, entertain, and motivate the reader. Before you compose you ask yourself these three questions:

1) What do I want my readers to know about the school bond issue?

2) What do I want my readers to feel about this school bond issue?

3) What do I want my readers to do?

In writing you focus on the domains of knowledge, feeling, and action. This is the bridge between your thinking and the members of the community who will be reading the piece. What you have done so far is worthwhile even if you don't go the next step and compose anything. You have done some serious thinking on paper. Up to this point, you were only generating ideas without being critical of the relative merit of the words used to express them.

Having read over your notes, you now sort them out according to topic. In our example, you might sort out the notes that pertain to the needs of the school system, the good that the bond issue will do for children's education, the benefits to the economy, and the small amount it will cost each household. This results in what is called the "Topical Draft." I found that this made more sense than trying to write an outline before I had done the thinking on paper. I always find it easier to order things I had already written rather than trying to read the future and guess what I will discover. You wrote the generating notes so you wouldn't forget your thoughts. Now you want to organize your thoughts so the readers will comprehend your reasoning and not forget the points you make. In this draft, you are trying to get ideas that are already generated organized into logical categories. The ideas didn't come to you in logical order, but now that you have them written down, you can arrange them in some logical form. The possible arrangements are almost limitless, so you pick the one you think will move the readers to vote for the bond issue.

Ask yourself the following questions to help organize the material for this composition.

1) **What are you trying to say in this article?** The school issue bond is important for the present and the future.

2) **What is the one big point you want to make?** The reader should get out and vote "yes" for the school bond.

3) **What is the problem you are confronting?** I believe many people are not aware how important the formative years are for children, and how much the quality of their education determines what kind of future citizens they will make. Adversaries who preach one gospel, "Hold down taxes," may be penny-wise and pound-foolish. To stint on our children's education is a sure way to bankrupt a country.

4) **What is your solution?** You think all citizens should feel that school children are their children. Every American should feel responsible for the education children are getting and do something positive to make sure it is a good one. Voting for the school bond issue is a step in the right direction.

5) **What is your strong point?** You have been a principal in the public schools for nearly 20 years, and you have countless stories to tell about the influence good schools and committed teachers have on the young. These stories are powerful and can convince citizens they should work together to pass this school bond.

If I were writing the article, I would choose three stories that would really touch the reader, and make an impassioned conclusion. If when I was in third grade, they decided to save money on the schools and crammed 50 students into a classroom, I would never have had the individual attention that helped me to go on to graduate school and become an educator. I'm glad our parents and grandparents were wise enough to pass bond issues in their day.

Imagine all that will be done before you write a connected text with paragraphs. What a difference this makes! In the old days, when I sat down to write a paper, it took me forever because I would write a sentence, then rewrite it, then change the word order again, look up a word for spelling, worry about a comma, etc. I lost the forest because I was looking at individual trees. Now with this method, I am ready to label the material, separate it into logical chunks, and start actually writing. I have a beginning, a middle, and an end. I now write my rough draft with minimal corrections. All I am doing is crafting a paper in which the order and organization of my original thoughts flow with some logic.

In this same phase, I now rewrite what I have put in my first draft, often cutting out large chunks. I know now that I have much too much material for the space allotted so I cut out much good stuff in order to make what is left more pungent, powerful, and moving. I rewrite more easily the next time through, and I make corrections as I go along. Now I have a first draft.

SECOND DRAFT

In the second draft, which is often referred to as revising, you can change the order of words, sentences, paragraphs, or sections, and make corrections that will tighten the article, making it clearer and more concise. The order of your thinking and the best order to move the reader may not be the same. I call the first, the logical order and the second, the psychological order. In the generating phase you were only interested in what you thought and you organized your thoughts logically; now you are more interested in how you will capture the attention of the reader and keep him or her reading on. This psychological order is the main thrust of the second draft. Now you are becoming reader-centered, whereas before you were writer-centered. If you can't keep the interest of the reader throughout the article, you won't accomplish your goal. When you write for an audience, you have to remember the customer or reader is always right. If the readers don't find your material informative, understandable, interesting, and persuasive, they won't read further and you won't get a "yes" vote for the school bond. The reader can put your article down and stop reading at any time.

Remember the Greeks insisted on *ethos* and *pathos*, as well as *logos*. When you do this second draft, you want to make sure you have personalized the article so the reader will know it is meant for him or her. You want to establish yourself as someone worthy to be believed. You want to tell stories and give concrete examples so the reader will be moved to act, and finally, you want to present the kind of reasons that appeal logically to the reader's mind. You want him or her to conclude that to vote for the school bond makes absolute sense and to vote against it would be self-defeating. And in the last sentence in the article, you simply ask the reader to vote for the school bond.

When I write an article with the goal of trying to persuade the readers to do something, I always start by telling the readers who I am and why it is worth their time to keep reading. Then I briefly outline what I am going to say, and then say it. Finally, I tell them what I have just said in a summary form and I close reminding them why I said it—to get them to do one particular thing. In our example, it would be to ask them to vote "yes" on the school bond. This is the outline I find it easiest to use when I am trying to persuade readers to do something or change their minds about something.

Notice that this chapter itself follows this persuasive form. I am writing this chapter with the hope that I can persuade you to stop thinking of writing as finding the correct, perfect, most apt words to express some well-thought-out ideas, and instead to think of writing as thinking on paper. The first goal of writing is not to craft a manuscript that will persuade someone to do something. The reason we write in the first place is for ourselves, so we can see our thoughts on paper. We want to make sense of our world, find meaning in it. We understand that only after we have been able to find meaning or significance in something will we be able to compose a paper and express our thoughts to others. We may seldom or never write a paper for publication, but it is absolutely necessary that we use our powers to think daily. Writing is the best way to help us think new thoughts, discover new relationships, and grasp the whole picture. I write so I may think. I think best with a pencil in my hand (or a piece of chalk if I have a chalkboard); I bet you do too.

EXPRESSING IDEAS

To conclude this section, we will look briefly at the final stage, *expressing ideas*. When you finish the second draft of your paper on the school bond issue, you take a rest or a change of scenery before you start the third and last phase. You have roughly two more hours to spend on this last phase and you now want to focus on expression and communication. (Note how many steps come before this.)

Now you focus on things like format, style, grammar, tone, and accessibility. We have come to performance or "show time," a time to put yourself on stage. This is like giving a speech to a target audience, only you are writing instead of speaking. In a real sense, you assume a persona or a "voice." You are going to play the role of a veteran principal. If you are an experienced principal, you have a big advantage over almost all your readers. You know schools, teachers, parents, students, staff, textbooks, teaching styles, learning styles, disciplinary problems, and what schooling is all about. You have something worthwhile to say. How will you make your ideas accessible, understandable, sharp, and persuasive? You take your second draft and see if you can't use some scissors and paste. The use of the word processor has been a real boon to this phase of the work. In my writing, the big thing I have to do is "cut." I over-write and as a result have too many digressions, repetitions. After many years in the classroom, a teacher-writer has a tendency to be repetitious. *Repetitio est mater scientiae.* Repetition is certainly the mother of knowledge, but you don't want to beat a dead horse. That means cutting out some good metaphors, stories, examples for the sake of brevity and clarity.

When you are focusing on the expression of ideas, you are rewriting. All rewriting means rethinking, so you may find some better ideas and replace original material with new stuff that comes up as you rewrite. What helps me is to imagine a reader asking me a question, "What do you mean by the 'expression of ideas', I thought you were doing that from the beginning?" Then I answer this question, clarifying that I am now focusing on the expression of ideas that I already have down on paper, and I am thinking of "selling" my ideas to the reader. Now I am geared toward the reader. No longer am I using the paper to generate ideas. I have already composed my generated ideas and now I am trying to polish them up for the reader. I am performing for others. In the first two stages I was mostly writing for myself.

Even when I compose with the idea of publishing, I write speaking out loud to some principal I imagine sitting in front of me. My wife often comes in and asks, "Who are you talking to?"

When it comes to the expression of ideas, I focus even more deeply on the words I would choose if I could be speaking directly to that principal.

Another benefit I get from this third phase is seeing where I have made "lyric leaps"—stating two ideas or propositions without explaining the connection between them. The connection was in my head, but I never bothered to make it explicit. This is a common mistake, to think the reader can read your mind and discover what you meant to say. In this last polishing I try to reread the draft, making believe I am a principal who comes to this material out of the blue and is trying to understand my ideas. How can I make it easier for him or her? That is what I mean by being accessible. Having taught over 2500 principals helps me to get in touch with their minds. I know what level of language they communicate in, and I am familiar with their technical language. I write up to the principals, not down to them. I am aware that there are principals reading my book who are much smarter than I am, and other excellent principals who find it difficult to grasp abstract ideas. I don't write for the middle. I write for the top with the firm conviction that examples and context will be of great service to those whose vocabulary is less rich. I learn most from books that challenge me and stretch my thinking. I think others do also.

When you have completed the two hours allotted to this expression of ideas, you will have a third draft. It is a good idea, if you have the time, to sleep on this draft. The next day, read over the manuscript aloud, listening to how it sounds. You will be amazed how many small but important changes will pop out at you. These are not big changes—the repositioning of a word here or there, a couple of grammatical errors, and a few repetitive phrases.

You have accomplished the task—a finished product of 1200 words written for the op-ed page of your local paper. It is wonderful if you have someone you trust to critique the paper for you. My great gift has been a wife who can really edit. She can read my articles and make corrections in spelling, grammar, style, tone, and rhythm that enhance the material tremendously.

You have spent just a little over seven hours on a paper that consists of about 1200 words. Is that too much time? It all depends. The way I figure it is if I could get a hundred people to sit down with me one-on-one and listen to my plea for them to vote "yes" on the school bond, I bet I could get a lot of the undecided ones to do it. However, this would even take more hours. So if 200 or more people read my article, I will really be reaching a lot of people and it will be time well spent. Some of my readers will be persuaded by my message and will vote for the school bond. I will be making a difference in my county. I will be helping thousands of students, hundreds of teachers and parents. I think that would be worth seven hours of my time. It would take me that long to play 18 holes of golf and the only benefit to society would be my killing countless snakes.

Now you are finished with the paper, it has a life of its own. Let it go. The editors at the newspaper will decide whether to publish it. If they publish it, they will probably make a few changes of their own without distorting your meaning. When the article is printed, some people will disagree with what you say, many will skip it altogether, but you will be amazed how many people will read it and give some thought to what you have said. For too long we have given credence to people speaking out on education who haven't the vaguest idea of what modern schools are or should be. I really think it would be worth seven hours of your time to write a piece for the local paper, as well as to find other ways to get your ideas promulgated. Decision makers should know what principals think. Principals make a big difference in their schools; I would love to see them make a bigger difference in the community. More writing will help a great deal. Writing not only helps principals think better, it makes it possible for principals to share their wisdom and experience with others.

When the Steward Principal spends time doing this thinking or reasoning on paper, he or she will be much better able to make the daily decisions. It would be wonderful if more of them went the next two steps—composing and expressing these thoughts so others could study them and improve their own reasoning. Steward Principals have much that is worth communicating in writing.

SUMMATION

In this chapter, we attempted to show how important it is that principals spend their time *thinking on paper*. We reviewed the reasons for spending so much of our time in training principals on how to write better—namely, why written expression is so important to the role of the Steward Principal. We recommended that principals read Domain 17 in *Principals For Our Changing Schools* since the material is well-covered there. Our claim was that writing is first and foremost a symbolic activity of meaning-making. We chose to emphasize the prime function of writing which is understanding even before communicating. We reviewed Prewriting, Writer's Block, Generating, Composing, and Expressing Ideas.

QUESTIONS FOR REFLECTION

1. What does the statement: "Thinking in writing is a form of understanding" add to the statement: "Writing is a means of communication"?

2. What can a mastery of written expression do to help principals lead their schools better?

3. Would you agree with India Podson when she says, "Despite the obvious link between good writing and effective school leadership, today's principal preparation programs pay little attention to written expression? If so, why so; if not, why not?

4. How does thinking with a pencil in hand help us make sense of our world?

5. My wife and I used "thinking on paper" to help us make a key decision in our lives. How could you use this method in your important decision making?

6. Why do we sometimes get writer's block? How can we avoid or overcome this problem?

7. If we divide the task of writing into a) generating ideas, b) composing, and c) expressing our ideas, we won't waste so much time in the beginning searching for the one "right" word. Writing should be a lot more fun than it is for most of us. Do you agree? If so, why so; if not, why not?

8. When you reach the stage of "expressing ideas" you are at the performance end of the process. Now you must try to polish the writing and sharpen its appeal. Why does it help to have a good editor at this point?

9. Format, style, grammar, spelling, tone, and accessibility are keys to good writing but they are also the obstacles that keep us from writing more often. Why do they scare most of us?

10. What does "reasoning for discovery" mean and how can it be enhanced when we try to "think on paper"?

11. Reasoning by questions—what, why, why not—can teach us to see the whole picture and avoid jumping to conclusions. How does writing help to answer the three questions?

9

PHILOSOPHICAL AND CULTURAL VALUES

The ultimate test of what a truth means is the conduct it dictates or inspires. —William James

In Domain 18 of *Principals for Our Changing Schools*, James W. Garrison and his development team address the most profound problem confronting public education in the United States. People cannot run a successful organization unless they share a common vision, and Garrison and his two co-team members, David J. Parks and Mary Jane Connelly, show that in public education we lack such a common vision.

The many groups who have an interest in public education—politicians, parents, teachers, students, administrators, the business community, taxpayers with and without children of their own in public school, professors in schools of education, church leaders, law enforcement agents, textbook and standardized test producers, and others—all appear to have differing visions for public schools. It is not surprising that these differing visions play out into differing goals.

The point that Garrison makes is that principals are forever being faced with demands from all these groups. The principals know they cannot satisfy all the needs of these disparate groups. The parents who want more "tracking" so their gifted sons and daughter will not be held back by the less gifted students, are opposed by educational theorists who claim that tracking has a deleterious effect on student learning. The business community whose goal is graduates who will be efficient workers are often opposed by parents who want their children to be caring, committed, and concerned neighbors and citizens. The citizens who want to hold down school costs believe the principal should get rid of all the fancy extras like counseling and guidance, special education specialists, art and music, and physical education teachers. They have one goal: save money by sticking to the basics. They are opposed by child advocates who make a strong case for helping special needs children early while remediation is most effective. We could go on with example after example, but no principal reading this book will be surprised at what we have been stating. Principals know that they are in a difficult position. Although they are being granted more discretion each year, they are confronted by splintered groups, each of which demands something different and often contradictory to the demands of others. Prayer in school versus no prayer in school. Parental censorship of library books versus allowing the media specialists to determine what is and what is not suitable for the library. Sex education versus no sex education.

Many principals feel totally unprepared to cope with these discordant demands. Neither the interested parties themselves nor the principals can fully grasp the connections underlying the demands the groups make on school goals, the cultural values the groups espouse, and the basic philosophical positions in which these values have their foundation.

DOMAIN 18

Garrison and his team offer a definition that will help us grasp the serious problem underlying this set of knowledge and skills that the Steward Principal must master.

Philosophical and Cultural Values: Acting with a reasoned understanding of the role of education in a democratic society and in accordance with accepted ethical standards; recognizing philosophical influences in education; reflecting an understanding of American culture including current social and economic issues related to education. (38)

The authors wisely state that all the philosophical analysis needed could never be learned in one preparation program. Rather they suggest that principals must continue to study society and philosophy to keep in touch with emerging values and perspectives so they can be in a position to analyze them and compare them with their personal philosophies.

Because there is so much good material contained in Domain 18, I am tempted to summarize it for the reader. Instead I strongly recommend that you carefully study Domain 18 in *Principals For Our Changing Schools* and try to grasp the connections between the demands you receive daily, the cultural values inherent in these demands, and the underlying philosophical positions from which the interested groups make their demands. What I will try to do is help you to form a more clearly delineated philosophical position for yourself. I know it sounds preposterous, but the busier the principal, the more he or she would save time by spending more hours reflecting on everyday experience, slowly developing a set of values and an underlying philosophy. Every person was meant to be a philosopher. Principals who have thought through their own philosophical positions will inevitably be the better leaders.

THE STEWARD PRINCIPAL ANSWERS
FOUR BASIC QUESTIONS

Forty years ago when I started to teach in a School of Education I was confronted by a serious problem. Trained as a Clinical Psychologist, I was not prepared to teach what in those days was called the Philosophy of Education. The bad news was I had never studied the Philosophy of Education; the good news was I had been trained by the Jesuits, so I had a solid background in Scholastic Philosophy. I was busy preparing for many different classes, but I found myself stealing time to read more about the philosophy of education. It became apparent to me that the key to improving schools was to find a philosophy of education that would help me to satisfactorily answer four basic questions: *Who Am I? What Is The World? How Can I Live And Work With Others? What Is To Know?* Steward Principals need to constantly reflect on these four questions as they shape and reshape their own philosophy.

Who Am I?

I thought then and I still think that any Philosophy of Education worth its salt should have a cogent answer for this most basic of all questions. I was willing at various stages of my development to accept the Thomistic answer, the Aristotelian, Socratic, or Platonic answers. They all had something good to say. I could agree with parts of all of them but I couldn't accept all of any of them. Later philosophers had something to offer as well. Grotius, Hobbes, Locke, Newton, Jefferson, Madison, and Voltaire were sons of the Enlightenment, and they were so flashy I almost got taken in by their superficial thinking. Again they fell short. I was being critical because the question *Who Am I?* was so important that I just couldn't accept a partial answer. Neither should any principal. If I don't figure out who I am, then I can't really answer the next question, *What Is The World*. If I don't know who I am, and what is the world in which I live, how can I know anything else? How can I figure out how to live and work with others? More basic still, if I don't know who I am as a human person, then I can't know my world, my fellow humans, and I can't even understand what it means to know something.

I studied Integral Liberalism, Critical Theory, Poststructuralism, Pragmatism, and Feminism. None of them gave me a satisfactory answer to my first question. Each of them had something worthwhile to say, but they all lacked the depth and breadth of the answer I sought. In many ways I found great literature to be a better source for the answers to these questions. The philosophers seemed so removed from the real daily struggles of life. I still haven't found the complete answers I seek. However, I have come a long way from the time forty years ago when I first sought to know what schools should be all about. I know now that schools should give students the tools for their life-long search to answer these four questions. Maybe I will die never having a totally satisfactory answer. Perhaps the fact that I continually sought for the answer will be enough. Schools that stifle students' desires to answer these questions for themselves do much damage. Schools that give them the answers do even worse.

Shakespeare lets King Lear ask the $64,000 question: "Who is it will tell me who I am?" Any good educational philosophy must offer a way to pursue the answer to that fundamental question. In Domain 18, the authors offer as samples five philosophies or Theories of Education. I read them carefully and found them wanting.

I thought I knew who I was when I reached my fortieth birthday. I was a human person just a little less than the angels and a little more than the beasts, and I had a little of both of them in me. Over the last 35 years, I have begun to see that I am quite a bit less than the angels, and only a very little bit away from the animals. I don't think that is too pessimistic, except perhaps that it insults the animals. Animals, unlike humans, don't kill their own wantonly. In this century we humans have achieved something truly horrendous. We have killed 100,000,000 of our fellow humans. No other animal species has ever perpetrated a crime of that magnitude. I am a human person similar to all other human persons on spaceship earth and yet uniquely myself so that I cannot be mistaken for any other human by those who really know me. If earth is a spaceship and we humans are its crew, then I as a human must take responsibility for this spaceship. I must be a steward of the earth and I must teach all other humans that they too should be responsible for the earth and for the welfare of others.

I Am a Human Person Like All Other Humans

When I started to study psychology in 1945, I was amazed how the social scientists were battling to prove that there was no such thing as a human nature. They were so afraid of Galton's Theory of genetic determinism that they bent over backwards to try to prove that heredity played little or no serious part in the structure and function of a human person. Like Margaret Mead who saw only what she was sent to see in adolescent girls in Samoa, other psychologists and anthropologists taught us that cultural determination was the answer. They taught that we humans are all born like a blank page, and our culture and environment do all the writing on us. Cultural determinism carried the day in the forties and fifties. I was puzzled. The Jesuits' philosophy had taught me human nature was distinctive and universally distributed in all the habitable areas of the earth. I really thought to be born human meant something special. It shocked me to read one Sociology study after another that claimed little resemblance between humans in different cultures and locales.

In trying to answer the question *Who Am I?* I flip-flopped for years, unable to decide whether we humans were mostly formed by memes (cultural determinants) or genes (biological determinants). Today, with new breakthroughs in molecular biology and the deeper study of the brain and nervous system, I am beginning to realize that genes play a real part in our structure and function as humans. There is a genetic map that depicts humans that is different from that of other animals. This in no way negates the influence exerted on us by our culture. I'm glad I didn't take an unequivocal position on this question in the 40s or 50s. The Steward Principal is justly suspicious of theories that put too much stress either on genes or on memes.

So What Does It Mean To Be a Human Being?

Anthropologist Don Brown wrote a book entitled, *Human Universals* (39). In it, he summarizes the common human traits that most social scientists today accept. He calls these characteristics the traits of Universal People. As a principal, it may help you in forming your own philosophy of education to know that scientists now believe that we humans are much more alike than we are different. To me it means that every student has potential, some of which we may not notice. So we follow the maxim: although it is not sin to fail, it is sin to lower expectations. With a trillion connections in the three-pound human brain, it is no wonder we haven't taken advantage of all the possibilities.

We know that the genetic endowment of humans consists of 23 pairs of chromosomes that together hold approximately fifty thousand genes. How closely related are humans of all kinds? The average unrelated strangers differ genetically by approximately a tenth of one percent. In other words, I differ genetically from a native Albanian, Eskimo, or Turk or any stranger in the U.S. by 50 genes out of a possible 50,000. A human person has only a six percent genetic difference from a rhesus monkey.

We differ genetically from chimpanzees by only two percent. An afternoon of unbiased observation of a cage full of chimps will give you the strange feeling that you are more closely related than you might want to admit. We humans as a class are very close in our genetic make-up, but we are also genetically close to the higher mammals.

Because we humans are bipedal—that is, we walk on two feet instead of four—two things follow. We have our arms and hands free to use tools, and we have a pelvic problem. In order to support our erect position, our birth process is difficult, and we are born earlier in our development than other animals. Thus the majority of the brain's development occurs outside the womb. This means the infant is exposed to and influenced by many different environments, events, and people. And because the environment is different for each person, the specific abilities that each of us develops from our genetic pool differ considerably. We are very much alike genetically (genes). We differ markedly in our environments (memes), and we directly fashion ourselves by our personal choices (schemes). We are each one of a kind, like all others, yet like no other person who has ever lived. How does that influence the way we learn?

We humans can't fend for ourselves when we are born. Unlike the parents of other animals who can almost immediately reclaim their place in the group after their offspring are born, human mothers and fathers find that taking care of a newborn is nearly a full-time job for at least three or four years. What makes us humans special is precisely this closely bonded mother-father-child unit. This family pattern is found in all groups of humans everywhere. When this process starts to fall apart, something dire always happens.

All humans begin life with the same basic emotions, the same color vision, the same time orientation. We have our cultural knowledge embedded in a language that has a grammar and a set of phonemes. Every human child in the first year of life experiments with all the sounds found in every known language. The language they select as primary is the one that is modeled for them and taught to them, usually by the mother. Fortunate is the baby whose mother speaks correctly, lovingly, and frequently to her child. We all speak using our oral and nasal cavities. With language comes the ability to think and speak in abstractions. We all use symbolic speech. Unfortunately, humans can and do use their language skills to lie and deceive as well as to communicate their true feelings and beliefs. The more you have traveled, the more you realize that humans manage to express much more than their words indicate through nonverbal gestures, which are similar around the world. Words may be the coin of exchange for communicating reasons for things, but gestures are the coin of exchange for emotional interchanges.

As humans we place high priority on different kin categories. We use separate terms for father, mother, sister, brother and spend much time and energy being concerned with these relationships. The family is of maximum importance. We also have separate words for age, gender, and status groups. The teenage boy says, "He is the rich old man who hired Mary's older brother."

As humans we all appear to be both excited and repelled by sexual attraction. At different periods in our history, we spend more or less time and energy talking about sex. It is a high interest subject to teenagers, for obvious reasons. In our day, for reasons I don't fully understand, sex seems to have an exaggerated importance for a vast number of our fellow humans. It sells beer and cigarettes as well as cars and TVs. All peoples have elaborate rituals to govern sexual acts and there are standards for genital modesty. In almost all societies, people refrain from making love in public. This taboo is close to disappearing in our culture.

Humans are group seekers. They spend a large part of their lives in groups. We have cousins by the dozens and regularly visit aunts, uncles, grandparents, and family friends. The extended family is of great importance in most parts of the world. Although the systems differ, it appears that all humans have an organized system for bringing up children. Today's schools play an expanding role in bringing up children in industrially advanced countries. Why?

Children the world over have childhood fears; they have attachments (Linus's blanket). They recognize people by their faces. They live with parents in a sheltered place. The adults know how to use fire and tools for getting and preparing food and building shelters.

Humans use the same basic emotions and communicate mostly via facial expressions and tone of voice. They cooperate in family raising, which has high priority. When this cooperation breaks down, humans everywhere seem to have a set of regulations and procedures that they use for conflict resolution. Violence is the last resort.

We all have rituals for a spiritual life and a set of beliefs to explain the mysterious. We have myths and explanations about the origin and conduct of the world in which we live. Art, dance, and poetry are often used to express the mysteries.

When people no longer accept mystery in their lives, they turn to magic.

Robert Ornstein in his fascinating book, *The Roots of Self*, (40) cautions us that with all this in common, each human person isn't created equal to others on almost any dimension from height to weight, to skin color, to eye color. The best society can do is offer every person an equal opportunity to develop his or her abilities as distributed to them through genetic and environmental sources.

As a low-weight infant (under six pounds) I was born with a serious handicap. Statistically, low weight infants have a high probability of succumbing to a heart attack, among other ills, in their adult life. I have had a couple of heart attacks, diabetes, and cancer but I was lucky to have lived in parts of the United States in which medical help was available that could help me survive. I was given more than an equal opportunity but I used up a lot of valuable society resources. I owe tremendous debts to the countless people who helped me overcome my genetic and environmental deficits. My hope has always been to pay back society even if only in token form for these gifts. If I lived in most parts of this earth I would not be writing books at 76 years of age. Helping principals seems to me the best way I can show my gratitude because Steward Principals do more to help children survive and grow than anyone except good parents.

As humans we are so much alike, it is absurd to seek out differences so we can fight over them. Humans have killed 100,000,000 of their fellow humans in wars during this century. If we used the resources wasted on wars to help our brothers and sisters born or brought up challenged in one way or another we would have a kinder and gentler world. I believe we are all born equal in the sight of God, but many humans play on an uneven playing field and the "call" to the fortunate is to provide as much as possible an equal opportunity for all. When public schools are run correctly, they are agencies in which this offering of "equal opportunity" becomes a reality. For that reason I have dedicated my life to helping principals, teachers, and parents to improve public schooling.

> Once upon a time a holy man was praying. As he prayed he noticed a procession of people passing by who were obviously crippled, beaten, and hungry. "Great God," he cried. "How is it that a loving creator can see such things and do nothing about them?" And out of the long silence God said, "I did do something about them, I made you."

So How Am I Different From Everyone Else?

This is the easier part of the question, *"Who Am I?"* As a human, I belong to the species of animals who have the most individual uniqueness. Although we humans are like all other humans in countless ways, we are also so different from any other human that we literally are one of a kind. We are unique.

That makes it harder for us to really know who we are. We are unique, but we generally are pretty vague about what we are really like. "Oh that we could know ourselves as others know us." We are unique: biologically, psychologically and psychiatrically. We are born with different biological endowments, into different cultures, with different family structures, family position, and social world, and each of these radically influence our development. The possibilities are countless. Don't forget we are changing biologically, psychologically, and psychiatrically every minute from birth until death. Moreover, our significant others are changing a pace, as are our physical and social environments. Is it any wonder we find it almost impossible to get a good fix on who we are as a person? The Greeks had it right when they said all education could be summarized by one injunction, "Know yourself."

So we as humans are each on a journey or pilgrimage of self-discovery. We don't walk alone. Just as in the *Canterbury Tales*, each of us pilgrims has a story to tell and we want desperately to be heard. Each of us must first learn to listen to the stories of others, then we can learn to tell our ever-unfolding life story. The better we listen to others and learn to tell our life stories, the more we will be fulfilling our "calling" to live fully and become all we are capable of becoming. We acknowledge that we will always be imperfect—a life in progress. We cannot ever fully know ourselves as others know us. Nor can we fully become the uniquely human person we have the capacity to become. We are always on the road, putting one step ahead of the other, accepting the vicissitudes of the human journey. We never give up hope that we can continuously decrease our imperfection, even as we know that full perfection eludes us.

As principals, this question will help you see how you yourself, each teacher, parent, or child is a unique pilgrim. It will aid you as you frame the role that you and your school will play, helping individuals and groups of pilgrims on their way. Your school will help them avoid the tendency to label and stereotype others even as others strive to label them.

WHAT IS THE WORLD?

If we are to live in this world for four or five score years, it becomes essential that we know more about our surroundings or environment. Doesn't it strike you as strange that for so many years we taught students to memorize the names of state capitals, their farm and manufacturing products, mountains and rivers, but nary a word about real environmental problems? Students learned little or nothing about air quality, water purity, ozone protection, hazardous waste, or pollution. Of course, we didn't have the knowledge we now have.

In planning a curriculum for the 21st century, we will certainly place heavier emphasis on the crisis of sustainability—the fit between humans and their habitats. If, as we said, we are all traveling on Spaceship Earth and have a real responsibility to work for its sustainability, we will have reasons not only to know the names of the earth's rivers, we will recognize them as integral parts of our living planet and its essential water supply. More than that, we will see how the purity of river water in any part of the globe will directly impinge on the purity of every other body of water. This ecological vision of the earth and its sustainability will have to be high on our agenda for the foreseeable future. No other issue of politics, economics, or public policy will remain unaffected by the crises of resources, population, climate change, species extinction, acid rain, deforestation, ozone depletion, and soil loss. Sustainability concerns itself with the terms and conditions of human survival, and we are finally beginning to educate at all levels with this in mind.

We are changing our curriculum and the process of educating the young precisely because we are learning a better answer to this question, *"What is the world?"* We are beginning to realize that whether Americans have social security payments in 2050 is of less importance than whether they will have pure air to breathe and clean water to drink. I didn't believe it when first told that water in the not too distant future may become much more expensive and precious than petroleum; oxygen more valuable than gold. Who would have believed back in 1894 that we would be killing other humans in the desert over petroleum?

The Sustainability Crisis cannot be solved by the same kind of education that helped create the problems. Schools and colleges are part of the problem. What passes for environmental education is still mostly regarded as a frill to be cut when the budgets get tight.

David Orr in his book *Ecological Literacy* (41) discusses what the limits of earth have to do with the content and process of education and the way we define knowledge. He believes as I do that schools are potential leverage points for the transition to sustainability. He offers four suggestions that I think will be of interest to principals who are developing their own philosophy.

1) Schools must acquaint students with the deeper causes of the Sustainability Crisis that confronts them. To do this, schools must increase their teaching of the humanities. The problems of sustainability are rooted in the human condition, and their solution will require people with greater philosophical depth and

perspective. Poststructuralism and Pragmatism just won't cut it. Neither will Critical Theory or Feminism. Integral Liberalism as it is now taught falls far short of helping us answer the four basic questions. Raw Capitalism is one of the main causes of the earth's unsustainability. Steward Principals should be searching for philosophical foundations that will enable them to answer the question: *What is the World?*

2) Sustainability demands a different kind of curriculum that encourages the development of ecological competence throughout the population. We need experts, but also a population that is both ecologically literate and competent. The goal of ecological competence develops the practical art of living well in particular places. With his interest in the practical arts, Dewey was on to something long before the Sustainability Crisis was on the agenda. School people should return to a respect of the practical arts. The native Americans knew them, so did our founding fathers. Somehow we let them slip away as we became "takers" rather then "leavers". As consumers we lose sight of the earth's fragility, limitedness, and need for nurturing.

3) We must acknowledge that ecological sustainability implies a recovery of civic competence. There is no possibility, according to Orr, of our building a sustainable society without an active, engaged, informed, and competent citizenry. In the environmental movement to date, citizens have forced governments and large economic interests to do things they are not otherwise inclined to do. The environmental movement is a democratic movement, but it will not remain such unless schools are committed to fostering widespread civic competence.

4) Orr recognizes that education is not just about society, it is about persons. At the individual level, education's goal is something like the Greek model of Paideia or that of the Renaissance person of wide

understanding, competence, and commitment to the common good. To my way of thinking, this may be the most important contribution schools can make. Steward Principals need to fight the narrowing demands of an economy which seeks workers trained to be effective and efficient in putting the earth's nonrenewable resourcs to use without being concerned about the earth's sustainability. For our times, we will need a broadly educated citizenry who can cope with changing environments and will not be chained to one worldview. Sustainability demands a people who are in close touch with their world as it is, and who can change the way they behave when it becomes clear that the present way of living is counterproductive. It is hard to get a petroleum engineer interested in utilizing renewable present-day solar energy, even as he is daily drawing out of the earth solar energy trapped eons ago. He can't grasp the fact that it is a limited oil source he is tapping . A Paideia-like humanistic education can give students the necessary flexibility to fit into their physical world, rather than try to force their world to suit their rigid needs.

HOW CAN I LIVE AND WORK WITH OTHERS?

After grappling with the questions: *Who am I?* and *What is the World?*, it is logical that we ask ourselves the next question, *How can I live and work with others?* As Steward Principals I am sure you have your own ideas on this subject. Many principals are convinced that schools are learning to help students live more peacefully together. I hear more and more about negotiation and conflict resolution in the schools. Purists would complain that these are subjects that should be handled in the home, not in the school. I can sympathize with their view but I am also aware that it is impossible to teach 30 third graders when many of them have not yet learned to live and work peacefully together. They can't learn in school if they are unable to solve their problems except with violence. School has always been a civilizing agent but in the past it had a great deal more help from the family, church, and neighborhood. Steward Principals need to ask the same question today, *"How can I live and work with others?"* How can the school help students live and work with others? We can get some help if we look back into our history.

THE BIG TEN

I reached back to 1894 for the report of the Committee of Ten to illustrate the kinds of conclusions that arise when a group of educators share a similar philosophy. The Committee of Ten insisted that all high school students—regardless of whether they were going on to college—should study history, civil government, and geography all taught as one. They wanted history and English "intimately connected" with constant cross-referencing to other countries and eras, to literature and art. They wanted more time for foreign language starting in the elementary grades. They called for rigorous continuing teacher education taught by university scholars. Teachers should be encouraged, and given the necessary means, to extend their classes beyond the narrow limits of the school and the text book. Today we are reinventing some of these ideas and claiming they are newly-minted coins.

The Committee of Ten was chaired by Charles William Elliot, the president of Harvard, and included six university scholars, three high school principals, and was rounded out by none other than William T. Harris, the U.S. Commissioner of Education. These were men and women who themselves had been privileged to follow a course of Liberal Arts, and they wanted the Paideia-type education to be available to all high school students. They advocated four years of foreign language in addition to English language and literature, three to four years of math and science, and two to four years of history. They felt that young Americans taking on the profession of citizen needed a demanding curriculum, not the feeble courses offered in too many high schools at the time. The report decried the "dry and lifeless system of instruction by text book." They claimed that facts alone were repellent; schooling should be aimed at developing in the students the invaluable mental power called judgment. They were opposed to merely covering the "matter." They didn't want the students to be exposed to countless unconnected facts whose relevance to their lives was nebulous at best. They thought it was better to cover a small amount of material and then to reflect on it in dialogue with other students. They believed that students could enhance their grasp of subjects in seminars, debates, re-inactments, field trips, museum work, mock legislatures and conventions. The Committee wanted the students engaged in active inquiry in original sources, studies in depth, and individual and group projects. All possible teaching aids should be used: engravings, photographs, maps, globes, and the "magic lantern" (the old-timer's overhead projector). To accomplish these goals, the Committee felt school hours needed to be longer and more flexible. Can you imagine that type of thinking in 1894?

I ask you to pass judgment on the ideas the Committee of Ten set forth. Could they have been written today? Aren't many of the innovations being hyped today just partial spin-offs from their more profound approach to high school education? They wanted to see all students prepared not just as workers, but as citizens and well rounded human persons who appreciated life, who knew how to live with others as well as work with them.

THE NAUGHTY NINE

Just 17 years after the report of the Committee of Ten was released, a group of nonacademic educators with a totally different philosophy came on the scene in 1911 and argued that if we followed the suggestions of the Committee of Ten, a multitude of high school students would drop out of school. This is the same kind of argument offered today whenever any group wants to elevate school standards and expectations. What a shame!

With a tremendous wave of immigration sweeping over the country at the turn of the century, U.S. schools were finding it more and more difficult to manage the influx of new students, many of whom spoke little or no English. They found themselves in the business of teaching the rudiments of English and civics and not much else. This may have had something to do with why this new Committee of Nine on the Articulation of High School and College issued a report that totally negated the report of the Committee of Ten.

The Committee of Nine, made up primarily of public school administrators, faced a huge "drop out" problem. The sons of immigrants were quitting school at 12 and 14 to work in the factories. My father was one of these new immigrants who had to leave school in eighth grade to get a factory job. He did this not to buy a car but to help put food on the table for his mother and seven siblings. He hated to leave school. The proof of it was that he spent over 20 years of his adult life attending night classes. Why didn't the schools adjust their schedules so these young people who had to go out to work could continue their education?

The Committee of Nine made a terrible mistake that we continue to make. They insisted that school's "holding power" depended on meeting the interests that "each boy and girl had at the time." They thought it was wrong to focus on the liberal arts, which they presumed had only one purpose: to prepare students for college. They were aware that only 10% were going on to college. This insistence on the liberal arts would lead students away from "pursuits for which they are adapted" toward those "for which they are not adapted and in which they are not needed." Schools therefore should focus on industrial arts, agriculture, and "household science." The truth is that my father and the majority of his peers were very well-adapted to learn the liberal arts. They were not given the chance. We can see how the "why" of school is so important. If the goal is merely to produce semi-skilled laborers, then one can follow the lead of the Committee of Nine. If the "why" includes preparing the students to be good citizens and well-rounded persons as well as trained workers, then one should follow the lead of the Committee of Ten.

It is easy to criticize the Committee of Nine from our vantage point. Hind sight is 20-20. We now see clearly that it would have been better to keep students in school and offer them a serious academic program, as recommended by the Committee of Ten, even if they didn't go on to college. A generally educated citizenry can vote wisely, learn new work skills easily, and function happily as well-rounded human persons. Most immigrant children didn't leave school because they didn't have the capacity to follow a demanding curriculum. They left for economic reasons. Their families needed their support. Today—a hundred years later—we are reaping the harvest of this unfortunate decision by the Committee of Nine. In our highly technical age, unskilled workers are paid so little they must work at two or more jobs to rise above the poverty level. They have little time to enjoy their rights or exercise their duties as citizens, and they are far from being well-rounded educationally. It was a bad decision that eight generations later led to the current gap between the rich and the poor and the shrinking of the middle class.

This was another instance of the economic state of the country dictating its educational policy. Whenever a government sacrifices the education of its young members in favor of some other social good, the bad effects of this decision come back to haunt us. This should give us pause as we look at decisions we are making today about schooling. There is no investment that pays better dividends than the investment in the education of our children.

The Committee of Nine was merely echoing a philosophy that is still ascendant in our country: the anti-intellectual movement. This effort to fight the "intellectuals" led to another disastrous report in 1918. The National Education Association's Commission on the Reorganization of Secondary Education wrote a report that was widely distributed by the U.S. Office of Education. This commission, made up solely of education administrators and lacking totally in academics, recommended no academic subjects in its list of seven things high schools ought to teach: health, command of fundamental processes, "worthy" home membership, "worthy" use of leisure, vocation, citizenship, and ethical character. No one can fault these ideals. They certainly should be taught, but not at the cost of a loss of foreign languages and literature, English literature, math, science, history, etc. We must not forget the three distinct purposes of schooling espoused by the Committee of Ten: for work, for public affairs, and for private culture. We have been putting two goals, socializing the masses and job training, ahead of a well-rounded education, only to find that we can't socialize the masses or prepare them for work in the electronic age without a heavy dose of the liberal arts. The main purpose of schooling must be learning to learn, and even learning to love to learn. This can't be accomplished if we shy away from intellectually challenging academic material. I worry about the 70 percent of our young people who don't graduate from a four-year college. They too deserve to get in high school what the Committee of Ten recommended. They need help in learning to live and work with others. Most of them have much greater potential than we realize.

WHAT IS TO KNOW OR WHAT IS INVOLVED IN THE PROCESS OF KNOWING ?

To answer the fourth basic question, we start with Mortimer Adler's explanation of human activity. In his book, *Aristotle for Everybody* (42), Adler tells us human activity has three very important directions: *making, doing,* and *knowing.* We can say that man and woman have three dimensions—Man and Woman the *Makers,* Man and Woman the *Doers,* and finally, Man and Woman the *Knowers.*

MAN AND WOMAN'S THREE DIMENSIONS

In the first of these dimensions, we have Man and Woman the *Makers.* Here we have human persons as artisans or artists. They produce all kinds of things: computers, bird houses, baked products, cars, alcohol, cigarettes, and firearms. It is not just when men and women produce statues or paintings that we should call them artists. That is too restrictive a use of the word "art." Anything in the world that is artificial as opposed to natural is a work of art—something a man or woman made.

When we consider man and woman as Makers, we talk about their productive thinking—the kind of thinking that is involved in making things. We also think of humans as Makers using the kind of knowledge we call skill—knowledge or know-how. When people are Makers, they are motivated by the beautiful. They want their productions to be considered beautiful. Perhaps this is why we started to use the word "art" in such a restrictive way. Actually, anything a man or woman makes that is pleasant to the eye and useful can be called beautiful. I often say my wife has made a beautiful cake.

School children delight in school projects in which they are encouraged to play the role of Makers. They rejoice when their group's project looks beautiful. Tired of just passively assimilating facts from text books, they feel liberated when they can make a poster or a model to illustrate some lesson. My memories of elementary and high school are few as far as the classroom experience is concerned, but I can remember most of the projects I worked on.

The next dimension takes us to Man and Woman the *Doers*. Somebody will ask, what is the difference between *making* and *doing*? When we talk about doing, we are referring to man or woman as the moral and social being—someone who can do right or wrong; someone who by what he or she does or does not do either achieves happiness or fails to achieve it; someone who finds it necessary to associate with other human beings in order to do what he or she feels impelled to do. With man and woman as *Doers*, their prime goal is to do good. The practical knowledge involved in being a doer is directed toward doing the right thing. They have to think about the means and ends of human activity and to know what is right or wrong for them to do in the conduct of their lives.

When I was young, we received a mark on our school report cards under the heading of Conduct or Deportment. It had nothing to do with the academic subjects, but my father said it was the most important mark on the report. In the mark, the teacher gave her estimate of how good or bad our conduct or deportment was in the classroom during that marking period. When I got a less than satisfactory mark in that area, my father was down on me for a long time. He would say, "I can understand that you might not understand something in math or history, but I can't understand why you couldn't *conduct* yourself in a gentlemanly manner. I am very disappointed in you." I still feel the sting of his remark as I type this paragraph. You can be sure I got a satisfactory mark in Conduct on the next report.

If as *Makers* we are seeking to produce something beautiful, as *Doers* we are striving to be good. To be good, I must learn to control my desires and my actions. *Doing* begins when practical thinking is put into action. My father was right: I could be good in school (deport or conduct myself well) if I learned to curb my impulses and care for others.

The third and final dimension is Man and Woman the Knowers. If we use *productive thinking* in our making, and *prac-*

tical thinking in our doing, we use *theoretical thinking*—thinking for the sake of knowing—when we act as Man and Woman the Knowers. We will take some time to develop this idea of theoretical thinking because it seems to be seeping out of our consciousness. We are so busy becoming *Makers* and *Doers*, we have neglected the importance of theoretical thinking. For the Steward Principals I can think of nothing more important than becoming excellent theoretical thinkers or *Knowers*. Only *Knowers* have the capacity to develop a vision.

At two great universities near where I live, Duke and the University of North Carolina, the administrators are working feverishly to improve the intellectual climate of their schools. Word has it that the students are too preoccupied with parties and sports and not sufficiently serious about their studies. When this is brought to the attention of the students, they become defensive and insist that they take heavy class loads and do everything the professors demand of them. The administration has to acknowledge that the students are bright and they do fulfill their academic obligations, but the administration thinks that the students lack intellectual curiosity. They use productive thinking and practical thinking, but they seem to shy away from thinking for thinking's sake—theoretical thinking. I'm afraid many faculty members at both institutions suffer from the same malady. The fact that the administration and faculty have so much trouble explaining to the students what they mean by a truly academic atmosphere indicates that they themselves have given up being *Knowers* in favor of being *Makers* and *Doers*. Since they cannot explain what it means to think for thinking's sake, all they can do is point to universities like Oxford, Cambridge, Harvard, Princeton, MIT, UC Berkeley, and ask, "Why can't we be like them?" If the faculty has given up the intellectual life in favor of publishing for tenure sake, then their criticizing the student body is like the pot calling the kettle black. If the faculty was really challenging the bright students to pursue the intellectual life, the students would not be partying as much as they are. A subtle anti-intellectualism has always characterized Americans. We pride ourselves on being *Makers* and *Doers*. That is not enough for the 21st century. We all have to become serious *Knowers*—thinkers who don't shy away from the theoretical.

WHAT IS THEORETICAL THINKING?

Thinking begins with the formation of ideas based on information received through the senses. Modern research teaches us that we have many more than the original five senses. Sensations are the input the mind receives from the outside world. Ideas are the output the mind produces as a result of what it receives. Thinking goes further. It relates or connects these ideas. It joins them together, separates them, and sets one idea against another. By these further activities of thinking, the mind produces knowledge not only about perceived or imagined objects we can remember, but also of objects that do not fall within our sensory experience. Arithmetic, algebra, and geometry are good examples of such knowledge.

Can a sensation be true or false? No, but a conclusion drawn from a sensation can be true or false. This reminds me of the joke that asks: "What is a sweater?" The answer is: "A sweater is what you put on when your mother is cold." Notice the mother who had the sensation of being cold extrapolated, thinking: if I am cold, my son or daughter must be cold and therefore, I will tell him or her to put on a sweater. Now the conclusion could be true or false. The son or daughter may have been running around playing a game of tag and feels hot rather than cold. Therefore, the mother's conclusion was untrue or wrong. The fact that she felt cold didn't jibe with the subjective thermal state of her offspring. The mother was accurate in judging her own thermal state. If she felt cold, she felt cold.

Even when your senses deceive you, as they often do, the sensation is neither true nor false. A dog resting in the shadows may look black to you. But in the sunlight, you see the dog is really brown. Your sensing of the dog in the shadows was not untrue. If you were to paint the picture of the dog in the shadows, you should paint it showing the dog to be black, because that is the way he looks under those circumstances. It would be untrue if you testified in court that the dog in the shadows was actually a black dog. All the sensation does is reflect what appears to be the case. It certainly appeared to you that the dog was black at that time in that place. The black or brown dog distinction can only be true or false when you add your thought and make a judgment, saying, "I have no doubt that was a black dog I saw." That is an untrue statement, and the opposing lawyer will immediately prove that you were wrong. He will pull out pictures of the same dog sleeping in the sunlight to show it was a brown dog. The untruth was in the thinking judgment, not in the sensation. That dog was black.

Language plays a big part in human thinking and knowing. Every common noun, and almost every adjective and verb in our language names an object we can think about because we have formed an idea about it. Not all the objects we can think about are objects we can also perceive, remember, or imagine. Dogs and cats, for example, are objects we can perceive and also think about when they aren't present. In physics we learned to think about small particles inside the atom like neutrons, positrons, and even quarks, which we cannot see.

Like sensations, ideas can neither be true nor false. If you and I were talking and out of the blue, I said the word "dog." You couldn't respond by saying either "yes" or "no." You would probably ask, "What are you talking about?" But if when I said "dog" I also pointed to a particular animal lying in the front yard, that would signify a judgment. I am expressing a judgment: that particular animal lying there is a dog. You would respond by saying something like this, "Yes, I wonder where he comes from." What was true in this case is the statement that I implicitly made when I said, "dog" and pointed to the animal in the yard. It wasn't just the idea of "dog," it was the judgment expressed by my pointing. I really said "That is a dog out there in the yard." If it wasn't a dog you could correct me and say, "No, that is a large cat."

So the idea of dog isn't true or false, it is the statement or sentence in which I connect the idea to some object that can be perceived—that dog in the front yard. To summarize, we can't be in error when we just think about the dog or see the dog lying in the shadow as black rather than brown. It is only when we add "is" or "isn't" that we can be in error or in truth. So in our thinking and speech we can be true or false only when we go beyond one idea and begin to connect two or more ideas. "That is a dog." "That isn't a dog." These are statements that can be true or false.

I know this sounds almost simplistic, but I believe this distinction is the foundation of all thinking and knowing. It is indispensable to lifelong learning and should be treated in every classroom. When Aristotle tells how the mind produces thought, he distinguishes among three levels of thought. Simply put, he tells us that from the raw material of sense experience (sensations), the mind forms *ideas*. *Ideas* in turn are the raw material out of which the mind forms *judgments* in which something is affirmed or denied (is or isn't). As single ideas are expressed in speech or writing by single *words*, so judgments are expressed by *sentences*, declarative sentences in which "is" or "is not" is included. "That is a dog lying there in the front yard." That can be true or false. Suppose my friend disputes my statement and we walk out together and discover it was not a dog but rather a large cat. Then my prior statement (expressed judgment) was untrue. I may have an accurate idea of a dog but I have applied it incorrectly to the animal in the front yard.

The third level of thought Aristotle calls *reasoning* or *inference*. When one statement becomes the basis for asserting or denying another statement, the mind moves up to the third level of thought. At this level, thinking involves giving reasons for what we think. At this level, what we think can be true or false, it also can be either *logical* or *illogical*.

Steward Principals would profit greatly from a course in logic. If Newton is the father of the law of gravity, and Einstein the father of the law of relativity, Aristotle is the father of the law of contradiction: the first law of logic. He didn't invent logic, but he wrote the book on it. Human beings are hard-wired to think logically but the wires often get loose, resulting in some of the greatest folly you could imagine. Steward Principals would do a great service to teachers and students if they insisted on a formal study of logic starting at least by fourth grade. Man the Knower must follow the laws of logic if he is to find the truth and be able to communicate it.

The prime law of logic is the law of contradiction. Stated simply, it sounds almost silly, but believe me, its violation causes great pain and grief in this world of ours. The law of contradiction says: a thing—whatever it may be—cannot exist and not exist at the same time. It either exists or it does not exist, but not both at once. You can hear politicians, TV commentators, learned professors as well as children and teens making contradictory statements daily. Worst of all they don't even know they are doing it. In the same paragraph, they will make statements that contradict each other. For example, politicians will say, "We should get rid of the federal Department of Education and spend the money on local education, but to ensure that local schools do their job we should make them meet national standards." When people talk about getting "back to basics" in school, I really wish they meant getting back to logic, without which we cannot use inference and learn new truth.

Ernest Dimnet in, *The Art of Thinking,* says, "Americans cannot realize how many chances for mental improvement they lose by their inveterate habit of keeping up six conversations when there are twelve people in the room. To sum up, the child notices grown-ups and begins to think their thoughts; he goes to school, and too often education imposes other people's thoughts upon him instead of helping him go back to his own; once out of school, he makes money, or arrives, or amuses himself; there is no question of thinking any more, unless we call thinking using one's mind to attain practical ends. Altogether, life does just the reverse of what it is supposed to do; it travels away from thought, and the process begins when we are ten years old." (43)

We live in a world in which everyone is expected to have an opinion on everything. Opinion polls are a good example. The President of the United States gives an hour-long State of the Union speech and immediately thereafter a pollster asks a group of people to comment on what the president said. Few of the people questioned have any knowledge whatsoever about the issues the President discussed, but they do have opinions. Aristotle warns us that answers that don't consist of knowledge are merely opinions. An opinion is no better than the evidence the speaker can adduce in its favor. Opinions approach knowledge if they have the weight of the evidence on their side. The responses recorded in most opinion polls are a pooling of ignorance. Former first lady Nancy Reagan used an astrologer to guide her in her advice to her husband, the president. For some period, this country was at the mercy of an astrologer who determined at what time the president could or could not address the nation or travel to a meeting. Now polls containing flimsy opinions by people who have no knowledge of the issues determine which way the leaders should proceed. Oh, how we need to go back to Aristotle to discover how to think!

In using the Socratic method in elementary and high schools, I have found that few students are afraid to offer opinions on a variety of subjects, regardless of their unfamiliarity with the subject being discussed. When they are challenged and asked to give reasons for their opinions, they often act hurt and merely say, "That's how I feel about it." This is the equivalent of saying, "I have no evidence for my opinion and that shouldn't matter." Worse still, I find students afraid to confront each other and to ask opinion-sharers for evidence to bulwark their opinions. They seem to subscribe to the idea that everyone has a right to his or her opinion, and no one should be uncivil enough to ask them to justify their opinion. When this occurs, the seminar drones on with people offering contradictory opinions, and all agreeing with the contradictions and contraries.

This is not the way to use the third level of thinking. Men and women need first of all to learn how to know or to think if they are to be good *Makers, Doers,* and *Knowers.* Continued use of the seminar method is one of the best means to teach logic. As humans we were made to be *Makers* and *Doers* but we are especially characterized by our ability to be *Knowers.* We can't become real Knowers unless we can share our burgeoning knowledge with other learners to test its validity. We become Knowers by *observing, classifying things in nature and subjecting them to experimentation based on hypotheses, which flow from theories.* If our hypotheses are confirmed, we know our knowledge is valid. We also become Knowers by *reading widely in science and literature* to see what others have done in their observations, classifications, experimentations, and validations. Finally, we learn most in my opinion through *human conversations* in which we subject our opinions to the group with the hope that they will help us either confirm or reject the opinions we are sharing.

Mortimer Adler in *The Paideia Proposal,* points out,

"The teacher's role in discussion (seminars) is to keep it going along fruitful lines—by moderating, guiding, and correcting, leading, and arguing like one more student! The teacher is first among equals. All must have the sense that they are participating as equals, as is the case in a genuine conversation." (44)

The Steward Principal is aware that the school cannot cram students with all the knowledge and skills they will need during their adult life , but schools can and must train students in the art of thinking. As the Steward Principals work out their own answers to the four basic questions confronting them, they will be able to help all the stakeholders: students, teachers, principals, other staff to become successful *Makers, Doers*, and *Knowers*.

SUMMATION

In this final chapter, I have tried to offer to the Steward Principal the best gift I have. Stewardship is about service based on a balance of power, a primary commitment to the larger community, a shared opportunity for stakeholders to define the school's purpose and what kind of culture or philosophy it will have. The Steward Principal will have great influence on the school in shaping and forming with the stakeholders the philosophy and culture of the school.

In this chapter we have reviewed some of the more basic ideas in philosophy to help the Steward Principal carry out this phase of school leadership. We reviewed briefly the definition of Philosophical and Cultural Values as offered in Domain 18 of *Principals For Our Changing Schools* and encouraged the reader to pursue the ideas set forth by Garrison and his team. We espouse the idea that Steward Principals must be philosophers if they are to lead in the formation of an overall vision for the school. With this in mind, we explored the four basic philosophical questions: *Who am I? What is the world? How can I live and work with others? What is to know?* Steward Principals reflect long and deeply on these questions in order to help all stakeholders form the school philosophy. We saw in the history of Education a pursuit of philosophical foundations offered by the Big Ten, and we saw them jettisoned by the Naughty Nine.

The conclusion of the chapter is devoted to this important question, *What is to Know?* We differentiated among our roles as

Makers, Doers, and *Knowers* and tried to show how the Steward Principal can make sure that the school leads students not only to a practical knowledge but also to a theoretical knowledge. This will keep them always curious and open to knowing more, even if they don't see an immediate practical application for the knowledge. Steward Principals who are working on their own philosophy of education can help students become better *Knowers* as well as *Makers* and *Doers.* To be proficient in these activities, the students—like the principals—will have to become thinkers who are never afraid to ask the deeper philosophical questions.

QUESTIONS FOR RELECTION

1. There are four basic questions on which your philosopohy of life and your philosophy of education hang. Who am I? What is the world? How can I live and work with others? What is to know? We must grapple with these questions for our whole life. Do you agree? How will our answers to these questions affect the way we run our schools?

2. Too much meddling with school policy is done by people who aren't even aware of how the four basic questions impinge on schooling. How can principals enlighten the public about the connections?

3. In the early part of the century, social scientists worked hard to prove that there was no such thing as "human nature." They traveled the globe selecting data that would confirm their hypothesis. Why did they do this? They had a good point they were trying to make.

4. Hitler scared all of us with his theory of Aryan supremacy. We bent backwards to deny the influence of genetics on humans. Now we are swinging back to the point where we can admit three causes for human anatomy and behavior: genes, memes, and schemes. What do we mean by that? How does it change our answer to the question, "Who am I?"

5. We humans are each on a journey of self-discovery. We don't walk alone. What role does school play in helping students to answer the question, "Who am I"?

6. What would a curriculum centered on sustainability do to help students answer the question, "What is the world"?

7. How did the Committee of Ten and the Committee of Nine answer the same question in two different ways? Why? What does it say about their philosophical positions?

8. If you had to learn how to live and work with others what kind of an education would you choose for yourself and your children? The answer by Committee of Nine or Ten? Why?

9. Adler tells us human activity has three very important directions: the three are making, doing, and knowing. We all are called to be makers, doers, knowers. How does our philosophy of education take this into account?

10. The prime law of logic is the law of contradiction. What does it say about our education when the politicians and the media have no fear of feeding us contradictory statements since they believe with good evidence that the rank and file don't realize the laws of logic are being twisted into sophistries?

EPILOGUE

As a principal, ask yourself the following three questions: How can I serve the school to the best of my ability? Is it possible to do something in and with the school that will be of real value and service to something larger than myself and my immediate family? Is it possible for me as a principal to be safe and secure while pursuing my freedom and searching for ways to be of service?

Every six weeks, a new educational program is announced that is guaranteed to improve the school. There is something of value in every one of them. The problem is, where do you as a principal start? Which one of the 925 "how to improve the school suggestions" do you begin to implement? How do you do what you ought to be do and in what order?

In this book I have taken nine of the Domains of Knowledge and Skill recommended in *Principals For Our Changing Schools*, and tried to make them "user friendly" for the busy principal. In *The Principal As Steward*, I covered the following areas: Student Guidance and Development, Staff Development, Measurement and Evaluation, Resource Allocation, Motivating Others, Interpersonal Sensitivity, Oral and Nonverbal Expression, Written Expression, and finally, Philosophical and Cultural Values. To stitch the nine domains together, I used the concept of Stewardship as the integrating thread. To improve your school, your proficiency in the nine domains will help you be a Steward in the best sense of the word. Granted, the stakeholders must accept a responsible role in the changing school or it just won't change. No principal can possibly change a school against the wishes of the teachers, students, parents, or Central Office, yet if the principal plays the role of a true Steward, there is a high probability that a critical mass of the stakeholders will begin to think of the school as theirs, and begin to go the extra mile to make it the best school possible.

I love the story of the mother who reprimanded her six-year-old son for constantly following his eight-year-old brother so closely. The older brother had complained that the young one was a pest following him everywhere. After telling the young brother to give his older brother some space, the younger one replied, "I don't really follow him around like he said. It's just that everywhere I want to be, he gets there before me."

In a school in which the principal is a master of the nine domains and has the attitude of a Steward, all the stakeholders just seem to want to go where the principal goes. When the principal and all the stakeholders--searching for freedom, security, and service--find that they can achieve these goals together better than alone, the principal has become a Steward.

In an earlier book, *The Principal's Edge*, I covered the first nine domains of knowledge and skill recommended by the National Policy Board in *Principals For Our Changing Schools*. The first nine domains: Leadership, Information Collection, Problem Analysis, Judgment, Organization Oversight, Implementation, Delegation, Instruction and the Learning Environment, and Curriculum Design are also keys to becoming a Steward Principal. In the earlier book, I make the point that a principal who mastered these domains would have an edge in running an efficient and effective school. I have great faith in the research work done by the National Policy Board in compiling the data for *Principals For Our Changing Schools*. I recommend that all principals familiarize themselves with this volume. It contains the input of thousands of practicing principals who were asked what a good principal needed to know and be able to do. I don't think there is a better source of information for principals available. My two books are only commentaries on this major opus. I wrote them hoping I could lure princpals into becoming acquainted with the source: *Principals For Our Changing Schools*.

The National Policy Board singled out 21 Domains of Knowledge and Skill for principals. But in my book I have handled only 18 of the 21. I omitted the final three: Legal and Regulatory Applications, Policy and Political Influences, and Public Relations. Any experienced principal is aware of the importance of these three areas of knowledge and skill. I didn't omit them because I thought they were unimportant.

My reason for settling on 18 of the 21 Domains is quite simple. I really didn't feel competent to handle the last three. I felt a lawyer experienced in school law would be best able to handle Domain 19: Legal and Regulatory Applications. I omitted Domain 20: Policy and Political Influences, for two reasons. First, I lack knowledge and experience in this area, and second my blood pressure rises to unhealthy levels when I think too long on this subject. I am aware of the damage that is done to students, teachers, and principals by politicians who, knowing little and caring less about the mission of the public schools, use these schools as footballs in their game of power seeking. I know it is wrong of me to fasten on the negative. There are politicians who do care and want only the best for the students, but I still worry about micro-managerial decisions being made by people of good will who are too far removed from the "smell of the chalk" to know what is best for the school. Since school systems will be politically controlled for the next millenium, principals must learn the system and understand how best to use it for the good of the students. I hope principals will have some say in the future about not only how their own school should operate but also how to free school systems from political meddling. A good start would be opting for appointed rather than elected school board members.

Finally, I omitted Domain 21 even though I realize that today more than ever principals must improve in their ability to handle media and public relations. I do believe that many of the domains we covered, especially the two in this book on communication, will help principals in this task.

For more insight and clarification of these domains, I recommend a new series of books, THE SCHOOL LEADERSHIP LIBRARY, edited by David Erlandson and Alfred Wilson (45). There are 21 books in this series, each one devoted to one of the domains recommended by the National Policy Board for Educational Administration.

In this book, I have suggested that Stewardship is an umbrella idea that offers the means of achieving the fundamental change needed by our schools. The spirit of Stewardship should permeate the entire school. Principals who recognize this fact will function most effectively as the leaders of their schools.

REFERENCES

(1) *Prisoners of Time*, Report of the National Educational Commission on Time and Learning. April, (1994), U.S. Government Printing Office. Washington, D.C. 20402-9328. page 15.

(2) Erik Erikson, *Childhood and Society*, Second edition, (1963), W.W. Norton & Company Inc. New York. pages 252–253

(3) Gilligan, M.D. James, *Violence: Our Deadly Epidemic and Its Causes*, 1996, G.P. Putnam's Sons, New York. page 110.

(4) *Principals For Our Changing Schools*, (1993), Edited by Scott D. Thomson. National Policy Board for Educational Administration, 205 Hill Hall, University of Missouri, Columbia, Missouri, 65211.

(5) Comer, M.D., James, *School Development Program*, Child Study Center, 230 South Frontage Road, P.O. Box 3333, New Haven, CT 06510-8009.

(6) *op. cit., Principals For Our Changing Schools*, page 10-9.

(7) *Learner Centered Psychological Principles*: Guidelines For School Redesign And Reform, 1993, American Psychological Association. First St. N.E. Washington, DC, 20002-4242.

(8) Senge, Peter M. *The Fifth Discipline*, Doubleday, New York, 1990, page 7.

(9) *op. cit., Principals For Our Changing Schools*, page 11-3

(10) Cervantes, S.M., *Don Quixote of La Mancha*. Mentor Books, New American Library, New York.

(11) *op. cit., Prisoners of Time*, page 7.

(12) *ibid*, page 36.

(13) *ibid*, page 29.

(14) Vella, Jane, *Learning to Listen Learning to Teach*, Jossey-Bass, San Francisco, 1994, page 7.

(15) Mitchell, Ruth, *Testing for Learning*, Free Press, New York, 1992, page 2.

(16) *ibid*, page 172.

(17) *op. cit.*, *Principals For Our Changing Schools*, page 12-3.

(18) Gardner, Howard, *The Unschooled Mind*, Basic Books, New York, 1991, page 245.

(19) *op. cit.*, *Test for Learning*, page 109.

(20) Johnson, Bil, *Performance Assessment Handbook, vol. 1,* Eye on Education Pub. Inc., Princeton, NJ, 1996, page.

(21) Adler, Mortimer, *The Paideia Proposal*, Macmillian Pub. Co., New York, 1982, page 54.

(22) *op. cit.*, *Performance Assessment Handbook, vol. 1,* page 90.

(23) *ibid*, pages 47 and 48.

(24) *op. cit.*, *Principals For Our Changing Schools*, page 14-3.

(25) Greenleaf, Robert K.,*Servant Leadership*, Paulist Press New York, 1977, page 13.

(26) *op. cit.*, *Principals For Our Changing Schools*, page 15-3.

(27) De Pree, Max, *Leadership is an Art*, Dell Pub. Co. New York, 1990, page 22.

(28) *op. cit.*, *Principals For Our Changing Schools*, page 15-6.

(29) McGregor, D.M., *The Human Side of Enterprise*, McGraw-Hill, New York, 1960. page 88.

(30) McCall, Jack, *The Principal's Edge*, Eye on Education, Princeton, NJ, 1994, page 142.

(31) *op. cit.*, *Principals For Our Changing Schools*, page 16-3.

(32) Goleman, Daniel, *Emotional Intelligence*, Bantam Books, New York, 1995, page 261.

(33) *op. cit.*, *Principals For Our Changing Schools*, page 17-3.

(34) *ibid*, page 17-5.

(35) *ibid*, page 17-7.

(36) Howard, V.A. & Barton, J.H., *Thinking on Paper,* Wm. Morrow Co. New York, 1986, page 20.

(37) *ibid*, page 28.

(38) *op. cit.*, *Principals For Our Changing Schools*, page 18-3.

(39) Brown, Don, *Human Universals*, McGraw-Hill, New York, 1991, page 55.

(40) Ornstein, Robert, *The Roots of Self*, Harper, San Francisco, 1995, page 32.

(41) Orr, David, *Ecological Literacy*, State University of New York, Albany, 1992, page 84.

(42) Adler, Mortimer, *Aristotle for Everybody*, Macmillan Co. New York, 1978, page 54.

(43) Dimnet, Ernest, *The Art of Thinking*, Fawcett Pub. Co. Greenwich, CT, page 80.

(44) *op. cit.*, *The Paideia Proposal*, page 54.

(45) Erlandson, David and Wilson, Alfred, editors, *The School Leadership Library*, 1996, Eye on Education, Larchmont, NY.

FIGURES

Figure #1 in *Principals For Our Changing Schools*, page 10-1.

Figure #2 *ibid*, page 11-1.

Figure #3 *ibid*, page 13-1

Figure #4 in Hackman, J.R. and Oldham, G.R. (1976). Motivation through the design of work: Test of a theory. *Organizational Behavior and Human Performance, 16*, 250–279. © Copyright 1976 by Academic Press.

Figure #5 in *Principals for our Changing Schools*, page 15-11.

Figure #6 *ibid*, page 16-9.